Contemporary
European
Architects

Volume V

Philip Jodidio

Contemporary **European** Architects

Volume V

TASCHEN

KÖLN LISBOA LONDON NEW YORK PARIS TOKYO

Page 2 | Seite 2
Rudy Ricciotti: Le Stadium, Vitrolles, France | Frankreich, 1994–95
© Photo: Paul Raftery/Arcaid

© 1997 Benedikt Taschen Verlag GmbH
Hohenzollernring 53, D-50672 Köln

Edited by Christine Fellhauer, Cologne
Design: Sylvie Chesnay, Paris
Cover Design: Mark Thomson, London
French translation: Jacques Bosser, Paris
German translation: Franca Fritz, Heinrich Koop, Cologne

Printed in Italy
ISBN 3-8228-8070-1

Contents | Inhalt | Sommaire

6   New but Aware of the Past
European Architects in the mid 1990s

Neues, im Bewußtsein der Vergangenheit
Europäische Architekten Mitte der 90er Jahre

Nouveau, mais conscient du passé
Architectes européens du milieu des années 90

52   Wiel Arets
60   Ben van Berkel
66   Mario Botta
80   Coop Himmelb(l)au
88   Sir Norman Foster
98   von Gerkan, Marg und Partner
106   Zvi Hecker
114   Herman Hertzberger
120   Josef Paul Kleihues
134   Jean Nouvel
140   Christian de Portzamparc
146   Reichen & Robert
154   Rudy Ricciotti
160   Thomas Spiegelhalter

170   Biographies | Biographien
174   Bibliography | Bibliographie
175   Index
176   Credits | Fotonachweis |
        Crédits photographiques

New but Aware of the Past
European Architects in the mid 1990s

Neues, im Bewußtsein der Vergangenheit
Europäische Architekten Mitte der 90er Jahre

Nouveau, mais conscient du passé
Architectes européens du milieu des années 90

With a few years' hindsight, it is possible to identify the late 1980s as a period of exuberant experimentation in contemporary architecture. From the last gasp of the "Post-Modern" pastiche to the skewed volumes of deconstruction, things quite literally went off in every possible direction. Collapsing real estate markets from California to Japan, a growing sense of social dysfunction particularly in Europe, and a natural swing of the pendulum from euphoria to doubt, all played their role in the changing taste of the 1990s. Today's challenge is not so much to provide an astonishing form as it is to renovate existing structures or to build a new generation of modern buildings distinguished by their almost austere functionalism. For some observers this style may closely resemble the modernism or the brutalism of the 1950s. Indeed a quick look at the design and fashion of the present might well confirm the existence of a '50s revival. Yet the mood of the 1990s is very different from the technological optimism of the post-War years.

As every rule must have its exceptions, so the minimalist architecture of the present is contradicted by opposing trends. Fractured shapes are still very present, especially when they are justified by an underlying logic. Perhaps this is a key to the real inclination of the present. The forms of architecture are now, more than in the recent past, determined by stronger forces, be they economic or technical. It is the economy which dictates that old buildings now be reused more than before. In the somewhat less than immortal words of the candidate Bill Clinton, "It's the economy, stupid." Simplicity in design is in fact very much in harmony with the time of industrial "downsizing." Energy self-sufficiency, also related to cost consciousness, is another force behind new architectural design, but the natural laws governing "green" architecture sometimes lead to more complex forms. Finally, more sophisticated materials and construction techniques do make possible spectacular designs such as the new Erasmus Bridge in Rotterdam (Ben van Berkel, 1990–96), but here too, it is the laws of nature that permit the architect to provide an economically feasible solution to a complex technical problem. Modesty and even austerity have become governing principles in

Aus einem Abstand von mehreren Jahren erscheinen die späten 8oer Jahre im Rahmen der zeitgenössischen Architektur als eine Zeit überschwenglicher Experimentierfreude. Nach dem postmodernen Pasticcio und den schiefwinkligen Baukörpern der Dekonstruktion entwickelten sich die Dinge im wahrsten Sinne des Wortes in alle möglichen Richtungen. Der Zusammenbruch der Immoblienmärkte von Kalifornien bis Japan, ein vor allem in Europa ständig wachsendes Gefühl sozialer Funktionsstörungen und der natürliche Schwung des Pendels von der Euphorie zum Zweifel – dies alles war für den Geschmackswandel in den 90er Jahren mitverantwortlich. Heute besteht die Herausforderung nicht mehr in der Schaffung möglichst verblüffender Formen, sondern in der Umgestaltung von Altbauten oder im Bau einer neuen Generation moderner Gebäude, die sich vor allem durch einen nahezu asketischen Funktionalismus auszeichnen – ein Stil, der an die klassische Moderne oder den New Brutalism der 5oer Jahre erinnert. Nach einem Blick auf das Design und die Mode der heutigen Zeit erscheint es tatsächlich so, als ob die 5oer Jahre wieder auferstehen. Aber im Gegensatz dazu unterscheidet sich die Stimmung der 90er Jahre sehr deutlich vom technologischen Optimismus der Nachkriegszeit.

Aber da jede Regel ihre Ausnahme benötigt, steht die minimalistische Architektur der Gegenwart im Widerspruch zu gegenläufigen Trends. Gebrochene Formen spielen auch heute noch eine bedeutende Rolle, vor allem, wenn sie durch eine tiefere Logik gerechtfertigt werden. Vielleicht ist dies der Schlüssel zum wahren Trend der Gegenwart. Die Formen der Architektur werden heute, stärker noch als vor wenigen Jahren, von mächtigeren Kräften bestimmt – egal, ob wirtschaftlicher oder technischer Natur. Es ist die Wirtschaft, die vorschreibt, daß heute wesentlich mehr ältere Gebäude einer neuen Nutzung zugeführt werden als bisher – oder, um es mit den nahezu unsterblichen Worten des Kandidaten Bill Clinton zu sagen: »It's the economy, stupid.« Und tatsächlich paßt die heutige Schlichtheit im Design perfekt zu einer Zeit der industriellen »Schrumpfung«. Der Wunsch nach autarker Energieversorgung, kombiniert mit Kostenbewußtsein, kann als weitere Kraft hinter der neuen

Avec quelques années de recul, nous pouvons considérer aujourd'hui la fin des années 1980 comme une période de l'histoire de l'architecture contemporaine marquée par une création exubérante. Des derniers soubresauts du pastiche postmoderniste aux volumes éclatés du déconstructivisme, les architectes se sont littéralement lancés dans toutes les directions imaginables. L'effondrement des marchés immobiliers de la Californie au Japon, le sentiment grandissant des dysfonctionnements sociaux, particulièrement en Europe, et l'inévitable retour de balancier qui ramène de l'euphorie au doute, ont tous joué un rôle dans le changement du goût architectural dans les années 1990. Aujourd'hui, le défi n'est pas tant d'imaginer des solutions formelles qui étonneront les commanditaires que de rénover des bâtiments existants ou d'édifier une nouvelle génération d'immeubles modernes qui se distinguent par leur fonctionnalisme presque sévère. Pour certains observateurs, ce style pourrait bien se rapprocher de très près du modernisme ou du brutalisme des années 50. Un rapide coup d'œil au design et à la mode d'aujourd'hui confirme d'ailleurs ce retour aux années 50. Cependant l'atmosphère des années 90 est très différente de l'optimisme technologique de l'après-guerre.

Chaque règle connaît ses exceptions. L'architecture minimaliste actuelle se trouve confrontée à des tendances opposées. Les formes fracturées sont encore très présentes, en particulier lorsqu'une logique interne les justifie. Peut-être est-ce là une des clés de la tendance actuelle. Plus encore que dans un récent passé, les formes de l'architecture sont aujourd'hui déterminées par des contraintes plus fortes, qui peuvent être économiques ou techniques. C'est l'économie qui veut que l'on rénove aujourd'hui davantage de bâtiments anciens que naguère. Comme le faisait remarquer à sa façon le candidat présidentiel Bill Clinton lors de sa première élection «C'est l'économie, idiot.» La nouvelle simplicité de conception est en fait en harmonie avec le downsizing (réduction) actuellement à la mode dans l'industrie. L'autosuffisance énergétique, également liée à la prise de conscience des coûts, est une autres des contraintes qui pèsent sur les nouvelles approches architecturales, même si

Wiel Arets, AZL Headquarters, Heerlen, The Netherlands, 1991–95. Facing Akenstraat, this concrete facade of the new building is located directly next to the older, brick section of the AZL Headquarters.

Wiel Arets, AZL Hauptgebäude, Heerlen, Niederlande, 1991–95. Die zur Akenstraat zeigende Betonfassade des Neubaus liegt unmittelbar neben dem ursprünglichen AZL-Gebäude, einem Backsteinbau.

Wiel Arets, siège social d'AZL, Heerlen, Pays-Bas, 1991–95. Donnant sur l'Akenstraat, la façade de béton du nouveau bâtiment touche pratiquement celle de l'ancien siège en briques.

contemporary architecture, but as always, talented creators emerge who are able to make the best of such constraints.

Adding on – Starting over

Born in Heerlen, The Netherlands in 1955, Wiel Arets graduated from the Technical University of Eindhoven in 1983. A former Diploma Unit Master at the Architectural Association in London (1988–92), he is Dean of the Berlage Institute, Postgraduate Laboratory of Architecture in Amsterdam (1995–98). Like Ben van Berkel, who was born in 1957, and who has also worked at the AA in London, Arets is one of the outstanding representatives of the younger generation of Dutch architects now emerging. A recent critique of his work published in a Dutch architectural magazine affirmed that he "has given his own interpretation to the familiar language of early modernism ..." and that "he stands aloof from everything that has been written and said about the neo-modernist mainstream of Dutch architecture." "His appropriation of formal elements from the work of Tadao Ando," according to this critic, "is unique and abnormal in Holland."[1] Although partial, this analysis of the style of Wiel Arets does prepare the observer to encounter his AZL Headquarters (Heerlen, The Netherlands, 1991–95). AZL Beheer Heerlen is the former retirement fund for Limburg's mine workers, and they commissioned Arets to renovate and expand their offices in 1991. He chose to "plug" the new building for 220 people into the existing 1941 brick headquarters. A reinforced concrete structure, the elongated volume of the new building runs perpendicular to the older offices, with extensions connecting directly into them. With this design, Wiel Arets creates not only a symbiotic relationship between past and present, but also a metaphor for contemporary office design. As he says, "... plugging plays a major role in switching on and off the machinery belonging to the advanced office automation to be implemented here."

Faced with a similar design challenge, the Austrian architects Coop Himmelb(l)au chose a much more radical design, at least in outward appearance. They were commissioned to remodel and add to an existing warehouse for the Austrian Research

Architektur vermutet werden – aber manchmal führen die Gesetze der Natur, die die »grüne« Architektur bestimmen, auch zu komplexeren Formen. Schließlich erlauben verbesserte Materialien und neue Konstruktionstechniken besonders spektakuläre Entwürfe wie die neue Erasmusbrücke in Rotterdam (Ben van Berkel, 1990–96). Aber auch in diesem Fall sind es die Gesetze der Natur, die dem Architekten für ein kompliziertes technisches Problem eine wirtschaftlich machbare Lösung ermöglichen. Bescheidenheit und sogar Strenge haben sich zu Leitprinzipien der zeitgenössischen Architektur entwickelt; aber wie immer finden sich auch in dieser Zeit talentierte Baumeister, die in der Lage sind, das Beste aus solchen Beschränkungen zu machen.

Ergänzung – Neubeginn

Der 1955 in Heerlen (Niederlande) geborene Wiel Arets beendete 1983 sein Architekturstudium an der Technischen Hochschule Eindhoven. Arets, ein ehemaliger Diploma Unit Master der Architectural Association in London (1988–92) und jetziger Dekan des Berlage Postgraduierteninstituts für Architektur in Amsterdam (1995–98), zählt zusammen mit dem 1957 geborenen Ben van Berkel, der ebenfalls an der AA studierte, zu den auffälligsten jüngeren niederländischen Architekten. Eine kritische Beschreibung seiner Arbeiten, die vor kurzem in einem niederländischen Architekturmagazin zu finden war, bestätigt, daß er »die bekannte Sprache der frühen Moderne auf ganz persönliche Weise interpretiert ...« und »dabei Distanz zu allem wahrt, was über den neo-modernen Mainstream in der niederländischen Architektur geschrieben und gesagt wurde.« Weiter schreibt der Kritiker: »Seine Verwendung formaler Elemente der Arbeiten Tadao Andos ist in Holland ungewöhnlich und einzigartig.«[1]

Diese – zugegebenermaßen parteiische – Stilanalyse bereitet den Besucher auf eine Begegnung mit Arets' AZL Hauptgebäude (Heerlen, Niederlande, 1991–95) vor. Die AZL Beheer Heerlen verwaltet die frühere Pensionskasse der Limburger Bergarbeiter und beauftragte Arets 1991 mit der Renovierung und Erweiterung ihrer Büros. Der Architekt entschied sich dafür, das neue Ge-

les lois naturelles qui semblent gouverner l'architecture «verte» aboutissent parfois à des formes plus complexes. Enfin, des matériaux et des techniques de construction plus sophistiqués permettent la réalisation de projets spectaculaires comme le nouveau pont Érasme (Ben van Berkel, 1990–96), bien que là encore, ce soient les lois de la nature qui permettent à l'architecte d'apporter une solution économiquement réalisable à un problème technique complexe. La modestie, et même l'austérité, sont devenus des principes moteurs de l'architecture contemporaine. Comme à toutes les périodes, cependant, émergent un certain nombre de créateurs de talent capables de tirer le meilleur parti de telles contraintes.

Ajouter – Reconstruire

Né à Heerlen, aux Pays-Bas, en 1955, Wiel Arets a achevé ses études d'architecture à l'Université Technique d'Eindhoven en 1983. Ancien responsable de la classe de diplôme de l'Architectural Association de Londres (1988–92), il est doyen de l'Institut Berlage, laboratoire post-universitaire d'architecture d'Amsterdam (1995–98). Comme Ben van Berkel, né en 1957, et qui a également travaillé à l'AA Londonienne, Arets est l'un des plus brillants représentants de la jeune génération montante d'architectes néerlandais. Récemment, une étude sur son travail parue dans un magazine d'architecture néerlandais notait: «Il donne une interprétation du langage familier du modernisme historique qui lui est propre..., et se tient à l'écart de tout ce qui a été écrit et dit sur le courant néo-moderniste de l'architecture néerlandaise.» Selon le même critique, «son appropriation d'éléments formels empruntés à Tadao Ando est unique et hors normes pour les Pays-Bas.»[1] Bien que partielle, cette analyse du style de Wiel Arets prépare cependant assez bien l'observateur à la découverte du siège de AZL (Heerlen, Pays-Bas, 1991–95). AZL Beheer Heerlen est l'ancien fond de pension des mineurs du Limbourg, qui a demandé à l'architecte de rénover et d'agrandir ses bureaux. Arets a choisi de «brancher» le nouveau bâtiment – conçu pour 220 personnes – sur le vieux siège social en brique qui date de 1941. En béton armé, le volume allongé du nouveau

Center (Seibersdorf, Austria, 1993–95). Given the reputation of Coop Himmelb(l)au principals Wolf D. Prix and Helmut Swiczinsky for challenging the existing order in architecture, it is not altogether surprising that their approach to this remodeling job has placed "an emphasis on dynamism and not a static state." In a short 1978 manifesto entitled "The Future of the Splendid Desolation," they wrote: "Contemporary architecture will be honest and true, when streets, open spaces, buildings and infrastructures reflect the image of urban reality, when the devastation of the city is transformed into fascinating landmarks of devastation." More catastrophically they intoned the rules of a new religion: "Architecture gains meaning in proportion to its desolation. This desolation comes from the act of using. It gains strength from the surrounding desolation. And this architecture brings the message: Everything you like is bad. Everything that works is bad. Whatever has to be accepted is good."[2] Fortunately, the messianic tone of the rhetoric of Coop Himmelb(l)au does not really translate into built form. Thus, much as early modernism was emptied of its political message quite soon, so Coop Himmelb(l)au has actually gone on to building real buildings with real people in them who are not particularly eager to be submitted to more desolation than what they already have to put up with in any modern city. Echoing the varying disciplines of those who were to work in the Seibersdorf building, from environmental engineers to mathematicians, in a concept of "simultaneity" of the old and the new, the architects say that "highly differentiated parts of the building are mixed together, not wildly, but as mentioned, simultaneously." Outstanding representatives of the so-called deconstructivist movement, Coop Himmelb(l)au have not actually built a large number of projects, with the notable exception of the old master paintings pavilion of the Groninger Museum (with Alessandro Mendini; Groningen, The Netherlands, 1990–94). They did participate in the seminal 1988 exhibition at the Museum of Modern Art, "Deconstructivist Architecture," with their Vienna Rooftop Remodeling and the Hamburg Skyline project. Although the skewed forms of deconstruction are no longer at the forefront of

bäude für 220 Mitarbeiter in das ursprüngliche Hauptgebäude, einen Ziegelbau aus dem Jahr 1941, »einzustöpseln«. Der langgestreckte neue Baukörper aus Stahlbeton verläuft rechtwinklig zu den alten Gebäuden, wobei seine Ausläufer eine direkte Verbindung zwischen beiden Teilen schaffen. Mit diesem Entwurf schuf Arets nicht nur eine symbiotische Verbindung von Vergangenheit und Gegenwart, sondern auch eine Metapher auf herkömmliches Bürodesign. Er sagt dazu: » ... das Einstöpseln spielt eine entscheidende Rolle beim Ein- und Ausschalten der komplizierten Büroautomation, die hier durchgeführt werden soll.«

Mit einer ähnlichen Herausforderung konfrontiert, entschied sich die Wiener Architektengemeinschaft Coop Himmelb(l)au für einen deutlich radikaleren Entwurf – zumindest in bezug auf das äußere Erscheinungsbild. Das Büro erhielt den Auftrag, für das Österreichische Forschungszentrum in Seibersdorf ein altes Lagerhaus umzubauen und zu erweitern (1993–95). Wer den Ruf der Coop Himmelb(l)au-Gründer Wolf D. Prix und Helmut Swiczinsky und ihre Lust an der Herausforderung der bestehenden Architekturordnung kennt, den konnte es nicht verwundern, daß ihr Ziel bei diesem Umbau darin bestand, »den Dynamismus zu betonen, und nicht statische Zustände.« In einem kurzen Manifest mit dem Titel »Die Zukunft der Splendid Desolation« schrieben sie 1978: »Die zeitgenössische Architektur wird erst dann ehrlich und wahrhaft sein, wenn Straßen, offene Räume, Gebäude und Infrastrukturen das Bild der urbanen Realität widerspiegeln, wenn sich die Verheerung der Städte in faszinierende Wahrzeichen der Verheerung verwandelt hat.« Die Grundsätze ihrer neuen Religion intonierten sie noch apokalyptischer: »Eine Architektur gewinnt an Bedeutung proportional zu ihrer Verwüstung. Diese Verheerung entsteht aus dem Akt des Benutzens. Sie bezieht ihre Stärke aus der umgebenden Zerstörung. Eine solche Architektur vermittelt die Botschaft: Alles, was man mag, ist schlecht. Alles, was funktioniert, ist schlecht. Alles, was akzeptiert werden muß, ist gut.«[2] Glücklicherweise ließen sich ihre messianischen Töne nicht in gebaute Formen umsetzen – und ebenso wie die frühe Moderne sehr schnell ihre politische Stoßkraft verlor, gingen Coop Himmelb(l)au letztendlich dazu über,

Coop Himmelb(l)au, Research Center, Seibersdorf, Austria, 1993–95. An existing warehouse structure, converted to office use collides with a new element.

Coop Himmelb(l)au, Forschungszentrum Seibersdorf, Österreich, 1993–95. Das ehemalige Lagerhaus, das zu Büroräumen umgebaut wurde, »kollidiert« mit einem neuen Bauelement.

Coop Himmelb(l)au, Centre de recherches, Seibersdorf, Autriche, 1993–95. Le nouveau bâtiment entre littéralement en collision avec l'entrepôt existant, transformé en bureaux.

bâtiment se développe perpendiculairement aux anciens bureaux, avec des extensions qui s'y connectent directement. Ainsi, Wiel Arets crée non seulement une relation symbiotique entre le passé et le présent, mais également une métaphore du bureau contemporain. Comme il l'écrit: «...le branchement joue un rôle majeur dans la mise en ou hors circuit des systèmes d'automatisation des tâches de bureaux mis en œuvre dans ce lieu.»

Confrontés à un défi similaire, les architectes autrichiens Coop Himmelb(l)au ont choisi une solution beaucoup plus radicale, du moins dans son apparence extérieure. Ils ont été commissionnés pour remodeler et agrandir un entrepôt existant pour le Centre de Recherche autrichien (Seibersdorf, Autriche, 1993–95). Étant donnée la réputation bien établie des principaux associés de Coop Himmelb(l)au – Wolf D. Prix et Helmut Swiczinsky – de remettre en question l'ordre architectural existant, il n'est pas vraiment surprenant que leur approche de ce remodelage mette «l'emphase sur le dynamisme, et non sur un état statique.» Dans un bref manifeste datant de 1978 intitulé «Le Futur de la désolation splendide», ils écrivaient: «L'architecture contemporaine sera honnête et authentique lorsque les rues, les espaces ouverts, les bâtiments et les infrastructures refléteront l'image de la réalité urbaine, lorsque la dévastation de la cité sera transformée en de fascinants monuments à la dévastation.» Plus catastrophistes encore, il entonnaient les règles d'une nouvelle religion: «L'architecture gagne en sens proportionnellement à sa désolation. Celle-ci vient de l'acte d'usage. Elle se nourrit de la désolation environnante. Et cette architecture délivre le message que tout ce que vous aimez est mauvais. Tout ce qui fonctionne est mauvais. Tout ce qui doit être accepté est bon.»[2] Il est heureux que le ton messianique de cette rhétorique ne se traduise pas vraiment dans leurs réalisations. Ainsi, de même que le premier modernisme a été vidé assez rapidement de son message politique, Coop Himmelb(l)au en est venu à édifier de vrais immeubles pour de vrais utilisateurs pas particulièrement anxieux d'être soumis à une désolation supérieure à celle qu'ils doivent déjà affronter dans n'importe quelle ville actuelle. En écho aux divers spécialistes appelés à intervenir sur l'immeuble de Sei-

architectural thought, there is a natural delay between the emergence of a theory and its appearance in built form. The exuberance of the Seibersdorf project would seem to be a bit out of tune with the times, but the architects do go to some lengths to explain these forms in terms of the activity of the center. At almost any time in recent architectural history, however, contradictory styles have existed simultaneously.

The German firm of von Gerkan, Marg und Partner does not have much to do with Coop Himmelb(l)au, in terms either of style or of scale of their respective projects. With approximately 200 employees, von Gerkan, Marg und Partner is equipped to deal with large challenges such as their recently completed New Leipzig Fair (Leipzig, Germany, 1993–96). Especially up until World War I, Leipzig was a home to the most important international trade fair. The Machine Tool Hall with its 21,000 square meters was the largest German exhibition building of its time. The Automobile Hall designed by the Leipzig architects Crämer & Petschler in 1928, with a clear span of 100 meters and a columnfree length of 140 meters, was a favored location for Nazi mass rallies. Because of the destruction wrought during World War II, and the immobility of the Soviet authorities, Leipzig's place as a fair center was given up to other cities like Hanover, which today boasts the largest German facilities, receiving 2.3 million visitors in 1995. A competition to build new fair buildings, organized by the city in 1991 with fourteen invited architects' teams, was won by von Gerkan, Marg und Partner. Their hall is 80 meters wide, with an apex reaching up 30 meters, and a length of 243 meters. Although this does not match the clear span of 115 meters and the column-free length of 420 meters of the 1889 Galerie des Machines in Paris, the architects affirm that the Leipzig structure "responds to the Galerie's ingenious structure with contemporary building methods." Indeed, the Leipzig Fair brings to mind the great glass buildings of the past such as Joseph Paxton's Crystal Palace. Although this group of structures, offering an indoor exhibition area of 102,500 square meters, does make use of modern technology, it recalls through both the history of Leipzig and that of past exhibition halls that it is very

reale Gebäude für reale Menschen zu bauen, die keinen besonderen Wert darauf legen, einer noch größeren Verwüstung ausgesetzt zu werden, als sie sie in jeder modernen Stadt erleben können. Der Entwurf spiegelt die verschiedenen Fachdisziplinen derjenigen wider, die in dem Seibersdorfer Gebäude arbeiten sollen, von Umweltingenieuren bis Mathematikern. Zum Konzept der »Gleichzeitigkeit« von Altem und Neuem erklären die Architekten: »In diesem Bauwerk sind völlig unterschiedliche Teile miteinander vermischt, nicht wahllos, sondern – wie bereits erwähnt – gleichzeitig.« Als herausragende Vertreter des Dekonstruktivismus haben Coop Himmelb(l)au nur relativ wenige ihrer Projekte realisieren können, unter denen der Pavillon für die Sammlung der Alten Meister im Groninger Museum (mit Alessandro Mendini, Groningen, Niederlande, 1990–94) besonders herausragt. 1988 wurden ihre Entwürfe – darunter ein Dachausbau in Wien und ihr Hamburg Skyline-Projekt – im Rahmen der bahnbrechenden Ausstellung »Deconstructivist Art« im Museum of Modern Art gezeigt. Obwohl die schiefwinkligen Formen der Dekonstruktion nicht länger an vorderster Front der architektonischen Gedankenwelt stehen, gibt es eine natürliche Verzögerung zwischen der Entstehung einer Theorie und deren Erscheinen in gebauter Form. Der Überschwang des Seibersdorfer Projekts erscheint in der heutigen Zeit zwar ein wenig deplaziert, aber die Architekten sind bemüht, diese Formen mit den Aktivitäten des Zentrums und dem Nebeneinander von Alt und Neu zu erklären. Dabei haben zu fast jedem Zeitpunkt der neueren Architekturgeschichte widersprüchliche Stile gleichzeitig nebeneinander existiert.

Das deutsche Büro von Gerkan, Marg und Partner verbindet nur wenig mit Coop Himmelb(l)au – sowohl in stilistischer Hinsicht wie auch in bezug auf den Umfang ihrer Projekte. Mit seinen etwa 200 Mitarbeitern ist von Gerkan, Marg und Partner in der Lage, sich auch großen Herausforderungen wie dem vor kurzem beendeten Bau der Neuen Messe Leipzig (1993–96) zu stellen. Vor allem bis zum Ersten Weltkrieg war Leipzig die Heimat der bedeutendsten internationalen Handelsmesse, und die dortige Werkzeugmaschinenhalle galt mit ihren 21 000 m² als

bersdorf – des ingénieurs en environnement aux mathématiciens – et dans le cadre d'un concept de «simultanéité» ancien/nouveau – les architectes font remarquer que «des parties extrêmement différenciées du bâtiment sont mélangées, non de façon désordonnée, mais simultanée.» Représentant notable du mouvement déconstructiviste, Coop Himmelb(l)au n'a pas, pour l'instant, réalisé un très grand nombre de projets, à l'importante exception près du pavillon des maîtres anciens du musée de Groningue (avec Alessandro Mendini, Groningue, Pays-Bas, 1990–94). Ils ont participé à l'exposition historique de 1988 du Museum of Modern Art de New York, «Deconstructivist Architecture,» avec leur célèbre projet de remodelage du dernier niveau d'un immeuble viennois, ou celui du panorama urbain de Hambourg. Bien que les formes éclatées de la déconstruction ne soient plus à l'avant-garde de la pensée architecturale, on constate comme toujours un délai naturel entre l'émergence d'une théorie et son apparition sous forme construite. L'exubérance du projet de Seibersdorf peut sembler de ce fait un peu décalée par rapport à l'époque, mais les architectes expliquent assez longuement leurs formes en termes d'activité de ce centre de recherche ou de juxtaposition de l'ancien et du nouveau. Pratiquement à toutes les périodes de l'histoire de l'architecture récente, il est vrai que des styles contradictoires ont coexisté.

L'agence allemande von Gerkan, Marg und Partner ne possède guère de points communs avec Coop Himmelb(l)au, que ce soit en termes de style, ou d'échelle de projets. Avec 200 collaborateurs environ, von Gerkan, Marg und Partner sont équipés pour prendre en main des réalisations aussi importantes que la nouvelle Foire de Leipzig (Leipzig, Allemagne, 1993–96) qu'ils viennent d'achever. Ville particulièrement prospère jusqu'à la Première Guerre mondiale, Leipzig a longtemps été le siège d'importantes foires internationales. Le Hall des machines-outils (21 000 m²) était le plus grand bâtiment de foire en Allemagne pour son époque. Celui de l'automobile, conçu par les architectes locaux Crämer & Petschler en 1928, avec une portée de 100 m et une longueur de 140 m sans la moindre colonne porteuse, a servi aux manifestations de masse nazies. Les des-

Von Gerkan, Marg und Partner, New Leipzig Fair, Leipzig, Germany, 1993–96. An aerial view and an interior image of the main hall give an idea of the dimensions of this project, and underline its connection to 19th century iron and glass architecture.

Von Gerkan, Marg und Partner, Neue Messe Leipzig, Deutschland, 1993–96. Ein Luftbild und eine Innenansicht der zentralen Glashalle vermitteln einen Eindruck von den Dimensionen dieses Projektes und verdeutlichen seine Beziehung zur Glas- und Stahlarchitektur des 19. Jahrhunderts.

Von Gerkan, Marg und Partner, Nouvelle Foire de Leipzig, Allemagne, 1993–96. La vue aérienne et l'intérieur du hall principal traduisent bien les dimensions de ce projet, et soulignent ses liens avec l'architecture de fer et de verre du XIXᵉ siècle.

Josef Paul Kleihues, Hamburger Bahnhof, Berlin, Germany, 1992–96. Only one of the two planned vaulted galleries, accompanying the existing railway station architecture, was actually built.

Josef Paul Kleihues, Hamburger Bahnhof, Berlin, Deutschland, 1992–96. Aus Kostengründen konnte bisher nur eine der beiden geplanten Ausstellungs-hallen, die den alten Bahnhof flankieren sollen, fertiggestellt werden.

Josef Paul Kleihues, Hamburger Bahnhof, Berlin, Allemagne, 1992–96. Seule l'une des deux galeries à verrières voûtées prévues a été pour l'instant construite, pour compléter la transformation en musée de cette ancienne gare.

much inscribed within a tradition. Although large glass volumes have remained a constant feature of contemporary architecture, particularly in atriums, the kind of referenced link to the past underlined by von Gerkan, Marg is something of an innovation in recent times. Such a design is undoubtedly economical, respectful of the history of its own genre, and practical for its purpose, which is to offer large spaces to trade fairs.

Still in Germany, Josef Paul Kleihues has recently completed a first phase of the renovation and expansion of the old Hamburger Bahnhof (Berlin, Germany, 1992–96). Built in 1846–47 as a railroad station linking Berlin and Hamburg, this structure is just to the east of the former line dividing East and West Berlin. Shut down in 1884 and transformed into a transportation and building museum (1904–06), the Hamburger Bahnhof suffered severe bomb damage during World War II. Placed off limits by the Allied Control Commission, the building was put under the control of the West Berlin Senate in 1984. Restored, it was used for a number of contemporary art shows, including the 1988 exhibition "Zeitlos" (Timeless). Josef Paul Kleihues won a restricted 1989 competition to convert the former station into a museum facility, which now houses the Erich Marx collection of contemporary art. Parallel to the original glass-covered concourse, the architect designed a pair of 80 meter long halls, but due to a lack of funds only the eastern gallery has thus far been built. Although it seems an almost ideal location for the works of Beuys, Kiefer, Twombly, Rauschenberg or Warhol that it houses today, Josef Paul Kleihues has placed great emphasis on what he calls the "Hamburger Bahnhof identity." In other words, while succeeding in translating the shapes of the past into a usable modern facility, he felt that it was essential to conserve the substance of the earlier incarnations of the architecture. It is interesting to note that Kleihues, who opted in his Chicago Museum of Contemporary Art for precisely the kind of neo-modernist austerity mentioned above, would here be so respectful of a more distant past. Both cases highlight a new quality of contemporary architecture, which might be simply called "humility" if it were not for the flamboyant personality of many of the "stars" of the profession.

größtes deutsches Ausstellungsgebäude ihrer Zeit. Die 1928 von den Leipziger Architekten Crämer & Petschler entworfene Automobilhalle besaß eine freie Spannweite von 100 m und eine säulenfreie Länge von 140 m und wurde von den Nationalsozialisten gern für Massenkundgebungen benutzt. Aufgrund der Zerstörungen des Zweiten Weltkriegs und der Unbeweglichkeit der sowjetischen Behörden mußte Leipzig seinen Platz als Messezentrum an Städte wie Hannover abgeben, das heute (mit 2,3 Millionen Messebesuchern 1995) über die größten Einrichtungen dieser Art verfügt. 1991 gewannen Gerkan, Marg und Partner den Wettbewerb für den Bau einer neuen Messe, zu dem die Stadt 14 Architektenteams eingeladen hatte. Ihre Halle ist 80 m breit, mit einem Scheitelpunkt von 30 m und einer Länge von 243 m. Obwohl diese Maße nicht an die Dimensionen der 1889 erbauten Galerie des Machines in Paris heranreichen (mit einer freien Spannweite von 115 m und einer säulenfreien Länge von 420 m), bestätigen die Architekten, daß ihr Leipziger Bauwerk »den genialen Entwurf der Galerie mit heutigen Konstruktionsmethoden beantwortet«. Tatsächlich erinnert die Neue Messe Leipzig an großartige Glasbauten der Vergangenheit, wie etwa Joseph Paxtons Crystal Palace. Obwohl sich dieser Komplex mit einer Ausstellungsfläche von 102 500 m² moderner Technologie bedient, steht sie unzweifelhaft im Einklang mit der Tradition – sowohl durch die Geschichte Leipzigs als auch der früherer Ausstellungshallen. Auch wenn große Baukörper aus Glas, vor allem als Atrium, zu den typischen Merkmalen der zeitgenössischen Architektur zählen, stellt diese von den Architekten bewußt unterstrichene Verbindung zur Vergangenheit in der heutigen Zeit eine Innovation dar. Ein derartiger Entwurf ist zweifellos ökonomisch, voller Respekt für die Geschichte des eigenen Genres und praktisch, da er seinen Zweck erfüllt – nämlich große Räume für Ausstellungen zur Verfügung zu stellen.

Ein anderer deutscher Architekt, Josef Paul Kleihues, stellte vor kurzem die Sanierung und Erweiterung des alten Hamburger Bahnhofs (Berlin, 1992–96) fertig. Der 1846–47 speziell für die Zugverbindung zwischen Berlin und Hamburg errichtete und 1884 wieder geschlossene Hamburger Bahnhof liegt auf einem

tructions de la fin de la Seconde Guerre mondiale, et l'immobilisme des autorités communistes firent perdre à Leipzig son rôle de centre de foires au profit de villes comme Hanovre qui possède aujourd'hui les plus vastes équipements d'Allemagne dans ce domaine et a reçu 2,3 millions de visiteurs en 1995. Lancé par la ville en 1991, le concours pour la construction des nouveaux bâtiments de la foire a vu la participation de quatorze architectes invités et la victoire de von Gerkan, Marg und Partner. Leur hall mesure 80 m de large pour une longueur de 243 m et une hauteur de 30 m de hauteur. Bien que ces chiffres n'égalent pas et de loin la portée libre de 115 m et la longueur sans colonne de 420 m de la Galerie des machines à Paris (1889), les architectes affirment que la construction de Leipzig «rappelle l'ingénieuse structure de la Galerie mais avec des méthodes de construction contemporaines.» Il est certain que la nouvelle Foire de Leipzig fait penser aux grands bâtiments de verre du passé, comme le Crystal Palace de Joseph Paxton. Bien que cet ensemble qui représente une surface d'exposition couverte de 102 500 m² ait fait appel aux technologies modernes, il manifeste par ses liens avec l'histoire de Leipzig et celle des halls d'exposition du passé son inscription dans une tradition déjà longue. Même si les grands volumes sous verrière appartiennent également à l'architecture de notre temps – particulièrement sous la forme d'atriums – la référence au passé soulignée par von Gerkan, Marg und Partner est une innovation récente. Un tel projet est certainement économique, respectueux de l'histoire à sa façon, et fonctionnel dans les vastes espaces qu'il offre à l'exposition.

Toujours en Allemagne, Josef Paul Kleihues vient de terminer la première phase de rénovation et d'extension de l'ancienne Hamburger Bahnhof – la gare de Hambourg – (Berlin, Allemagne, 1992–96). Construite en 1846–47 pour la liaison ferrée Berlin-Hambourg, elle se trouve juste à l'est de l'ancienne ligne de partage entre Berlin-Est et Berlin-Ouest. Fermée en 1884 et transformée en musée du transport et de la construction (1904–06), elle souffrit d'importants bombardements pendant la Seconde Guerre mondiale. Placée hors limites par la Commission de contrôle des forces alliées, elle fut rendue au Sénat de Berlin-

One of the largest combined renovation and construction jobs in recent years in western Europe was the project carried out by the Paris-based architects Reichen & Robert for the Nestlé Center (Noisiel, France, 1993–95). A 14 hectare complex including some 41,000 square meters in renovated buildings and 19,000 square meters of new offices and other facilities for about 1,800 people, the Nestlé Center was completed at a cost of 800 million French francs, of which about 620 million was for construction. Bernard Reichen and Philippe Robert have extensive experience in both renovation work and new construction. Their projects include the Halle Tony-Garnier (Lyon, France, 1988) and the Pavillon de l'Arsenal (Paris, France, 1988), both of which involved rehabilitation of old industrial-type buildings. They also built the American Museum in Giverny, France (1992). In Noisiel, located near Marne-la-Vallée just outside Paris, they faced a particularly challenging site, with a number of historic structures, including Jules Saulnier's Moulin (1865–72), which is a listed building (Monument historique). The former Menier Chocolate Factory, which by 1887 was producing twelve million kilograms of chocolate a year, was acquired by Nestlé in 1988 when they bought Rowntree-Mackintosh. They decided in 1993 to bring together their various French affiliates on this large site on the banks of the Marne river. The intervention of Reichen & Robert on the Noisiel site had to do with improving the coherence of the use of spaces not originally intended as offices, and with adding new buildings that would not disturb the underlying harmony of one of the most interesting 19th century industrial sites in Europe. Modern without being banal, the new buildings on the site blend in with their older neighbors through devices such as their ample public spaces and large glazed areas. No attempt is made to imitate the late 19th century industrial architecture of the Menier factory, but neither do the modern buildings on the site declare their independence from a tradition that was in effect their point of origin, both stylistically and historically speaking. Nestlé's original intention in calling on Reichen & Robert had been to convert the site for rental to other firms, but the architects succeeded in persuading them that they could move in themselves for much the

Gelände, das sich direkt östlich der ehemaligen Demarkationslinie zwischen Ost- und Westberlin befindet. Das Gebäude wurde zwischen 1904 und 1906 in ein Museum für Transport- und Bauwesen umgewandelt, während des Zweiten Weltkriegs stark beschädigt und von der Alliierten Kontrollkommission zum Sperrgebiet erklärt, bevor man es 1984 der Aufsicht des Westberliner Senats unterstellte. Nach seiner Restaurierung diente der Hamburger Bahnhof als Veranstaltungsort für verschiedene zeitgenössische Kunstausstellungen, u.a. für die Ausstellung »Zeitlos« (1988). 1989 gewann Josef Paul Kleihues eine geschlossene Ausschreibung für die Umwandlung des ehemaligen Bahnhofs in ein Museumsgebäude, das heute die Sammlung Erich Marx (mit zeitgenössischer Kunst) beherbergt. Parallel zu der ursprünglichen verglasten Bahnhofshalle entwarf der Architekt zwei je 80 m lange Galerien, von denen aus Kostengründen bisher nur die östliche fertiggestellt werden konnte. Obwohl es sich dabei um nahezu ideale Ausstellungsräume für die Werke von Beuys, Kiefer, Twombly, Rauschenberg und Warhol handelt, legte Kleihues großen Wert auf die »Identität des Hamburger Bahnhofs«. Mit anderen Worten: Während es ihm einerseits gelang, die Formen der Vergangenheit in moderne, nutzbare Räumlichkeiten zu übertragen, war er auch der Überzeugung, daß die Substanz der früheren Architektur erhalten bleiben müsse. Interessanterweise entschied sich Kleihues, der für sein Chicago Museum of Contemporary Art einen Entwurf im bereits oben erwähnten, neo-modernen, strengen Stil schuf, bei diesem Bauprojekt für einen respektvolleren Umgang mit einer weiter zurückliegenden Vergangenheit. Beide Beispiele zeugen von einer neuen Eigenschaft zeitgenössischer Architektur, die man schlicht als »Bescheidenheit« bezeichnen könnte, wären da nicht die schillernden Persönlichkeiten vieler »Stararchitekten«.

Eines der größten Sanierungs- und Neubauprojekte, das in den vergangenen Jahren in Westeuropa durchgeführt wurde, war die von den Pariser Architekten Reichen & Robert vorgenommene Umwandlung einer alten Schokoladenfabrik in das Nestlé-Zentrum (Noisiel, Frankreich, 1993–95). Auf einem 14 ha großen Gelände gelang es ihnen, einen Teil der alten Gebäude mit etwa

Ouest en 1984. Restaurée, elle servit à diverses expositions d'art contemporain dont la célèbre manifestation «Zeitlos» (Intemporel) de 1988. C'est en 1989 que Josef Paul Kleihues a remporté un concours restreint pour la conversion de ce bâtiment en un musée qui abrite aujourd'hui la collection Erich Marx d'art contemporain. Parallèlement à la verrière originale, l'architecte a imaginé deux halls de 80 m de long. Les restrictions budgétaires n'ont permis que d'en construire un pour l'instant. Bien que le lieu soit idéal pour les œuvres de Beuys, Kiefer, Twombly, Rauschenberg ou Warhol que contient la collection, l'architecte a décidé de mettre en valeur ce qu'il appelle «l'identité de la gare de Hambourg». En d'autres termes, tout en réussissant à adapter les formes du passé à un usage contemporain, il a senti qu'il était essentiel de conserver la substance des premières incarnations de cette architecture. Il est intéressant de noter que Kleihues, qui pour son Museum of Contemporary Art de Chicago a choisi l'austère néo-modernisme mentionné plus haut, s'est montré si respectueux d'un passé plus distant. Ces deux exemples soulignent une des nouvelles qualités de l'architecture contemporaine qui pourrait tout simplement s'appeler «humilité», s'il ne fallait compter avec la personnalité flamboyante de nombreuses «stars» de la profession.

L'un des plus importants chantiers de rénovation et de construction de ces dernières années en Europe occidentale est le projet mené à bien par les architectes parisiens Reichen & Robert pour le Centre Nestlé (Noisiel, France, 1993–95). Ce complexe de 14 ha qui accueille près de 1800 personnes comprend des bureaux et divers équipement sur 41 000 m² en rénovation et 19 000 m² en construction neuve. L'ensemble a été réalisé pour 800 millions de francs environ, dont 620 pour la construction. Bernard Reichen et Philippe Robert possèdent une vaste expérience aussi bien de la rénovation que de la construction. Parmi leurs projets réalisés figurent la Halle Tony Garnier (Lyon, France, 1988), et le Pavillon de l'Arsenal (Paris, 1988), tous deux des rénovations de bâtiments de type industriel. Ils ont également édifié le Musée Américain de Giverny (France, 1992). À Noisiel, près de Marne-la-Vallée dans la grande banlieue de Pa-

Reichen & Robert, Nestlé Center, Noisiel, France, 1993–95. One of the largest reconversions of existing industrial space carried out in recent years in Europe.

Reichen & Robert, Nestlé-Zentrum, Noisiel, Frankreich, 1993–95. Eine der größten Umwandlungen von Industriebauten, die in den vergangenen Jahren in Europa durchgeführt wurde.

Reichen & Robert, Centre Nestlé, Noisiel, France, 1993–95. L'une des plus importantes reconversions d'installations industrielles récemment achevées en Europe.

Reichen & Robert, Nestlé Center, Noisiel, France, 1993–95. The architects worked extensively on the covered passageways which link the various elements of the Nestlé complex.

Reichen & Robert, Nestlé-Zentrum, Noisiel, Frankreich, 1993–95. Die Architekten beschäftigten sich intensiv mit den glasüberdachten Passagen, die verschiedene Teile des Komplexes miteinander verbinden.

Reichen & Robert, Centre Nestlé, Noisiel, France, 1993–95. Les architectes ont particulièrement soigné les passages couverts qui relient les divers composants de ce vaste complexe.

same cost as a modern office building, and with a much more congenial working environment.

In this last instance, as in the preceding ones, the close link established between the architecture of the past and that of the present is apparent. Rather than the superficial pastiche so popular in the post-modern period, the tendency now is to recuperate old spaces, or to use traditional ideas because they permit savings or a higher degree of comfort than purely new structures. If some new designs bring to mind the modernist architecture of an earlier time, it is because it has now become legitimate for younger architects to cite modernism as one of their essential historical references. For their predecessors, the tabula rasa declared by such seminal figures as Walter Gropius left little room for such interest in the past, even recent.

From Adulation to Education

One of the most popular areas for architectural experimentation in the 1970s and 1980s was the museum. From Los Angeles to Tokyo new institutions sprang up, and others added on to their existing buildings at a rate that could not be maintained with the new austerity of the 1990s. Of course, by that time any city that thought highly enough of itself had a brand new Gehry, Hollein or Isozaki-designed temple of art. Naturally, museums continue to be built, and some like Frank O. Gehry's Guggenheim Bilbao promise to be every bit as exciting as the best of the previous wave. A demand for new places of worship and of education seems to be taking up some of the "slack" left by the reduction in museum construction.

One of the outstanding figures of European architecture, and indeed a seasoned builder of museums (San Francisco Museum of Modern Art) and churches (Évry Cathedral, France), is Lugano-based Mario Botta. Two of his recent commissions illustrate the breadth of his style, often assumed to be largely based on round brick structures. The more successful of these is on a relatively small scale, but then Botta's reputation was originally formed by his private houses in the Ticino area of Switzerland. The Monte Tamaro is located close to the highway linking

41 000 m² Grundfläche zu sanieren und neue Verwaltungsgebäude mit 19 000 m² Grundfläche sowie weitere Einrichtungen für etwa 1 800 Mitarbeiter zu schaffen. Die Gesamtkosten beliefen sich auf 800 Millionen Francs, von denen etwa 620 Millionen Francs auf Bauarbeiten entfielen. Neben der Umwandlung und Sanierung alter Industriebauten (wie etwa der Halle Tony Garnier in Lyon, 1988, oder des Pavillon de l'Arsenal, Paris, 1988) errichteten Reichen & Robert auch diverse Neubauten wie das American Museum in Giverny (Frankreich, 1992). In Noisiel, in der Nähe von Marne-la-Vallée am Rande von Paris, stießen sie auf eine besondere Herausforderung: das Gelände der ehemaligen Menier-Schokoladenfabrik, mit zahlreichen historischen Bauten – einschließlich Jules Saulniers »Moulin« (1865–72), einem denkmalgeschützten Bauwerk (Monument historique). Die Firma Nestlé hatte die frühere Schokoladenfabrik, die 1887 zwölf Millionen Kilogramm Schokolade im Jahr produzierte, 1988 bei der Übernahme von Rowntree-Mackintosh erworben. 1993 wurde beschlossen, alle französischen Tochtergesellschaften auf diesem großen Gelände am Ufer der Marne zusammenzubringen. Bei der Umwandlung des Geländes mußten Reichen & Robert einerseits den Zusammenhalt der ursprünglich nicht als Verwaltungsräume geplanten Gebäude verbessern und andererseits neue Bauten hinzufügen, ohne dabei die Harmonie eines der interessantesten europäischen Industriegelände des 19. Jahrhunderts zu zerstören. Ihre modernen Neubauten passen sich aufgrund verschiedener Elemente – wie etwa der großzügigen Freiflächen oder der großen Glasflächen – nahtlos an die älteren Nachbargebäude an. Dabei wurde weder der Versuch unternommen, die Industriearchitektur des späten 19. Jahrhunderts zu imitieren, noch distanzieren sich die neuen Gebäude auf dem Gelände von einer Tradition, der sie sowohl in stilistischer als auch in historischer Hinsicht selbst entspringen. Nestlé beauftragte Reichen & Robert ursprünglich mit der Umwandlung des Geländes, um es an andere Firmen zu vermieten, aber den Architekten gelang es, die Firmenführung davon zu überzeugen, selbst auf das Gelände zu ziehen – und zwar zum Preis eines modernen Bürogebäudes, aber mit einer besseren Arbeitsumgebung.

ris, ils se sont trouvé confrontés à un site particulièrement délicat, et à un certain nombre de bâtiments historiques, dont le moulin de Jules Saulnier (1865–72), classé monument historique. Cette ancienne chocolaterie Menier, qui, vers 1887, produisait 12 000 tonnes de chocolat par an avait été acquise par Nestlé en 1988 lors de son rachat de Rowntree-Mackintosh. La société suisse décida en 1993 de réunir ses différentes filiales françaises sur ce vaste emplacement en bordure de Marne. L'intervention de Reichen & Robert avait pour objectif d'améliorer la cohérence d'espaces qui n'avaient pas été prévus à l'origine pour des bureaux, et de les agrandir par des constructions nouvelles sans troubler l'harmonie de l'un des plus intéressants sites industriels du XIXᵉ siècle d'Europe. Modernes sans être banales, les nouvelles constructions se fondent aux anciennes par le biais, entre autres, de vastes espaces communs ou de grandes surfaces sous verrière. Les architectes n'ont pas tenté d'imiter l'architecture industrielle du siècle précédent, mais leurs bâtiments modernes n'en nient pas pour autant leur dépendance d'une tradition à laquelle ils doivent en effet leur origine à la fois stylistique et historique. L'intention originelle de Nestlé en faisant appel à Reichen & Robert était de louer ces installations à d'autres entreprises, mais les architectes ont su convaincre l'entreprise qu'elle pouvait s'y installer pour à peu près le même coût que dans un immeuble de bureaux moderne, tout en offrant un environnement de travail beaucoup plus convivial.

Dans ce dernier cas, comme dans les précédents, le lien étroit entre l'architecture du passé et celle d'aujourd'hui est évident. Plutôt que de s'abandonner aux pastiches superficiels si populaires lors la période postmoderniste, la tendance actuelle est à la récupération d'espaces existants, ou à faire appel à des concepts traditionnels qui permettent des solutions économiques ou un plus haut niveau de confort que des constructions intégralement modernes. Si certains projets rappellent l'architecture moderniste à ses débuts, c'est parce qu'il est aujourd'hui légitime pour les architectes des nouvelles générations de citer le modernisme parmi leurs références historiques essentielles. Pour leurs prédécesseurs, la tabula rasa réclamée par des per-

Bellinzona to Lugano. Indeed, the cable car rising up to the 2,000 meter peak passes directly over that route. It is more than a coincidence if Mario Botta's Chapel on the Monte Tamaro is located directly next to the restaurant and service facilities of the lift. The architect had been called on by the village of Mogno in the Valle Maggia to rebuild their Church of St. John the Baptist, destroyed by an avalanche on April 25, 1986. The local opposition that delayed this project led Egidio Cattaneo, owner of the lift at the Monte Tamaro, to propose that Botta's church be built there instead.

The final design for the Monte Tamaro is naturally quite different than that planned for Mogno, although the two share a truncated cone as a main feature. The strong form of the Chapel projects out toward the spectacular valley running from Lugano to Bellinzona, permitting visitors not only to admire the view but also to reflect on the relationship of the church itself to the power of nature. One of the outstanding features of the Chapel is its rusticated stone cladding. As Botta explains, "I worked a great deal on the stone, even considering at one point the possibility of using stone quarried on the mountain itself. This would have partially obviated the difficulties involved in hauling the cladding up from the valley below. But the stone was too fragile it broke too easily. Instead I chose to use porphyry, which is rich in iron, and extremely hard. It is like steel, and it cannot be used as though it were aluminum or butter! I instructed the workers to use it as simply and as humbly as they could, but also to obtain the strongest result possible."[3] Aside from its architecture, the Chapel on the Monte Tamaro is of interest as well because of the unusual collaboration that evolved between the architect and a painter, the Italian Enzo Cucchi. It was Botta who called on him to create frescoes within the existing architectural forms. Although the task was not simple, because the main space involved measures 70 by 2 meters, Cucchi succeeded in creating forms – two elongated cypress trees whose tips touch under the passage leading to the Chapel, and cupped hands behind the altar whose power is entirely appropriate to this location. As Botta says, since meeting Cucchi with his dealer Bruno Bischofsberger

Bei den hier vorgestellten Beispielen kommt die enge Verbindung zwischen der Architektur der Vergangenheit und der Gegenwart deutlich zum Ausdruck. Im Gegensatz zum oberflächlichen Pasticcio, das sich in der Postmoderne großer Beliebtheit erfreute, geht der Trend nun dahin, alte Bausubstanz zu reaktivieren oder auf traditionelle Ideen zurückzugreifen, da diese zur Einsparung von Kosten beitragen und mehr Komfort bieten als vollkommen neu errichtete Gebäude. Falls einige neue Entwürfe an die moderne Architektur einer früheren Zeit erinnern, liegt das daran, daß die heutigen jungen Architekten die Moderne mittlerweile als einen ihrer wichtigsten historischen Bezüge zitieren dürfen. Ihren Vorgängern ließ die Theorie des Tabula rasa, die von solch zukunftsweisenden Persönlichkeiten wie Walter Gropius deklariert wurde, wenig Raum für ein Interesse an der Vergangenheit, nicht einmal der jüngsten Vergangenheit.

Von der Anbetung zur Bildung

Einer der beliebtesten Bereiche architektonischer Experimentierfreude in den 70er und 80er Jahren war der Museumsbau. Von Los Angeles bis Tokio schossen neue Institutionen wie Pilze aus dem Boden, während andere Museen ihre Gebäude in einem Tempo erweiterten, das von der neuen Sparsamkeit der 90er Jahre nicht aufrechterhalten werden konnte. Zu dieser Zeit besaß jede Stadt, die etwas auf sich hielt, einen brandneuen, von Gehry, Hollein oder Isozaki entworfenen Kunsttempel. Dennoch werden auch heute noch Museen gebaut, und Projekte wie Frank O. Gehrys Guggenheim Museum in Bilbao versprechen, mindestens genau so interessant zu werden wie jeder Bau des vergangenen Booms. Die Nachfrage nach neuen Orten der Anbetung und der Bildung scheint ein wenig von der »Flaute« aufzufangen, die durch den Rückgang im Museumsbau entstand.

Eine der herausragenden Persönlichkeiten der europäischen Architektur und erfahrener Baumeister von Museen (San Francisco Museum of Modern Art) und Kirchen (Cathédrale d'Évry, Frankreich) ist der in Lugano ansässige Mario Botta. Zwei seiner aktuellen Bauten verdeutlichen die Bandbreite seines Stils, der bisher häufig nur mit runden Ziegelbauten assoziiert wurde. Das

sonnages aussi importants que Walter Gropius ne laissait que peu de place à un intérêt similaire pour le passé, même récent.

De l'adulation à l'éducation

Le musée a été le lieu d'expérimentation architecturale le plus prisé au cours des années 1970 et 1980. De Los Angeles à Tokyo, de nouvelles institutions ont fait leur apparition tandis que d'autres s'agrandissaient à un rythme qui ne pouvait prétendre se maintenir dans l'austérité économique des années 90. Toute ville un peu consciente de son importance s'est cependant déjà offert un de ces nouveaux temples de l'art signés Gehry, Hollein ou Isozaki. Naturellement de nouveaux musées continuent à s'édifier, et certains comme le Guggenheim de Bilbao dû à Frank O. Gehry promettent d'être aussi passionnants que les plus brillantes réalisations de la vague précédente. La demande de nouveaux lieux de prière et d'éducation semble compenser, au moins partiellement, la baisse de chiffre d'affaires des agences d'architecture provoquée par la rétraction des budgets de construction de musées.

Constructeur de musées (San Francisco Museum of Modern Art) et d'églises (cathédrale d'Évry, France), Mario Botta est l'une des grandes figures de l'architecture européenne. Son agence est installée à Lugano. Deux de ses chantiers récents illustrent la variété de son style, souvent associé à des structures cylindriques en brique. La plus réussie de ses dernières créations est de taille relativement réduite, ce qui nous rappelle que sa réputation vient à l'origine de quelques petites résidences privées qu'il avait construites dans le Tessin. Le Monte Tamaro domine l'autoroute qui relie Bellinzona à Lugano. La télécabine qui escalade ce sommet de 2 000 m d'altitude passe d'ailleurs au-dessus de cette voie. Ce n'est pas un hasard si la chapelle que Mario Botta vient d'élever au plus haut de cette montagne voisine avec le restaurant et la gare de cette remontée. En effet, le village de Mogno, dans la Valle Maggia, avait fait appel à l'architecte pour reconstruire l'église Saint Jean-Baptiste, détruite par une avalanche le 25 avril 1986. Le projet ayant été retardé par des oppositions locales, Egidio Cattaneo, propriétaire de la

Mario Botta, Tamaro Chapel, Ticino, Switzerland, 1990–96. In a spectacular setting between Bellinzona and Lugano, this mountain chapel reaffirms the link between contemporary architecture and more ancient forms in an innovative way.

Mario Botta, Tamaro-Kapelle, Tessin, Schweiz, 1990–96. Die in einer großartigen Umgebung zwischen Bellinzona und Lugano gelegene Kapelle am Monte Tamaro zeigt auf originelle Weise die Beziehungen zwischen zeitgenössischer Architektur und wesentlich älteren Bauformen.

Mario Botta, Chapelle du Mont Tamaro, Tessin, Suisse, 1990–96. Dans un site spectaculaire entre Bellinzona et Lugano, cette chapelle de montagne réaffirme de façon novatrice le lien entre l'architecture contemporaine et les formes anciennes.

Mario Botta, Tinguely Museum, Basel, Switzerland, 1993–96. Seen from the opposite side of the Rhine, the new museum has a long, slightly curved access ramp, which looks out onto the river.

Mario Botta, Tinguely-Museum, Basel, Schweiz, 1993–96. Von der gegenüberliegenden Rheinseite aus sieht man die lange Eingangsrampe des neuen Museums, die den Besuchern einen Blick auf den Fluß ermöglicht.

Mario Botta, Musée Tinguely, Bâle, Suisse, 1993–96. Vue de l'autre rive du Rhin. On accède à ce nouveau musée par une longue rampe d'accès couverte et légèrement incurvée, en bordure du fleuve.

some years before, he had looked for occasions to collaborate with the painter. "I thought it would be good to work on the Monte Tamaro with a 'primitive' artist, one capable of avoiding the risks of mere decoration. You cannot go to the mountain in a chapel of this strength and simply decorate it. I think that Enzo understood that, and that he made a powerful gesture. He wanted to create a symbolic work, to carve into the wall itself. That is how we were able to collaborate on this project."[4]

Botta's second recent project in Switzerland may have posed more complex problems than the Monte Tamaro Chapel. Indeed, his new Tinguely Museum in Basel, built on the grounds of the pharmaceuticals giant F. Hoffmann-La Roche did not have a particularly favorable location. Directly next to the rail and highway lines connecting Basel to Bern, the museum also faces a particularly busy and wide avenue. The other two facades, on the Rhein and the small park of the Hoffmann-La Roche complex, seem more favorably situated, and it is no accident that the openings of the museum are in these directions, while Botta has chosen to block views toward the more urban surroundings. With its cladding of pink Champenay sandstone and its fortress-like volume, this institution does not at first seem well adjusted to the ephemeral or rather fragile nature of Jean Tinguely's sculptures. The main exhibition area on the ground floor, for example, is strongly articulated by very large overhanging beams. Indeed the nature of these beams was related to a peculiarity of the site. The museum was built over an underground water storage tank, and the beams carry the weight of the building over this invisible obstruction. The somewhat restricted configuration of the underground display rooms was also influenced by the water storage tank. Be that as it may, Botta explains that his intention was to create not a harmony, but rather a contrast with the work to be displayed. Where Tinguely's sculptures are almost haphazard assemblages of found materials like scrap metal, the museum is distinguished by its gray-stained oak floors, and walls in white plaster or Venetian black stucco. Simplicity is the byword, but in this instance, the simplicity seems to lapse on occasion into an inappropriate heaviness. In architectural terms, the long curving

erfolgreichere der beiden Projekte wurde in relativ kleinem Maß-stab ausgeführt – aber Botta begründete seinen Ruf ursprünglich mit seinen Privathäusern im Schweizer Tessin. Der Monte Tamaro liegt in unmittelbarer Nähe der Autobahnverbindung von Bellinzona nach Lugano; die Seilbahn zu diesem 2000 m hohen Gipfel verläuft quer über dieser Schnellstraße. Dabei ist es kein Zufall, daß Mario Bottas Kapelle auf dem Monte Tamaro unmittelbar neben dem Restaurant und den Serviceeinrichtungen des Lifts zu liegen kam: Der Architekt wurde von dem Dorf Mogno im Maggia-Tal mit dem Wiederaufbau der Kirche des heiligen Johannes beauftragt, die am 25. April 1986 von einem Erdrutsch zerstört worden war. Aber Egidio Cattaneo, der Führer der lokalen Opposition, die dieses Projekt erfolgreich verzögerte, ist zugleich Liftbesitzer am Monte Tamaro; er schlug vor, daß Bottas Kirche auf dem Berg entstehen sollte.

Der endgültige Entwurf für die Kapelle auf dem Monte Tamaro unterschied sich natürlich erheblich von Bottas Plänen für Mogno, obwohl beide von einem stumpfen Kegel als Grundform ausgingen. Die kraftvollen Formen der Kapelle überragen das imposante Tal zwischen Lugano und Bellinzona und bringen den Besucher nicht nur dazu, den großartigen Ausblick zu bewundern, sondern auch über die Beziehung des Kirchenbaus zu den Naturkräften zu philosophieren. Zu den besonderen Merkmalen der Kapelle gehören ihre Außenmauern aus Bossenquadern. Botta sagt dazu: »Ich habe mich lange mit der Wahl des Steines beschäftigt und sogar darüber nachgedacht, ob ich nicht Stein aus dem Berg selbst abbauen und verwenden sollte. Das hätte zumindest teilweise die Schwierigkeiten beseitigt, die wir beim Transport der Verkleidung aus dem Tal herauf hatten. Aber dieser Stein war zu zerbrechlich. Statt dessen entschied ich mich für Porphyr, der besonders hart und eisenhaltig ist. Dieser Stein wirkt wie Stahl und kann nicht einfach wie Aluminium oder Butter verwendet werden! Ich sagte den Arbeitern, sie sollten den Stein so einfach und anspruchslos wie möglich verarbeiten und nur auf ein besonders stabiles Resultat Wert legen.«[3] Die Kapelle auf dem Monte Tamaro ist aber nicht nur aufgrund ihrer Architektur interessant, sondern auch wegen der ungewöhnlichen

télécabine du Monte Tamaro proposa que l'église de Botta soit construite à cet endroit.

Le projet final de Monte Tamaro est naturellement assez différent de celui prévu pour Mogno, bien que tous deux aient adopté la forme du cylindre tronqué. La masse puissante de la chapelle se projette spectaculairement vers la vallée, permettant aux visiteurs non seulement d'admirer la vue mais de méditer sur les relations entre l'église et son environnement naturel. L'un des aspects remarquables de la construction est le rusticage de la pierre de parement. Comme l'explique Botta: «J'ai beaucoup réfléchi au problème de cette pierre, au point même d'envisager d'utiliser celle qui se trouvait sur le site lui-même, ce qui aurait en partie réglé les difficultés d'avoir à tout monter de la vallée. Mais elle était trop fragile, se brisait trop facilement. J'ai préféré utiliser un porphyre, riche en fer, et extrêmement dur. Il est aussi dur que l'acier, et ne peut certainement pas se traiter comme de l'aluminium ou du beurre! J'ai demandé aux maçons de le travailler aussi simplement et aussi humblement que possible, mais de tenter d'obtenir le résultat le plus fort possible.»[3] En dehors de son architecture, la chapelle du Monte Tamaro est également intéressante pour la collaboration inhabituelle qu'elle illustre entre un architecte et un peintre, en l'occurrence Enzo Cucchi. C'est Botta lui-même qui a fait appel à cet artiste pour créer les fresques qui se déploient sur son architecture. La tâche n'était pas aisée, en particulier parce que l'espace le plus difficile à traiter mesurait 70 x 2 m, mais Cucchi a réussi à créer des formes – deux cyprès allongés dont les sommets se rejoignent sous le passage menant à la chapelle, et des mains réunies en un geste de prière derrière l'autel – dont la force semble appropriée à la rigueur du lieu. Botta avait envie de collaborer avec cet artiste depuis sa rencontre avec celui-ci et son marchand Bruno Bischofsberger quelques années auparavant. «Je pensais qu'il serait bien de travailler à Monte Tamaro avec un artiste «primitif», capable d'éviter le risque de la simple décoration. On ne peut aller dans la montagne, dans une chapelle de cette force et de cette simplicité et simplement la décorer. Je pense qu'Enzo l'a compris, et qu'il a réalisé ici un geste plein de force. Il a voulu

passage overhanging the Rhine through which visitors enter the museum, and which the architect calls "La Barca", is the most spectacular and successful gesture to be seen here. The result of unusual generosity on the part of Hoffmann-La Roche, and on the part of Tinguely's widow Niki de Saint Phalle who gave most of the works, this new Basel museum is an exception that goes to prove that museum construction has now become a much more rarefied and exceptional kind of project. For governments often under severe fiscal pressure, it is no longer deemed responsible to invest considerable sums in museums, no matter how much they may generate in the long run in tourism and other ancillary revenue.

One of the most active architects in the world, Sir Norman Foster, whose current projects include the new Hong Kong airport and the renovation of the British Museum and the Reichstag, recently completed an exceptional teaching facility on the Sidgwick site of Cambridge University. His Faculty of Law building is unusual because of the great care taken to fit the new structure into a rich environment of modern buildings. Indeed, here Foster's Law building is located just a few meters from James Stirling's 1967 History Faculty to the west, and north of Hugh Casson's 1950s Selwyn College. By rearranging the ground levels around the neighboring structures in a respectful manner, Foster has created a continuity echoed in the very design of his building, for example in the reconstituted Portland stone facade opposite Casson's edifice. Distinguished by its long curving glass north facade, the Faculty of Law is also exceptional in its particularly energy-efficient design, permitting the use of a minimum amount of air conditioning in the lecture rooms below grade. Under contractual obligation to create a building with a minumum life-span of fifty years, Foster shows the face of a new modernity in Cambridge, which is capable of respecting both the environment and neighboring architecture, be it traditional or more recent.

A much more unusual teaching facility is Zvi Hecker's Heinz-Galinski School in Berlin. Born in 1931 in Poland, Hecker grew up in Samarkand and Krakow before moving to Israel in 1950.

Zusammenarbeit zwischen einem Architekten und einem Maler, dem Italiener Enzo Cucchi. Botta selbst beauftragte Cucchi, Fresken in die bestehenden architektonischen Formen zu integrieren. Obwohl diese Aufgabe nicht einfach war, vor allem, weil der auszumalende Raum 70 x 2 m mißt, gelang es Cucchi, passende Formen zu entwerfen – zwei spitz zulaufende Zypressen, deren Spitzen sich unter der zur Kapelle führenden Passage berühren, und eine Darstellung zweier geöffneter Hände hinter dem Altar, deren kraftvolle Ausstrahlung diesem Ort angemessen ist. Seit Botta vor einigen Jahren Cucchi und dessen Kunsthändler Bruno Bischofsberger begegnet war, suchte er nach einer Möglichkeit zur Zusammenarbeit mit diesem Künstler. »Ich dachte, es wäre passend, am Monte Tamaro mit einem ›primitiven‹ Künstler zu arbeiten, der in der Lage war, das Risiko einer reinen Dekoration zu vermeiden. Man kann nicht in die Berge gehen, eine Kapelle von dieser Kraft betreten und sie einfach nur dekorieren. Ich glaube, daß Enzo dies verstand und darum eine kraftvolle Arbeit schuf. Er wollte eine symbolische Darstellung entwerfen und sie in die Mauern meißeln. Auf diese Weise konnten wir an diesem Projekt zusammenarbeiten.«[4]

Bottas zweites aktuelles Bauwerk in der Schweiz dürfte größere Schwierigkeiten bereitet haben als der Bau der Tamaro-Kapelle – unter anderem deshalb, weil sein neues Tinguely-Museum in Basel, das auf dem Grund und Boden des Pharma-Giganten Hoffmann-La Roche entstand, nicht auf einem derart günstigen Baugelände erbaut werden konnte. Das Museum liegt nicht nur unmittelbar neben der Bahnstrecke und der Autobahn Basel–Bern, sondern darüber hinaus an einer vielbefahrenen breiten Straße. Die anderen beiden Seiten, in Richtung Rhein bzw. eines kleinen Parks des Hoffmann-La Roche-Geländes, wirken wesentlich attraktiver; daher ist es kein Wunder, daß die Öffnungen des Museums hauptsächlich in diese Richtungen weisen, während Botta den Ausblick auf die urbaneren beiden Seiten bewußt blockierte. Auf den ersten Blick scheint dieses Museum, mit seiner Verkleidung aus rosa Champenay-Sandstein und seinem festungsähnlichen Baukörper, für Jean Tinguelys ephemere, zerbrechlich wirkende Skulpturen kaum geeignet zu

créer une œuvre symbolique, qui s'intègre au mur lui-même. C'est ainsi que nous avons pu collaborer sur ce projet.»[4]

Le second projet suisse récent de Botta a sans doute posé des problèmes plus complexes que la chapelle du Monte Tamaro. Le nouveau musée Tinguely, à Bâle, construit sur les terrains d'un géant de l'industrie pharmaceutique, Hoffmann-La Roche, ne bénéficiait pas d'un site particulièrement favorable. À proximité directe de l'autoroute et des voies de chemin de fer Bâle-Berne, il donne également sur une grande avenue très fréquentée. Les deux autres façades, sur le Rhin et le petit parc du complexe Hoffman-La Roche, semblent mieux orientées, et ce n'est pas par hasard que les ouvertures du musée donnent dans ces directions, ni que Botta a décidé de clore la vue vers l'environnement plus urbain. Avec son parement en calcaire rose de Champenay et ses volumes de chateau fort, cette nouvelle institution ne semble à première vue guère en harmonie avec la nature assez fragile des sculptures de Jean Tinguely. Le principal espace d'exposition du rez-de-chaussée, par exemple, est fortement marqué par de lourdes poutres en porte-à-faux, dont la raison tient à l'une des contraintes du site. Le musée a été construit au-dessus d'un réservoir d'eau souterrain, et les poutres supportent le poids du bâtiment au dessus de cet obstacle invisible. Ceci dit, Botta explique que son intention n'était pas de créer une harmonie, mais plutôt un contrepoint avec les œuvres exposées. Alors que les œuvres de Tinguely sont des assemblages de matériaux trouvés, le musée fait appel à des sols en chêne teinté gris et des murs en plâtre blanc ou en stuc vénitien noir. La simplicité est de règle, mais semble ici parfois tomber dans une lourdeur peu appropriée. En termes architecturaux, le long passage en courbe dominant le Rhin et à travers lequel les visiteurs pénètrent dans le musée et que l'architecte appelle «la barca», est le geste le plus spectaculaire et le plus réussi. Fruit de la grande générosité du groupe Hoffman-La Roche et de Niki de Saint Phalle, veuve du sculpteur qui a fait don de la plupart des œuvres, ce nouveau musée bâlois est une exception qui illustre que la construction de musées s'est raréfiée et relève aujourd'hui des projets exceptionnels. Pour des gouvernements, soumis à la pression sévère

Sir Norman Foster, Faculty of Law, University of Cambridge, Cambridge, Great Britain, 1993–95. Inside the Squire Law Library, the long, curved glass facade gives users a view out onto the neighboring park.

Sir Norman Foster, Faculty of Law, University of Cambridge, Cambridge, Großbritannien, 1993–95. Durch die langgestreckte, geschwungene Glasfassade bietet sich den Benutzern der Squire Law Library ein Ausblick auf den benachbarten Park.

Sir Norman Foster, Faculté de droit, Université de Cambridge, Cambridge, Grande-Bretagne, 1993–95. Vue de l'intérieur de la Squire Law Library, la longue façade courbe en verre donne sur un parc.

Zvi Hecker, Heinz-Galinski-School, Berlin, Germany, 1992–95. An original composition, based on the form of the sunflower, brings to mind a fragmentation that is typical of the so-called deconstructivist architects.

Zvi Hecker, Heinz-Galinski-Schule, Berlin, Deutschland, 1992–95. Der auf der Form einer Sonnenblume basierende Entwurf erinnert in seiner »Zerstückelung« an typische Bauten der dekonstruktivistischen Architektur.

Zvi Hecker, école Heinz-Galinski, Berlin, Allemagne, 1992–95. Inspirée de la forme d'un tournesol, cette composition originale rappelle la fragmentation typique des architectes déconstructivistes.

He studied architecture at Krakow Polytechnic (1949–50) and the Technion, Israel Institute of Technology, in Haifa (1950–54), where he obtained a degree in engineering and architecture in 1955. He also studied painting at the Avni Academy of Art in Tel Aviv (1955–57). Named after Heinz Galinski, who was long the chairman of the Jewish community in Berlin, this new school is further proof of the architect's fascination with the forms of nature. His crystalline Aeronautic Laboratory on the Technion campus in Haifa (1963–66), the "Sunflower" commercial and residential center in Ramat Hasharon, Israel (1964–90) and the Spiral Apartment building he completed in Ramat Gan, Israel in 1990 all showed this tendency, but the school in Berlin is a particularly complex example of Hecker's interest in the shape of the sunflower. He relates this complexity to that of the city itself. As he says, "The school in Berlin is a city within a city. Its streets meet at squares and the squares become courtyards. The walls of the school house the school, but they also build walkways, passages and cul-de-sacs. The outside of the school is also the inside of the city, because the school is the city."[5] Like such figures as Frank O. Gehry, Zvi Hecker may be influenced by architects like Erich Mendelsohn, and although his complex, fractured forms may seem more in the style of 1980s deconstructivism than they are in the neo-modernist trend of the 1990s, his work, like the lightening bolt shape of Daniel Libeskind's Jewish Museum (Berlin, Germany), continues to be of current interest, particularly because it is based on historical reasoning, elaborat-

sein. So ist beispielsweise die Hauptausstellungsfläche im Erdgeschoß deutlich durch sehr große, auskragende Träger untergliedert – ein bauliches Detail, das sich allerdings durch eine Besonderheit des Baugeländes erklärt: Das Museum wurde über einem unterirdischen Wassertank errichtet, und die Träger stützen das Gewicht des Gebäudes über dieser unsichtbaren Konstruktion. Die etwas eingeschränkte Struktur der unterirdischen Ausstellungsräume erklärt sich ebenfalls durch den unterirdischen Tank. Botta erklärt, daß er ein Gebäude schaffen wollte, das nicht in Harmonie, sondern in Kontrast zu den ausgestellten Stücken steht. Während Tinguelys Skulpturen fast wie willkürliche Ansammlungen zufällig gefundener Materialien wirken, wird der Museumsbau von grau gebeizten Eichenböden und Wänden aus weißem Gips oder venezianischem schwarzem Stuck dominiert. Schlichtheit ist das Motto – aber in diesem Fall scheint diese Schlichtheit gelegentlich in eine unangebrachte Massigkeit zu entgleisen. In architektonischer Hinsicht ist die lange, geschwungene, über den Rhein auskragende Rampe, durch die der Besucher das Museum betritt und die der Architekt als »La Barca« bezeichnet, das beeindruckendste und gelungenste Detail des Entwurfs. Das neue Basler Museum, das durch die ungewöhnliche Großzügigkeit der Firma Hoffmann-La Roche und der Witwe Tinguelys, Niki de Saint Phalle, entstehen konnte, die einen Großteil der Exponate zur Verfügung stellte, kann als Ausnahme der Regel gelten, daß Museumsbauten in der heutigen Zeit selten und außergewöhnlich geworden sind. Für viele Regierungen, die sich nicht selten starkem steuerlichen Druck ausgesetzt sehen, gilt es als geradezu unverantwortlich, bedeutende Summen in Museen zu investieren – egal, ob solche Bauten langfristig den Tourismus ankurbeln oder zusätzliche steuerliche Einnahmen bringen könnten.

Sir Norman Foster, einer der meistbeschäftigten Architekten der Welt, zu dessen aktuellen Aufträgen der neue Flughafen von Hongkong, die Umgestaltung des British Museum und der Umbau des Reichstags in Berlin zählen, beendete vor kurzem auf dem Sidgwick-Campus der Universität Cambridge den Bau einer Lehreinrichtung. Ungewöhnlich an Fosters Faculty of Law

des contribuables, il ne semble plus désormais possible d'investir des sommes considérables dans des institutions muséales, quel que soit leur intérêt à long terme pour le tourisme et leurs revenus dérivés.

L'un des architectes les plus actifs du monde, Sir Norman Foster, dont les projets actuels comptent parmi eux le nouvel aéroport de Hongkong, la rénovation du British Museum et celle du Reichstag, vient d'achever un bâtiment universitaire exceptionnel sur le site de Sidgwick, pour l'Université de Cambridge. Cette faculté de droit est inhabituelle du fait du grand soin mis à l'intégrer dans son riche environnement de bâtiments modernes. Elle s'élève en effet à quelques mètres seulement de la faculté d'histoire de James Stirling (1967), à l'ouest, et du Selwyn College de Hugh Casson, au nord (années 50). En réaménageant avec respect les terrassements autour de ces voisins, Foster a créé une continuité qui fait écho à la conception même de son bâtiment, par exemple dans une façade en pierre de Portland reconstituée qui fait face à l'immeuble de Casson. Remarquable par sa longue façade nord courbe en verre, cette faculté est également exceptionnelle pour sa conception écologique qui permet de limiter le recours à l'air conditionné aux salles de lecture en sous-sol. Obligé par contrat de concevoir un immeuble dont la durée de vie soit de cinquante ans minimum, Foster affiche à Cambridge une modernité nouvelle capable de respecter à la fois l'environnement et l'architecture environnante, qu'elle soit traditionnelle ou plus récente.

Beaucoup plus inhabituelle est l'école Heinz-Galinski construite par Zvi Hecker à Berlin. Né en 1931 en Pologne, Hecker a grandi à Samarcande et Cracovie avant d'émigrer en Israël en 1950. Il a étudié l'architecture à l'École polytechnique de Cracovie (1949–50), au Technion, l'Institut Israélien de Technologie d'Haifa (1950–54) où il obtient un diplôme d'ingénierie et d'architecture en 1955. Il étudie également la peinture à l'Académie d'art Avni de Tel Aviv (1955–57). Portant le nom de Heinz Galinski longtemps président de la communauté juive de Berlin, cette nouvelle école est une preuve supplémentaire de la fascination de l'architecte pour les formes de la nature. Son cristallin laboratoire d'aéronautique du

Philippe Starck, Le Baron Vert, Osaka, Japan, 1990–92.
The rear of Starck's unusual monolithic structure faces
a cemetery, whose block-like monuments undoubtedly
influenced the French designer.

Philippe Starck, Le Baron Vert, Osaka, Japan, 1990–92.
Die Rückseite von Starcks ungewöhnlichem monoli-
thischen Bauwerk grenzt an einen Friedhof, dessen block-
artige Monumente den französischen Designer sicherlich
in seinem Entwurf beeinflußten.

Philippe Starck, Le Baron Vert, Osaka, Japon, 1990–92.
La façade arrière de ce monolithe donne sur un cimetière
dont les tombes massives ont probablement influencé le
designer français.

ed through the shapes of the natural world. These factors give
such architecture a legitimacy which it would lack if it were mere-
ly the result of formal experimentation.

Monolithic Modern

A 1996 exhibition at the Heinz Architectural Center of the
Carnegie Museum of Art in Pittsburgh focused attention on
"Monolithic Architecture." The point made by the exhibition
organizers, Rodolfo Machado and Rodolphe el-Khoury is that
many new buildings, imagined by such international figures as
Peter Eisenman, Rem Koolhaas, Rafael Moneo, Jean Nouvel or
Philippe Starck call on monolithic shapes which have been facili-
tated by the emergence of new design and construction techniques. Starck's unusual Baron Vert building in Osaka with its
slit windows, echoing paintings by the Italian artist Fontana is
situated next to a graveyard. Were the building itself not a metallic
green, its shape might call to mind those of the tombstones.
Indeed, Starck's Baron Vert seems like no other architecture
which has preceded it. Its mass seems more akin to that of an
object than to any traditional idea of the building, a fact which
may have to do with Starck's background in design.

A number of contemporary buildings can be grouped under
the heading of the monolith for differing, often contradictory reasons. What they share is an appearance of self-sufficiency, like
cities or world's unto themselves. The English architect Sir
Norman Foster has long nurtured the idea of towers which
might be large enough to form independent communities in
which residential and business functions would be mixed. His
most ambitious design of this type was the so-called Millennium
Tower (Tokyo, Japan, 1989). Frank Lloyd Wright imagined a tower
1 mile high, but Foster took the concept of the ultra tall building
a step further by actually delving into the formidable design
problems posed by a 170-story, 840 meter high tower to be built
in the Bay of Tokyo. With an estimated cost of £10 billion and
an impressive area of 1,039,206 square meters, the Millennium
Tower was a victim of the bursting of the real estate "bubble" in
Japan, but Foster maintains that he still hopes to construct some

ist vor allem die große Sorgfalt, mit der dieser Neubau in die vielschichtige Umgebung berühmter moderner Bauten eingepaßt wurde: Das neue Gebäude liegt nur wenige Meter östlich von James Stirlings History Faculty Library (1967) und südlich von Hugh Cassons 1950 entstandenem Selwyn College. Indem er die unterschiedlichen Bodenniveaus rund um die benachbarten Bauwerke auf respektvolle Weise anpaßte, schuf Foster eine Kontinuität, die sich auch im Entwurf seines Gebäudes wiederfindet, z.B. in der restaurierten Portland-Steinfassade gegenüber von Cassons Monumentalbau. Darüber hinaus zeichnet sich die neue Faculty of Law – deren auffälligstes Merkmal die langgestreckte, gewölbte Glasfassade gen Norden ist – durch ihren energiesparenden Entwurf aus, der es ermöglichte, nur die unterirdischen Hörsäle mit einer Klimaanlage auszustatten. Foster, der vertraglich zum Bau eines Gebäudes mit einer minimalen Lebensdauer von fünfzig Jahren verpflichtet wurde, zeigt mit diesem Gebäude das Gesicht einer neuen Moderne, die in der Lage ist, nicht nur der Umwelt, sondern auch der benachbarten Architektur – ob traditionell oder eher zeitgenössisch – mit Respekt zu begegnen.

Eine noch ungewöhnlichere Lehranstalt ist Zvi Heckers Heinz-Galinski-Schule in Berlin. Hecker, 1931 in Polen geboren, wuchs in Samarkand und Krakau auf, bevor er 1950 nach Israel ging. Er studierte Architektur an der Polytechnischen Universität Krakau (1949–50) und am Technion, Israel Institute of Technology, in Haifa (1950–54), wo er 1955 sein Diplom für Ingenieurbau und Architektur erhielt. Daneben studierte er von 1955–57 Malerei an der Avni Academy of Art, Tel Aviv. Die nach Heinz Galinski, dem langjährigen Vorsitzenden der Jüdischen Gemeinde Berlins, benannte Schule ist ein weiterer Beweis für die große Faszination, die die Formensprache der Natur auf Hecker ausübt. Schon sein kristallines Aeronautic Laboratory auf dem Technion Campus in Haifa (1963–66), das »Sunflower« Wohn- und Geschäftszentrum in Ramat Hasharon, Israel (1964–90) oder das Spiral-Apartmenthaus, das er 1990 in Ramat Gan, Israel, fertigstellte, zeugen von dieser Tendenz, aber das Berliner Schulgebäude kann als besonders komplexes Beispiel für sein Interesse an der Form der Son-

campus du Technion d'Haifa (1963–66), le centre commercial et résidentiel «Tournesol» de Ramat Hasharon, Israël (1964–90), ou l'immeuble d'appartements «Spiral» achevé à Ramat Gan, Israël, en 1990, illustrent tous cette tendance, mais l'école de Berlin est un exemple particulièrement complexe de son intérêt pour la forme du tournesol. Il relie cette complexité à celle de la ville, précisant: «L'école de Berlin est une ville dans la ville. Ses rues se croisent dans des places, et les places se transforment en cours. Les murs de l'école abritent l'école, mais déterminent également des cheminements, des passages, des impasses. L'extérieur de l'école est également l'intérieur de la ville, parce que l'école est la ville.»[5] Comme Frank O. Gehry, Zvi Hecker est peut-être influencé par des architectes comme Erich Mendelsohn, et bien que ses formes complexes et fracturées puissent sembler plus proches du déconstructivisme des années 80 que du néo-modernisme des années 90, son œuvre, comme la forme en éclair du Musée juif de Daniel Libeskind à Berlin n'en manque pas moins d'intérêt pour autant, en particulier parce qu'elle repose sur une réflexion historique passant par les formes de l'univers naturel. Ces facteurs donnent à cette architecture une légitimité dont elle manquerait si elle ne résultait que d'une expérimentation formelle.

Monolithisme moderne

En 1996, une exposition du Heinz Architectural Center du Carnegie Museum of Art de Pittsburgh a attiré l'attention sur ce qu'elle appelait la «Monolithic Architecture.» L'idée de ses organisateurs, Rodolfo Machado et Rodolphe el-Khoury, était que de nombreux immeubles récents imaginés par des créateurs d'origine aussi diverses que Peter Eisenman, Rem Koolhaas, Rafael Moneo, Jean Nouvel ou Philippe Starck faisaient appel à des formes monolithiques dont la mise en œuvre était facilitée par de nouvelles techniques de conception et de construction.
Le curieux immeuble «Baron vert» de Starck à Osaka avec ses fenêtres en fente, qui évoquent les œuvres du peintre italien Fontana, se trouve non loin d'un cimetière. Si l'immeuble n'était pas vert métallisé, sa forme pourrait rappeler celle d'une pierre

version of the building. It may now be more likely that another massive Foster-designed tower will take shape before the Tokyo project. The London Millennium Tower, announced at a press conference on September 9, 1996, would be a ninety-five-story 435 meter high office tower on the site of the Baltic Exchange, which was badly damaged by an IRA bomb in 1992. It would include office space as well as twelve levels of apartments in its north wing and seven in the south.

The spectacular rise of office towers in the Far East has undoubtedly revived the idea of the very tall building, thought some years ago to be an outmoded concept. Foster is just one of the architects favorable to such designs, with figures like Cesar Pelli, the author of the record-breaking 452 meter Petronas Twin Towers in Kuala Lumpur leading the way. Foster maintains that very tall buildings can be made to be energy efficient, and even argues that if they include residential units they might even reduce street-level traffic flow. This affirmation naturally requires that many people would live and work in the same structure, an assumption that current circumstances do not justify. Just as Frankfurt was quite proud to complete another Foster-designed tower (Commerzbank), which is currently the tallest office building in Europe, so the English architect maintains that London as a great financial center "must" regain the skyscraper title. This sort of reasoning guarantees that tall buildings will indeed remain on the architectural scene for some time to come.

Monolithic forms in contemporary design can take on very different appearances in other circumstances. Herman Hertzberger's Chassé Theater (Breda, The Netherlands, 1992–95), makes use of a curving roof to unite fundamentally disparate elements. Both the theater's site and the chaotic nature of the design and building process obliged the architect to seek unity in this overriding gesture. As Hertzberger has said, "The flytowers (large-scale theater towers) are the most prominent elements of the theater in both visual and urban terms, their chunky forms threatening to completely dominate the view toward the town. This gave rise to the idea of oversailing the entire conglomeration of spaces and masses, derived as this was from practical rather

nenblume gelten. Er vergleicht diese Vielschichtigkeit mit dem Bild einer Stadt. Hecker sagt: »Die Schule in Berlin ist eine Stadt in der Stadt. Ihre Straßen begegnen sich auf Plätzen, und die Plätze werden zu Hinterhöfen. Die Wände der Schule beherbergen die Schule, aber sie formen auch Passagen und Sackgassen. Das Äußere dieser Schule ist zugleich das Innere der Stadt, denn die Schule ist die Stadt.«[5] Wie auch Frank O. Gehry dürfte Zvi Hecker von Architekten wie Erich Mendelsohn beeinflußt worden sein; aber obwohl seine komplexen, gebrochenen Formen mehr an den Dekonstruktivismus der 80er als an die neomodernen Trends der 90er Jahre erinnern, sind seine Arbeiten – ebenso wie Daniel Libeskinds blitzförmiger Entwurf für das Jüdische Museum in Berlin – von aktueller Bedeutung. Dies gilt vor allem deshalb, weil sie auf einer historischen Argumentation beruhen und durch die Formen der Natur verfeinert wurden. Diese Faktoren verleihen einer derartigen Architektur eine Legitimität, die sie nicht besäße, wenn es sich nur um das Resultat formaler Experimentierfreude handeln würde.

Monolithische Moderne
Eine 1996 im Heinz Architectural Center des Carnegie Museum of Art in Pittsburgh stattfindende Ausstellung trug den Titel »Monolithic Architecture« (Monolithische Architektur). Damit wollten die Organisatoren der Ausstellung, Rodolfo Machado und Rodolphe el-Khoury, ihrer Ansicht Ausdruck verleihen, daß viele neue Bauten international anerkannter Persönlichkeiten wie Peter Eisenman, Rem Koolhaas, Rafael Moneo, Jean Nouvel oder Philippe Starck auf monolithischen Formen beruhen, die erst durch neue Design- und Bautechniken möglich geworden sind. Starcks ungewöhnliches Baron Vert-Gebäude mit seinen schlitzförmigen Fenstern, die an die Gemälde des italienischen Künstlers Fontana erinnern, liegt in Osaka unmittelbar neben einem Friedhof – und wenn das Bauwerk keine metallisch grüne Außenfassade besäße, würde es noch stärker an einen der Grabsteine erinnern. In der Tat wirkt Starcks Baron Vert wie keine andere Architektur zuvor: Die Masse des Bauwerks scheint eher einem Kunstobjekt als der traditionellen Auffassung von einem

tombale. Ce «Baron vert» ne ressemble en fait à aucune autre architecture existante. Sa masse semble plus proche de celle d'un objet que de l'idée traditionnelle que nous nous faisons d'un immeuble, et cette apparence est sans doute liée à l'expérience de designer de Philippe Starck.

Un certain nombre de constructions contemporaines peuvent se regrouper dans cette catégorie des «monolithes» pour des raisons diverses, parfois même contradictoires. Ils partagent une apparence commune de renfermement, offrant l'image de villes autarciques. L'architecte britannique Sir Norman Foster a longtemps réfléchi à des tours assez hautes pour abriter des communautés humaines autonomes dans lesquelles les fonctions d'habitat et de travail seraient mélangées. Son projet de ce type le plus ambitieux est la Millennium Tower (Tokyo, Japon, 1989). Frank Lloyd Wright avait déjà imaginé une tour de un mile de haut, mais Foster a approfondi le concept d'immeuble de très grande hauteur en s'attaquant aux formidables problèmes de conception posés par cette tour de 170 niveaux et de 840 m de haut destinée à la baie de Tokyo. Les 1 039 206 m² et les 10 milliards de dollars de cette Millennium Tower ont sombré dans les remous provoqués par l'éclatement de la bulle financière japonaise. L'architecte espère néanmoins toujours construire une version de ce projet, et il est plus que probable qu'il signera une nouvelle tour gigantesque avant que le projet de Tokyo ne voie le jour. La Millennium Tower de Londres, annoncée lors d'une conférence de presse le 9 septembre 1996, devrait élever ses 95 niveaux à 435 m de haut sur le site du Baltic Exchange, gravement endommagé par une bombe de l'IRA en 1992. Outre des bureaux, elle comprendra 12 étages d'appartements dans son aile nord, et 7 dans son aile sud.

La multiplication spectaculaire des tours de bureaux en Extrême-Orient a sans aucun doute relancé l'idée des immeubles de très grande hauteur, jugée démodée il y a quelques années encore. Foster n'est que l'un des représentants du petit groupe d'architectes intéressés par ce genre de projet, dont l'un des membres les plus éminents est Cesar Pelli, responsable des tours jumelles Petronas (Kuala-Lumpur) qui ont battu le record

Jean Nouvel, Galeries Lafayette, Berlin, Germany, 1993–96. A curved glass facade, which contrasts with the more rectilinear stone buildings typical of Berlin.

Jean Nouvel, Galeries Lafayette, Berlin, Deutschland, 1993–96. Die geschwungene Glasfassade steht in Kontrast zu den für Berlin typischen massiven Blockbauten.

Jean Nouvel, Galeries Lafayette, Berlin, Allemagne, 1993–96. La façade de verre en courbe contraste avec les alignements rectilignes des lourds immeubles de pierre et de brique berlinois.

Herman Hertzberger, Chassé Theater, Breda, The Netherlands, 1992–95. An overarching curved roof serves to unite disparate programmatic requirements.

Herman Hertzberger, Chassé Theater, Breda, Niederlande, 1992–95. Der Architekt vereint diverse programmatische Anforderungen unter einer geschwungenen Dachkonstruktion.

Herman Hertzberger, Chassé Theater, Bréda, Pays-Bas, 1992–95. Un toit enveloppant en forme de vague unit les différents éléments d'un programme disparate.

than architectural considerations, with the all embracing gesture of the undulating roof…This *modus operandi* may be likened to the way the component parts of a car engine are brought together in accordance with technical criteria and guidelines and then wrapped in the aesthetic garb of a motor car bonnet. The double wave of roof washing over the flytowers and cascading down over the foyer zone is there primarily to prevent any one component from predominating. The fact that the roof pulls together all the building's elements in effect makes it the principal facade."

The Museum of Contemporary Art (Chicago, Illinois, 1992–96) designed by the German architect Josef Paul Kleihues calls on a monolithic vocabulary related to strict modernist geometry. Located in the center of Chicago's most prestigious business, retail and residential neighborhood, the Museum stands out as being more closely related to the architectural history of modern Chicago than to more recent and more unorthodox movements. As Cheryl Kent wrote in the *Architectural Record*, "Deep into the 1990s, Kleihues's MCA seems to summarize a composure and restraint that has blessedly come to us after an era in which the over-the-top, program-be-damned hedonism of museums like Peter Eisenman's Wexner Center and Frank O. Gehry's Vitra Museum has been celebrated."[6] Kleihues himself cites Schinkel's Schauspielhaus and the Acropolis as being the antecedents of the MCA, which is in itself an indication of the

Gebäude zu ähneln – eine Tatsache, die mit Starcks Hintergrund als Designer erklärt werden könnte.

Eine ganze Reihe zeitgenössischer Bauten kann unter dem Begriff »monolithische Architektur« zusammengefaßt werden – wenn auch aus unterschiedlichen und häufig widersprüchlichen Gründen. Allen gemeinsam ist ein autarkes Erscheinungsbild, das an eine Stadt in der Stadt oder an eine eigene Welt denken läßt. Der englische Architekt Sir Norman Foster beschäftigte sich lange mit dem Konzept eines hohen Turms, der mit einer Mischform aus Wohn- und Geschäftsfunktionen als unabhängige Gemeinschaft funktionieren sollte. Sein ehrgeizigster Entwurf in dieser Hinsicht war der sogenannte Millennium Tower (Tokio, Japan, 1989). Während Frank Lloyd Wright von einem Turm von einer Meile Höhe nur träumen konnte, stellte sich Foster den gewaltigen Problemen bei der Konzeption eines extrem hohen Bauwerks und entwarf einen 840 m hohen Turm mit 170 Geschossen für die Bucht von Tokio. Mit geschätzten Baukosten in Höhe von etwa 25 Milliarden DM und einer beeindruckenden Gesamtfläche von 1 039 206 m² wurde der Millennium Tower jedoch ein Opfer der Immobilien-«Seifenblase« in Japan. Dennoch hegt Foster die Hoffnung, eines Tages eine abgewandelte Version des Gebäudes verwirklichen zu können. Aber zur Zeit erscheint es wahrscheinlicher, daß ein anderer, extrem hoher Foster-Entwurf noch vor dem Tokioter Projekt Gestalt annehmen wird: Der auf einer Pressekonferenz am 9. September 1996 vorgestellte London Millennium Tower – ein 435 m hoher Büroturm mit 95 Geschossen – soll auf dem Gelände der ehemaligen Baltic Exchange entstehen, eines Gebäudes in der Londoner City, das 1992 durch einen Bombenanschlag der IRA beschädigt wurde. Neben den Büroräumen sind in 12 Geschossen des Nordflügels und in 7 Geschossen des Südflügels Apartments geplant.

Zweifellos hat der aufsehenerregende »Aufstieg« von Bürohochhäusern in Asien dem Konzept des sehr hohen Gebäudes neues Leben eingehaucht, das noch vor wenigen Jahren völlig überholt zu sein schien. Foster ist nur ein Beispiel für die Architekten, die solchen Entwürfen positiv gegenüberstehen; Vorreiter dieser Gruppe ist Cesar Pelli, der Schöpfer des mit 452 m höch-

du monde de hauteur avec leur 452 m. Foster soutient que ce type d'immeuble peut contribuer à la maîtrise des dépenses d'énergie, et explique que même s'il comprend des appartements, il peut contribuer à diminuer la circulation automobile. Ceci suppose évidemment que de nombreuses personnes vivent et travaillent dans le même immeuble, ce que la situation économique et l'organisation actuelle des entreprises ne permet guère. Francfort étant assez fière de l'achèvement d'une autre tour de Foster, celle de la Commerzbank, actuellement le plus haut immeuble de bureaux d'Europe, l'architecte propose que Londres, grande capitale financière, reprenne le flambeau du gratte-ciel le plus élevé. Cette sorte d'attitude promet aux immeubles de grande hauteur de rester au premier plan de la scène architecturale quelques années encore.

Les formes monolithiques contemporaines peuvent aussi prendre d'autres apparences et s'adapter aux circonstances. Le Chassé Theater (Breda, Pays-Bas, 1992–95) d'Herman Hertzberger s'est recouvert d'un toit en forme de vague pour unifier des éléments fondamentalement disparates. Le site du théâtre comme la nature chaotique du projet et du chantier ont obligé l'architecte à rechercher une unité à travers ce geste spectaculaire. Il écrit: «Les tours des cintres sont les éléments les plus nettement proéminents du théâtre, en termes aussi bien visuels qu'urbains, leurs formes épaisses menaçant de dominer complètement la perspective vers la ville. D'où l'idée d'envelopper la totalité de cet agrégat de formes et d'espaces, né de considérations plus pratiques qu'architecturales, par un geste global qui prendrait la forme d'un toit ondulé ... Ce *modus operandi* peut être comparé à la façon dont les différents éléments du moteur d'une voiture sont regroupés selon des critères techniques, puis recouverts du vêtement esthétique d'un capot. La double vague de ce toit au-dessus des cintres et cascadant sur la zone du foyer est essentiellement là pour empêcher à tout élément de s'imposer. Cette couverture qui unifie tous les éléments de la construction devient en fait la façade principale.»

Le Museum of Contemporary Art de Chicago (Chicago, Illinois, 1992–96), conçu par l'architecte allemand Josef Paul Kleihues fait

directions of contemporary architecture, which seem today to be moving very much toward the mainstream. As the architect said, "I wanted a facade with no real ornaments. But I wanted a structure that would remember the tradition of ornaments in Chicago – the very beautiful terra-cotta elements you find in Frank Lloyd Wright's or Adler and Sullivan's buildings. The pyramidal structure of the cast aluminum panels carries with it that memory." The geometric austerity of Kleihues in Chicago is as closely related to the thought of Ludwig Mies van der Rohe as it is to that of Schinkel, which emphasizes the new-found capacity of architects to integrate not only the past, but also the lessons of modernism into their thought. As the commentator of *The New York Times* had it, "Modernism promoted novelty at the expense of historical continuity. The contemporary presents the new within a context of historical awareness." For Herbert Muschamp, "Chicago's new museum ... does put art back in a box, at the top of a Parnassian staircase that undoubtedly flatters artists even as it undermines contemporary art. The staircase is handsome, and so is the box. In its thoughtfulness and integrity, Kleihues's design evokes the golden age of Chicago architecture. But it makes no attempt to reach forward with the fumbling, restless desire of contemporary life."[7]

One of the most obviously monolithic structures to be completed recently in Europe is Rudi Ricciotti's Stadium (Vitrolles, France, 1994–95). Its blackened concrete form might just as well bring to mind the monolith in Stanley Kubrick's 1968 film "2001, A Space Odyssey" as other buildings, but this surprising exterior houses a very functional 6,000 square meters of space for rock concerts on a road linking the industrial zone of Vitrolles to the future "Technopole" of the Plateau d'Arbois. More a site for bauxite mines than for entertainment, Le Stadium stands out from its large parking lot, with an aluminum palm tree as its only visible concession to nature. Built on a former garbage dump, Ricciotti's building affirms its presence in an eerie, brutal way, an enigmatic object in the midst of an urban wasteland. As a venue for popular music frequented essentially by young people who are not from affluent backgrounds, Le Stadium stands as mute

sten Gebäudes der Welt, der Petronas Twin Towers in Kuala Lumpur. Außerdem vertritt Foster die Ansicht, daß sich auch sehr hohe Gebäude energiesparend konzipieren lassen, sogar, daß Hochhäuser mit integrierten Wohnungen den Straßenverkehr entlasten könnten. Dafür müßten natürlich viele Menschen im selben Gebäude leben und arbeiten – eine Voraussetzung, die unter den gegebenen Umständen kaum möglich ist. Ebenso wie die Stadt Frankfurt stolz darauf war, ein weiteres Foster-Hochhaus (die Commerzbank) fertigstellen zu können und damit das höchste Bürogebäude Europas zu besitzen, sollte London, nach Ansicht des englischen Architekten, als bedeutendes Finanzzentrum unbedingt versuchen, den Wolkenkratzer-Titel zurückzuerobern. Diese Art von Argumentation ist der Grund dafür, daß hohe Gebäude auch in näherer Zukunft nicht von der Architekturbühne abtreten werden.

In der zeitgenössischen Architektur können monolithische Formen – je nach Begleitumständen – ganz unterschiedliche Erscheinungsbilder annehmen. Herman Hertzberger bediente sich bei seinem Chassé Theater (Breda, Niederlande, 1992–95) einer geschwungenen Dachkonstruktion, um die grundverschiedenen Elemente seines Entwurfs darunter zu vereinigen. Denn sowohl das Gelände des Theaters als auch der chaotische Charakter der Planungs- und Bauarbeiten zwangen den Architekten, mit diesem beherrschenden Element nach Einheitlichkeit zu suchen. Hertzberger erklärte dazu: »Die Bühnentürme (großmaßstäbliche Theatertürme) bilden in visueller wie urbaner Hinsicht die herausragendsten Komponenten des Theaters. Ihre klobige Form drohte den Blick auf die Stadt vollkommen zu beherrschen. Dies brachte mich auf die Idee, das gesamte Konglomerat durch ein weiteres Element – die alles überspannende wellenförmige Dachkonstruktion – zu vereinigen, wobei diese Idee eher praktischen als architektonischen Erwägungen entsprang ... Diesen modus operandi kann man vielleicht mit der Art und Weise vergleichen, mit der die einzelnen Bestandteile eines Automotors in Übereinstimmung mit technischen Kriterien und Bestimmungen zusammengebracht und von der ästhetischen Form einer Motorhaube umhüllt werden. Die doppelte Dach-

lui aussi appel à un vocabulaire d'esprit monolithique qui se réfère à une géométrie moderniste stricte. Situé au centre du plus élégant quartier de Chicago, il est certainement mieux intégré à l'histoire architecturale de la ville que ne l'aurait été une réalisation d'un mouvement plus récent et moins orthodoxe. Comme l'a écrit Cheryl Kent dans «Architectural Record»: «Enraciné dans les années 90, le MCA de Kleihues semble résumer une posture et une retenue succédant avec bonheur à une période qui a vu glorifier des musées relevant un peu du n'importe quoi et d'un hédonisme du rejet du programme, comme par exemple le Wexner Center de Peter Eisenman ou le Vitra Museum de Frank O. Gehry.»[6] Kleihues lui-même cite la Schauspielhaus de Schinkel et l'Acropole comme précurseurs de son MCA, ce qui est en soi une indication des orientations de la tendance générale de l'architecture contemporaine. Comme l'ajoute l'architecte: «Je souhaitais une façade sans réels ornements. Mais je voulais une structure qui rappelle les traditions ornementales de Chicago – ces superbes éléments de terre cuite que l'on trouve sur les immeubles de Frank Lloyd Wright, ou d'Adler et Sullivan. La structure pyramidale des panneaux de fonte d'aluminium véhicule cette mémoire.» L'austérité géométrique de Kleihues à Chicago est aussi proche de la pensée de Ludwig Mies van der Rohe que de celle de Schinkel, et traduit la nouvelle capacité des architectes actuels à intégrer non seulement le passé, mais également les leçons du modernisme. Comme un critique du «New York Times» l'a noté: «Le Modernisme a promu la nouveauté au dépens de la continuité historique. L'architecture contemporaine introduit la nouveauté dans le cadre d'une conscience de l'histoire.» Pour Herbert Muschamp: «Le nouveau musée de Chicago... replace l'art dans sa boîte, au sommet d'un escalier parnassien qui flatte certainement les artistes même s'il mine l'art contemporain. L'escalier est élégant, de même que la boîte. Dans sa réflexion et son intégrité, le projet de Kleihues évoque l'âge d'or de l'architecture de Chicago. Mais il ne fait aucune tentative d'aller au devant de ce désir insatiable et maladroit qu'exprime la vie d'aujourd'hui.»[7]

L'une des constructions les plus ouvertement monolithiques

Josef Paul Kleihues, Museum of Contemporary Art, Chicago, Illinois, 1992–96. A geometric design which is an homage both to Karl Friedrich Schinkel and to Ludwig Mies van der Rohe.

Josef Paul Kleihues, Museum of Contemporary Art, Chicago, Illinois, 1992–96. Das geometrische Konzept ist eine Hommage an Karl Friedrich Schinkel und Ludwig Mies van der Rohe.

Josef Paul Kleihues, Museum of Contemporary Art, Chicago, Illinois, 1992–96. Une conception géométrique qui est un hommage à la fois à Karl Friedrich Schinkel et à Ludwig Mies van der Rohe.

testimony to the violence of much contemporary culture, taking its roots more in that culture than in traditions that are clearly removed from the experience of the building's users. It should also be noted that French municipalities have not entirely given up their taste for experimentation in architecture, born in good part during the Grands Travaux years of François Mitterrand. Other European towns on a par with Vitrolles might not have dared to build such an unexpected and powerful rock concert hall.

One of the architects featured in the "Monolithic Architecture" show in Pittsburgh was the Frenchman Jean Nouvel. A difficult personality, well known for his Institut du Monde Arabe and Fondation Cartier buildings in Paris, Nouvel also participated in the 1986 competition for a New National Theater in Tokyo, published on the cover of the Pittsburgh catalogue.[8] His Galeries Lafayette building, completed in 1996 (Berlin, Germany), is located at the corner of Friedrichstrasse and Französische Strasse on a prime site three blocks from the former Wall. "In Berlin," says Nouvel, "buildings are generally heavy and opaque. In contrast, I proposed a building where you can see through to the life inside." Indeed, much of the new architecture planned in Berlin in the recent wave of construction has adhered to the thick, predictable stone facades of another era. Nouvel points out that as significant a figure as Mies van der Rohe had proposed a glass tower to oppose the stone heaviness typical of Berlin. In this project, however, Nouvel's building has been coupled with stony designs by O.M. Ungers and Harry Cobb of Pei Cobb Freed. Its heart penetrated by luminous open cones, a facade printed with mirror patterns, the rounded mass of Nouvel's Galeries Lafayette, which is in fact in good part an office building, stands out in an audacious way against Berlin's new/old conformity.

Shapes on the Fringe
Holland's Ben van Berkel, based in Amsterdam, attended the AA in London, but he says, " I am from a different generation of architects than Rem Koolhaas and Zaha Hadid, and I am critical of that generation. I was taught by them at the AA, but I feel that they always tried very hard to develop a theory. The theory be-

welle, die sich über die Bühnentürme ergießt und bis über den Foyerbereich hinaus erstreckt, soll in erster Linie verhindern, daß irgendeine andere Bauform zu stark in den Vordergrund tritt. Die Tatsache, daß das Dach alle Gebäudeelemente unter sich vereinigt, macht es zur Hauptfassade.«

Das von dem deutschen Architekten Josef Paul Kleihues entworfene Museum of Contemporary Art (Chicago, Illinois) bedient sich einer monolithischen Formensprache, die stark an die strenge Geometrie der Moderne erinnert. Das im Herzen von Chicagos belebtesten Einkaufs-, Geschäfts- und Wohnviertel gelegene Museum zeichnet sich dadurch aus, daß es zur architektonischen Vergangenheit des modernen Chicago in engerem Bezug steht als zu jüngeren und unorthodoxeren Strömungen. Cheryl Kent schrieb dazu im »Architectural Record«: »Mitte der 90er Jahre scheint Kleihues MCA eine Ruhe und Zurückhaltung auszustrahlen, die glücklicherweise nach einer Ära über uns gekommen ist, in der der waghalsige, alle Lehren mißachtende Hedonismus solcher Museen wie Peter Eisenmans Wexner Center und Frank O. Gehrys Vitra-Museum gefeiert wurde.«[6] Kleihues selbst bezeichnet Schinkels Schauspielhaus und die Akropolis als Vorgänger des MCA, das sich seinerseits wiederum stark in Richtung des heutigen architektonischen Mainstream bewegt. »Ich wollte eine Fassade ohne auffällige Schmuckelemente. Aber ich wollte auch eine Konstruktion, die an die Ornamenttradition Chicagos erinnert – wie etwa die wunderschönen Terrakottaelemente, wie man sie an Gebäuden von Frank Lloyd Wright oder Adler and Sullivan findet. Die pyramidenförmige Anordnung der Gußaluminiumplatten führt diese Tradition fort.« Die geometrische Strenge von Kleihues MCA in Chicago steht in ebenso engem Zusammenhang mit der Gedankenwelt Ludwig Mies van der Rohes wie mit Schinkels Theorien und unterstreicht dadurch die neue Fähigkeit heutiger Architekten, nicht nur die Vergangenheit, sondern auch die Lehren der Moderne in ihre Überlegungen miteinzubeziehen. Der Kritiker der »New York Times«, Herbert Muschamp erklärte dazu: »Die Moderne förderte die Neuheit auf Kosten der historischen Kontinuität. Die heutige Architektur präsentiert das Neue in einem Kontext historischen

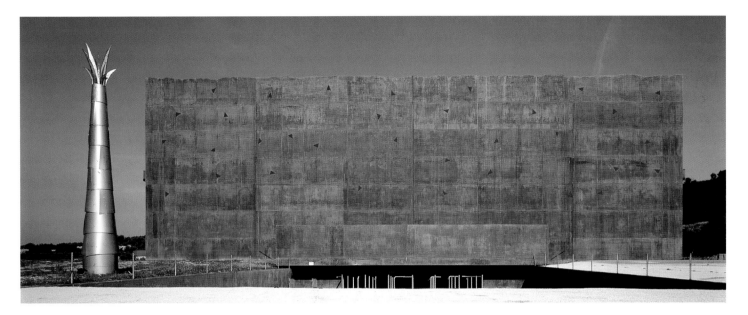

récemment achevées en Europe est le Stadium (Vitrolles, France) de Rudy Ricciotti. Cette masse de béton noir rappelle aussi bien le monolithe du film de Stanley Kubrick, «2001, Odyssée de l'espace» (1968), que certains autres bâtiments. Son extérieur surprenant abrite un espace tout à fait fonctionnel de 6 000 m² destiné aux concerts de rock, en bordure d'une route qui relie la zone industrielle de Vitrolles à la future Technopole du Plateau d'Arbois. Dans un site qui conviendrait mieux à une mine de bauxite qu'à un équipement culturel, le Stadium se dresse au milieu d'un parking, un palmier d'aluminium étant la seule concession visible accordée à la nature. Construit sur une ancienne décharge à ordures, le bâtiment de Ricciotti affirme sa présence d'une manière à la fois brutale et mystérieuse, objet énigmatique au milieu des friches urbaines. Lieu d'accueil de concerts de musique pop, surtout fréquenté par les jeunes de milieux populaires, il s'érige en témoignage muet d'une violence inhérente à une bonne part de la culture contemporaine, et dont les racines doivent peu à des traditions assez éloignées de l'univers de ses utilisateurs. Il faut noter en passant que les collectivités locales françaises n'ont pas abandonné leur goût pour l'expérimentation architecturale, stimulé en grande partie par la politique des Grands Travaux de François Mitterrand. D'autres villes européennes de la taille de Vitrolles n'auraient sans doute pas osé construire une salle de rock aussi inattendue et audacieuse.

Le Français Jean Nouvel faisait partie des architectes présentés dans l'exposition «Monolithic Architecture» de Pittsburgh. Personnalité difficile, célèbre pour son Institut du Monde Arabe et sa Fondation Cartier à Paris, il a également participé au concours de 1986 pour le Nouveau théâtre national de Tokyo, publié sur la couverture du catalogue de Pittsburgh.[8] Son immeuble pour les Galeries Lafayette berlinoises achevé en 1996 est situé sur un superbe emplacement à l'angle de la Friedrichstrasse et de la Französische Strasse, à quelques mètres de l'ancien mur. «À Berlin,» dit Nouvel, «les immeubles sont généralement lourds et opaques. Par contraste, j'ai proposé un immeuble à travers lequel vous pouvez voir jusqu'à la vie qui s'y déroule.» Il est vrai qu'une bonne part de l'architecture berli-

Rudy Ricciotti, Le Stadium, Vitrolles, France, 1994–95. The architect spent the entire budget intended for plants on a single aluminium tree.

Rudy Ricciotti, Le Stadium, Vitrolles, Frankreich, 1994–95. Der Architekt verwendete das gesamte, für die Bepflanzung der Außenanlagen zur Verfügung stehende Budget für eine einzige Palme aus Aluminium.

Rudy Ricciotti, Le Stadium, Vitrolles, France, 1994–95. L'architecte a consacré la totalité du budget prévu pour les plantations à un unique arbre géant en aluminium.

Ben van Berkel, Erasmus Bridge, Rotterdam, The Netherlands, 1990–96. Eloquent testimony to the inventiveness of current Dutch architects. Here Ben van Berkel enters a domain normally reserved to engineers.

Ben van Berkel, Erasmusbrücke, Rotterdam, Niederlande, 1990–96. Ein beeindruckender Beweis für den Einfallsreichtum der heutigen niederländischen Architekten. Mit dieser Brücke begab sich van Berkel auf ein Gebiet, das normalerweise Ingenieuren vorbehalten ist.

Ben van Berkel, Pont Érasme, Rotterdam, Pays-Bas, 1990–96. Témoignage éloquent de l'inventivité des jeunes architectes néerlandais d'aujourd'hui. Ben van Berkel s'est attaqué ici à un domaine habituellement réservé aux ingénieurs.

came the image of the theory. If there is a theory, we would apply it in a more tactile, a more physical way, in the sense that you rethink different typologies of organization or the use of materials. The point is that we are not working with an emblem of a theory or a representation of a manifesto. If you think of Bernard Tschumi, Rem Koolhaas and Peter Eisenman, their work was almost a kind of decorum of their own anti-architecture ... I think that it is possible to connect theory to making architecture that has a kind of magic. It is a question of rethinking questions like what is a facade, what is an entrance and how do you use materials."[9] Van Berkel's most visible recent project is his Erasmus Bridge (Rotterdam, The Netherlands, 1990–96). This resolutely asymmetrical bridge, with its inclined 139 meter high pylon giving an impression of delicate equilibrium, connects the center of

Bewußtseins. Chicagos neues Museum ... hat die Kunst wieder in einen Kasten gestellt – an das obere Ende eines Aufgang zum Parnaß, der zweifellos den Künstlern ebenso sehr schmeichelt, wie er die zeitgenössische Kunst untergräbt. Die Freitreppe ist ebenso nobel wie der Kasten. Die Besonnenheit und Integrität von Kleihues' Design weckt Erinnerungen an das Goldene Zeitalter der Chicagoer Architektur. Aber der Entwurf unternimmt keinen Versuch, sich mit den ungeschickten, rastlosen Sehnsüchten des heutigen Lebensstils auseinanderzusetzen.«[7]

Eine der offensichtlichsten monolithischen Konstruktionen, die in Europa in den vergangenen Jahren fertiggestellt wurden, ist Rudy Ricciottis Le Stadium in Vitrolles (Frankreich). Ricciottis massive Form aus schwarzem Beton erinnert zwar wie andere Gebäude auch an den Monolith in Stanley Kubricks »2001 – Odyssee im Weltall«, aber hinter diesem verblüffenden Erscheinungsbild verbirgt sich eine sehr funktionale Rockkonzerthalle von 6 000 m² Grundfläche. Le Stadium befindet sich an einer Straße, die das Industriegebiet von Vitrolles mit dem zukünftigen »Technopole« auf dem Plateau d'Arbois verbindet – also auf einem Gelände, das eher für Bauxitminen als für Freizeitvergnügen geeignet scheint. Die Halle ragt hoch über den großen Parkplatz hinaus und besitzt als einzige sichtbare Konzession an die Natur eine einzelne Palme aus Aluminium. Das auf einer ehemaligen Mülldeponie entstandene Gebäude zeichnet sich durch eine unheimliche, brutalistische Präsenz aus – ein geheimnisvolles Objekt inmitten eines städtischen Ödlands. Als Veranstaltungsort für Rock- und Popmusik, der hauptsächlich von jüngeren Leuten aus weniger vermögenden Verhältnissen frequentiert wird, ist Le Stadium ein stummes Zeugnis der Gewalt in vielen Bereichen zeitgenössischer Kultur und eher mit dieser Kultur verwurzelt als mit den Traditionen, die ganz eindeutig jenseits des Erfahrungsbereichs der Nutzer dieses Gebäudes liegen. Die französischen Behörden hatten ihre Lust zum Experiment noch nicht vollständig verloren, die hauptsächlich zu einer Zeit geweckt wurde, die durch François Mitterands Grands Travaux geprägt war. Andere europäische, mit Vitrolles vergleichbare Städte hätten den Bau einer solchenHalle vielleicht nicht gewagt.

noise de la vague récente de reconstruction a adhéré à la tradition ancienne des lourdes façades de pierre et de brique. Nouvel fait remarquer que Mies van der Rohe lui-même avait proposé une tour de verre par opposition à la lourdeur minérale typique de Berlin. Dans ce projet, cependant, le bâtiment de Nouvel se retrouve couplé à des projets minéraux de O.M. Ungers et Harry Cobb de Pei Cobb Freed & Partners. Pénétré jusqu'en leur cœur par des cônes ouverts qui laissent entrer la lumière, avec leur façade réfléchissante, les masses arrondies de ces Galeries Lafayette – en fait pour une bonne part immeuble de bureaux – se dressent avec audace face au conformisme berlinois, ancien et nouveau.

Formes en marge

Ben van Berkel, Hollandais installé à Amsterdam a étudié à l'A.A. de Londres, dont il est diplômé. Il tient cependant à préciser: «J'appartiens à une génération différente de celle de Rem Koolhaas et de Zaha Hadid, et suis critique vis-à-vis d'eux. J'ai suivi leurs cours à l'AA, et ai le sentiment qu'ils ont toujours cherché à mettre au point une théorie. Celle-ci est devenue l'image de la théorie. Si théorie il y a, nous devrions pouvoir l'appliquer d'une façon tactile, plus physique, au sens où elle devrait permettre de repenser différentes typologies d'organisation ou d'utilisation de matériaux. Le problème est que nous ne travaillons pas avec un emblème de théorie, une représentation de théorie ou un manifeste. Prenez Bernard Tschumi, Rem Koolhaas ou Peter Eisenman: leur travail est presque une sorte de décor de leur propre anti-architecture... Je pense qu'il est possible de connecter une théorie à la réalisation d'une architecture qui possède une sorte de magie. Il faut repenser des questions du type 'qu'est-ce qu'une façade', 'qu'est-ce qu'une entrée', 'comment utiliser les matériaux'.»[9] Le plus remarqué des projets récents de van Berkel est le pont Érasme (Rotterdam, 1990–96). Résolument asymétrique, avec son pylône incliné de 139 m de haut à l'équilibre délicat, il réunit le centre ville au nouveau quartier de Kop van Zuid. Par sa situation à l'extrémité de la rocade Boompjes qui draine presque toute la circulation automobile vers le centre de

the city with the Kop van Zuid development area. Because of its situation, at the end of the Boompjes drive which leads most external traffic into the city, the Erasmus Bridge is a highly visible symbol of Rotterdam's modernity. This visibility is accentuated by a carefully studied night lighting of the structure. According to the architect, it is precisely the height of the pylon, and the length deck, which has a free span of 284 meters, that determined the unusual angle of inclination of the pylon. As he says, "the conflict between forces and moments in the pylon results in parasitic bending, in which the angle in the uppermost section largely follows the line of moment." Although he was trained as an architect, Ben van Berkel worked briefly in the office of Santiago Calatrava after receiving his diploma at the Architectural Association in London in 1987.

Van Berkel's Wilbrink House (Amersfoort, The Netherlands, 1992–94), is on a very different scale. A relatively small house, it is located in an area that stands apart because of the diversity of its architecture. A neo-Moorish castle here stands in close proximity to modernist houses that for the most part exhibit their owners' love for their gardens. The Wilbrinks approached house building from a very different point of view. They told Van Berkel that they "hated" gardening, and resolved with him to make a statement against the pretentious architectural posturing of their area. The result was a house without a garden, and above all without a street-side facade. Instead, curious neighbors are greeted by an inclined plane covered with colored railway gravel. The goal, as the architect says, was to "make the house very introverted rather than showing off its architecture." Despite its unexpected entrance, the Wilbrink House is bright and open within. The architect says, "The light comes in very beautifully. We studied how the sunlight would fall before building the house. It has a very simple organization." Almost more important for Ben van Berkel than these factors, however, is the innovative structural approach he used for this house. "All the bricks in the Wilbrink House are glued, and that is totally new," he says. "This allows you to make a sloping wall without any supporting construction." The architect concludes, "I like to believe that you

Die Ausstellung »Monolithic Architecture« in Pittsburgh beschäftigte sich u.a. mit den Arbeiten des französischen Architekten Jean Nouvel. Der als schwierig geltende Nouvel, der mit seinem Institut du Monde Arabe und der Fondation Cartier in Paris einem breiteren Publikum bekannt wurde, nahm darüber hinaus an der Ausschreibung für das New National Theater in Tokio (1986) teil, wobei sein Wettbewerbsbeitrag den Katalog der Pittsburgher Ausstellung ziert.[8]

Nouvels 1996 fertiggestellte Galeries Lafayette befindet sich an der Ecke Französische Straße – Friedrichstraße in Berlin-Mitte, einer erstklassigen Lage, nicht weit von der ehemaligen Mauer. Nouvel erklärt: »In Berlin sind die meisten Bauten wuchtig und lichtundurchlässig. Im Gegensatz dazu entwarf ich ein Gebäude, durch das man hindurchsehen und das Leben im Inneren wahrnehmen kann.« Tatsächlich hielten viele Architekten der während des jüngsten Baubooms in Berlin entstandenen neuen Gebäude an den massiven Steinfassaden vergangener Zeiten fest. Nouvel erläutert weiter, daß eine so bedeutende Architektenpersönlichkeit wie Mies van der Rohe einen Glasturm entworfen hatte – als Kontrast zu der für Berlin typischen steinernen Wuchtigkeit. Nouvels Gebäude – von transparenten Lichtkegeln durchbrochen und auf der Fassade mit spiegelnden Mustern übersät – ist jedoch von »steinernen« Entwürfen von O.M. Ungers und Harry Cobb (von Pei Cobb Freed & Partners) umgeben. Seine runde, massige Galeries Lafayette, die größtenteils als Bürogebäude dient, ragt auf kühne Weise aus Berlins neuer bzw. alter Gleichförmigkeit heraus.

Formen am Rande

Der in Amsterdam ansässige Niederländer Ben van Berkel schloß 1987 seine Studien an der AA in London ab, sagt aber über diese Zeit: »Ich stamme aus einer anderen Architektengeneration als Rem Koolhaas oder Zaha Hadid und stehe dieser Generation kritisch gegenüber. Ich wurde von ihnen an der AA ausgebildet, aber ich glaube, daß sie immer zu sehr mit der Entwicklung von Theorien beschäftigt waren. In ihren Arbeiten wurde die Theorie zum Bild der Theorie. Wenn überhaupt eine

la ville, ce pont est un symbole hautement symbolique de la modernité de Rotterdam. Sa visibilité est accentuée par un éclairage nocturne étudié avec soin. La hauteur du pylône et la longueur du tablier – qui a une portée libre de 284 m – ont déterminé cet angle d'inclinaison inhabituel. L'architecte précise: «Le conflit entre les forces et les moments sur le pylône ont créé cette tension parasite, dans lequel l'angle de la section supérieure suit largement la ligne du moment.» Ben van Berkel a travaillé brièvement chez Santiago Calatrava, que ce pont peut évoquer.

Sa villa Wilbrink (Amersfoort, Pays-Bas, 1992–94) est un projet d'échelle évidemment très différente. Maison relativement petite, elle est située dans un quartier un peu particulier. Un château néo-mauresque se dresse à côté de maisons modernistes qui témoignent pour la plupart de l'amour de leurs propriétaires pour les jardins qui les entourent. Les Wilbrink ont approché le problème de la construction de leur résidence d'un point de vue très différent. Ils ont expliqué à van Berkel qu'ils «haïssaient» le jardinage, et décidé avec lui d'affirmer leur position face aux attitudes architecturales prétentieuses de leur quartier. Le résultat est une maison sans jardin, et surtout sans façade sur la rue. Les voisins ne voient qu'un plan incliné couvert de ballast coloré. L'objectif, selon l'architecte, était «de rendre la maison très introvertie, plutôt que de faire étalage de son architecture.» Malgré cette entrée inattendue, la villa est très ouverte et très lumineuse. «La lumière entre de façon merveilleuse. Nous avons étudié l'orientation du soleil. L'organisation de l'ensemble est très simple,» ajoute l'architecte. Mais plus important encore pour lui est l'approche structurale innovante qu'il a utilisée. «Toutes les briques sont collées, ce qui est totalement nouveau,» dit-il, «et permet de monter un mur incliné sans soutien particulier. J'aime croire qu'un architecte peut inventer, comme un scientifique. J'aime transgresser les idées et les redéfinir.»[10]

Il est certain que peu d'architectes actuels ont le goût ou le talent de travailler sur deux projets aussi différents que la villa Wilbrink ou le pont Érasme, mais Ben van Berkel, qui utilise abondamment l'ordinateur dans ses projets, représente une nouvelle génération de praticiens – âgés d'une quarantaine d'années –

Ben van Berkel, Wilbrink House, Amersfoort, The Netherlands, 1992–94. A unique process, which consists of gluing bricks together, permitted the architect to design walls that were not entirely vertical.

Ben van Berkel, Wilbrink-Haus, Amersfoort, Niederlande, 1992–94. Eine neuartige Bauweise, bei der Ziegelsteine miteinander verklebt werden, ermöglichte dem Architekten die Konstruktion schiefer Wände.

Ben van Berkel, villa Wilbrink, Amersfoort, Pays-Bas, 1992–94. Un procédé exclusif de collage des briques a permis à l'architecte d'imaginer des murs qui ne sont pas vraiment verticaux.

Thomas Spiegelhalter, Breisach House, Germany, 1992–93. Arrays of photovoltaic cells seen in this view emphasize the ecologically responsible nature of the architecture.

Thomas Spiegelhalter, Haus in Breisach, Deutschland, 1992–93. Die in dieser Abbildung sichtbaren großflächigen Solarzellen unterstreichen das umweltbewußte Konzept dieser Architektur.

Thomas Spiegelhalter, maison à Breisach, Allemagne, 1992–93. Des panneaux de cellules photovoltaïques expriment la sensibilité écologique de cette architecture.

can invent as an architect, like a scientist does. I like to transgress ideas and to redefine them."[10]

Admittedly, few current architects may have the taste or the talent to work on two such different projects as the Wilbrink House and the Erasmus Bridge, but Ben van Berkel, who makes extensive use of the computer in his designs, is a representative of a new generation of architects, today approximately forty years old, who are intent on redefining the limits of the profession. As in the case of some of their elders, they approach the history of modernist architecture just as they might earlier periods, as a resource on which they can draw to enrich their own creativity, while calling on the most contemporary techniques and materials. The fact that economic conditions oblige them to carefully work out every detail, and to spare no effort to complete their projects within strict budgets, may have contributed to the relatively austere style that seems to be popular, but it has not stifled their inventiveness.

Thomas Spiegelhalter was born in 1959 in Freiburg, Germany where he lives and works as a "sculptor, architect and communications designer." He writes, "I think the traditional division into art on this side and architecture on the other is quite obsolete and stifles communication between the various media." His recent house (Breisach, Germany, 1992–93) goes further than an association between art and architecture, however. Its 613 square meters of living and working spaces are divided on no less than sixteen "levels," grouped in three major sections in a spiral around a central glazed stairwell. Built for a couple with children who wanted an "ecologically responsive" building which could permit them to organize occasional concerts or exhibitions as well as house the family. On the roof of the house are 54 square meters of photovoltaic panels which generate energy and 13 square meters of tubular vacuum collectors for solar water-heating. This system is backed up by natural gas heating in periods of low sunshine. Spiegelhalter's interest in art or sculpture is evidenced in the unusual shape of this house, but also in his use of materials recovered in and near local gravel pits. Industrial or readily available materials are used with rough wood.

Architekturtheorie existiert, würde ich sie auf eine greifbare, physische Art und Weise umsetzen, wobei die Typologien der räumlichen Organisation oder die Verwendung der Materialien neu überdacht werden müßten. Der Punkt ist, daß wir nicht mit dem Symbol einer Theorie oder der Verkörperung eines Manifestes arbeiten. Die Arbeiten von Bernard Tschumi, Rem Koolhaas oder Peter Eisenman wirken beinahe wie eine Art Dekorum ihrer eigenen, anti-architektonischen Konzepte ... Ich glaube, daß es möglich ist, die Theorie mit einer Architektur zu verbinden, die eine Art von Magie ausstrahlt. Dazu müssen wir Fragen wie: ›Was ist eine Fassade?‹, ›Was ist ein Eingang?‹ oder ›Wie gehe ich mit Materialien um?‹ neu überdenken.«⁹ Van Berkels bekanntestes aktuelles Projekt ist seine Erasmusbrug in Rotterdam (1990–96). Diese kompromißlos asymmetrisch gestaltete Brücke mit ihrem 139 m hohen, geneigten Brückenpfeiler, der den Eindruck eines instabilen Gleichgewichts erweckt, verbindet das Stadtzentrum mit dem neuen Stadtteil Kop van Zuid. Durch ihre Lage am Ende der Boompjeslaan, über die ein Großteil des Fernverkehrs in die Stadt rollt, bietet die Erasmusbrücke ein herausragendes Symbol der Modernität Rotterdams. Ihre Augenfälligkeit wird nachts zusätzlich durch die ausgeklügelte Beleuchtung der Baustruktur betont. Dem Architekten zufolge ist der ungewöhnliche Neigungswinkel des Pylons durch dessen Höhe und die Länge der Brückentafel mit einer freien Spannweite von 284 m bedingt. Nach seinen Worten »führt der Konflikt zwischen Kräften und Drehmomenten im Pylon zu einer wie durch Störschwingungen bedingten Krümmung, wobei der Winkel im oberen Teilstück hauptsächlich der Linie des Drehmoments folgt.« Ben van Berkel arbeitete kurze Zeit im Ingenieurbüro von Santiago Calatrava, nachdem er 1987 sein Diplom an der Architectural Association erhalten hatte.

Bei van Berkels Wilbrink-Haus (Amersfoort, Niederlande, 1992–94) handelt es sich dagegen um eine ganz andere Größenordnung. Dieses relativ kleine Privathaus steht in einem Wohnviertel mit einer überraschend vielfältigen Architektur: Direkt neben einer Art Burg im Neo-Moore-Stil entdeckt man neo-moderne Häuser, aus denen die Liebe ihrer Besitzer für ihre

partis pour redéfinir les limites de leur profession. Comme pour certains de leurs prédécesseurs, le modernisme est pour eux une période historique qu'ils prennent comme une source mise à profit pour enrichir leur propre créativité, tout en faisant appel aux techniques et aux matériaux les plus contemporains. Le fait que les conditions économiques actuelles les obligent à travailler avec soin chaque détail dans le cadre de budgets serrés contribue peut-être à un style relativement austère qui semble actuellement populaire, mais n'a pas pour autant éteint leur inventivité.

Thomas Spiegelhalter est né à Fribourg (Allemagne) en 1959. Il y vit et travaille comme «sculpteur, architecte et designer en communications.» Il écrit: «Je pense que la division traditionnelle en art d'un côté et architecture de l'autre est pratiquement obsolète et étouffe la communication entre les différents médias.» Sa maison de Breisach (Allemagne, 1992–93) va cependant plus loin qu'une simple association entre art et architecture. Ses 613 m² d'espace de vie et de travail sont divisés en pas moins de 16 «niveaux,» regroupés en trois sections principales organisées en spirale autour de l'escalier central en verre. Construite pour un couple avec enfants qui voulait une maison «écologiquement pensée» permettant l'organisation occasionnelle de concerts ou d'expositions et une vie de famille confortable. La résidence Breisach aligne sur son toit 54 m² de cellules photovoltaïques et 13 m² de collecteurs tubulaires pour fournir le chauffage solaire. Un générateur à gaz peut chauffer la maison si l'énergie solaire est insuffisante. L'intérêt de Spiegelhalter pour l'art et la culture apparaît dans la forme curieuse de cette maison, mais également dans sa réutilisation de matériaux récupérés dans et près des gravières de la région. Il se sert également de bois brut, et de matériaux industriels ou facilement disponibles.

L'apparence très fragmentée de cette maison semble beaucoup plus proche de l'approche esthétique de Coop Himmelb(l)au ou de Zvi Hecker que de celle de Josef Paul Kleihues, architectes qui ont tous travaillé récemment en Allemagne ou en Autriche. Ils partagent néanmoins une volonté d'expression

The highly fragmented appearance of this house seems much closer to the esthetic approach of Coop Himmelb(l)au or Zvi Hecker than it might be to Josef Paul Kleihues, yet all of these architects have worked recently in Germany or Austria. What they may all share is a willingness to express powerful forms in architecture without apology. Their sophistication is spatial as opposed to really being esthetic, and this is an interesting contrast that they offer with the work of the French architect Christian de Portzamparc. The 1994 Pritzker Prize winner is perhaps best known for his Cité de la Musique (1984–95) complex on the north eastern periphery of Paris, yet one of his current projects is likely to win him far more acclaim. The LVMH Tower that he has designed for the French luxury goods conglomerate is to be located on 57th Street between Fifth and Madison Avenues. It is set on a narrow lot on the uptown side of the street, opposite the dark mass of the IBM Building. It is Portzamparc's third tower design after the Tour Crédit Lyonnais (Lille, France, 1991–95) and the Bandai Tower (1994), scheduled for Tokyo but not yet built. Portzamparc, as *The New York Times* has written, "is ambivalent about modernism. He reveres it as a humanist expression but deplores its dehumanizing impact. He appreciates novelty as a sign of urban life, but recognizes the need for continuity."[11] Continuity is defined in New York somewhat differently than it might be in Paris, for example. Yet Portzamparc's brand of lyrical modern architecture proves in Manhattan that it can find a valid expression in the city that, with Chicago, invented the skyscraper.

For the LVMH Tower, the French architect has turned complex zoning restrictions to his advantage, permitting the building to be higher than the neighboring (and rival) Chanel tower. He has also combined a sweeping curve in the facade, which is loosely inspired by the form of a flower with a silk-screen translucent white glass used to attenuate reflections from the IBM building, and green glass "to meet the stringent insulation coefficients" of New York's energy code. In a system first employed inside the concert hall of the Cité de la Musique, and then incorporated into the Bandai design, Christian de Portzamparc plans to use a light channel almost 100 meters long on the facade to wash the

Gärten spricht. Die Wilbrinks näherten sich dem Hausbau aus einer ganz anderen Perspektive. Sie erzählten van Berkel, daß sie Gartenarbeit »haßten« und kamen mit ihm überein, ein Statement gegen die hochgestochene architektonische Haltung ihrer unmittelbaren Umgebung abzugeben. Das Ergebnis war ein Haus ohne Garten, und vor allem ohne eine von der Straße aus erkennbare Fassade. Statt dessen werden neugierige Nachbarn von einer ansteigenden Ebene begrüßt, die mit gefärbtem Schotter bedeckt ist. Laut Aussage des Architekten wollte man »ein sehr introvertiertes Haus schaffen, und nicht mit dessen Architektur prahlen«. Aber trotz seines ungewöhnlichen Eingangs ist das Wilbrink-Haus im Inneren hell und offen. Van Berkel sagt dazu: »Der Lichteinfall ist wunderschön. Wir berechneten genau, wie das Sonnenlicht einfallen würde, bevor wir mit dem Bau des Hauses begannen. Das Gebäude ist sehr einfach aufgegliedert.« Aber noch wichtiger als diese Faktoren ist für van Berkel das neuartige Baukonzept, das er bei diesem Haus anwandte. »Sämtliche Ziegel des Wilbrink-Hauses sind miteinander verleimt. Diese Methode ist völlig neu: Sie erlaubt den Bau schräger Wände ohne jede Stützkonstruktion. Ich gebe mich gern der Illusion hin, daß man als Architekt ebenso wie ein Wissenschaftler etwas erfinden kann«, sagt Ben van Berkel. »Ich liebe es, Vorstellungen zu durchbrechen, um sie danach wieder neu zu definieren.«[10]

Zugegebenermaßen besitzen nur wenige der zeitgenössischen Architekten genug Talent und Geschmack, um zwei so unterschiedliche Projekte wie das Wilbrink-Haus und die Erasmusbrücke zu schaffen. Aber Ben van Berkel – der bei seinen Entwürfen häufig auf den Computer zurückgreift – kann als Repräsentant einer neuen, heute etwa vierzigjährigen Generation von Architekten gelten, die es sich zum Ziel gesetzt haben, die Grenzen ihres Berufsstandes neu zu definieren. Wie einige ihrer Vorgänger nähern sie sich der Geschichte der Moderne ebenso wie jeder anderen historischen Architekturperiode und betrachten sie als Inspirationsquelle, die sie zur Befruchtung ihrer eigenen Kreativität heranziehen können, während sie gleichzeitig auf modernste Bautechniken und -materialien zurückgrei-

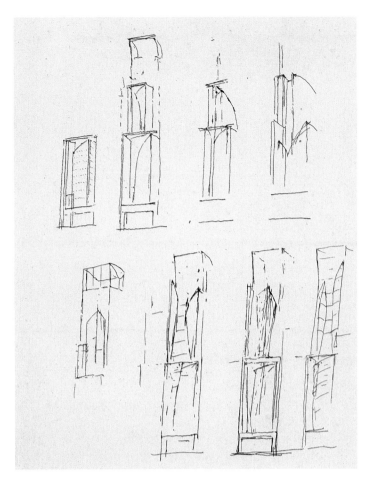

Christian de Portzamparc, LVMH Tower, New York, New York, 1995–98. A series of sketches by the architect show some of his ideas for the unusual facade of this building, located on 57th Street near Madison Avenue.

Christian de Portzamparc, LVMH Tower, New York, New York, 1995–98. Eine Reihe von Skizzen zeigen einige Gestaltungsideen des Architekten für die ungewöhnliche Fassade seines Bauwerks an der 57th Street in der Nähe der Madison Avenue.

Christian de Portzamparc, Tour LVMH, New York, New York, 1995–98. Cette suite de croquis de l'architecte montre quelques-unes de ses propositions pour la façade inhabituelle de cet immeuble situé sur la 57th Street, près de Madison Avenue.

de formes architecturales puissantes et sans compromis. Leur sophistication est spatiale, dans le sens où elle s'oppose à un pur esthétisme, ce qui représente un contraste intéressant avec l'œuvre de l'architecte français, Christian de Portzamparc. Ce Prix Pritzker 1994 est surtout connu pour sa Cité de la Musique (1984–95), important complexe en bordure du boulevard périphérique de Paris, mais l'un de ses projets actuels a toutes les chances de faire encore davantage parler de lui. La tour LVMH qu'il a conçue pour le groupe français de produits de luxe Louis Vuitton Moët Hennessy s'élèvera sur la 57th Street à New York, entre Fifth et Madison Avenues, sur un terrain étroit, face à la masse sombre de l'IBM Building. C'est la troisième tour de Portzamparc après celle du Crédit Lyonnais (Lille, France, 1991–95) et la Tour Bandai prévue à Tokyo mais non encore construite. Portzamparc, comme l'écrit le «New York Times «a une attitude ambivalente par rapport au modernisme. Il le révère comme expression humaniste mais déplore son impact déshumanisant. Il apprécie la nouveauté en tant que signe de la vitalité urbaine, mais reconnaît le besoin de continuité.»[11] La continuité new-yorkaise se définit de façon assez différente de celle de Paris, par exemple. Et pourtant l'architecture moderne lyrique de Portzamparc prouve à Manhattan qu'elle peut trouver une expression valable dans la cité qui, avec Chicago, a inventé le gratte-ciel.

Pour cette tour LVMH, l'architecte a su tourner a son avantage la réglementation très stricte du zoning, pour permettre à son immeuble de s'élever plus haut que sa voisine (et rivale), la tour Chanel. Il a également réussi à combiner la courbe enveloppante de la façade, librement inspirée de la forme d'une fleur, à un écran translucide de verre blanc qui atténue les reflets de l'immeuble IBM, et de verre vert «pour respecter les stricts coefficients d'isolation,» de la réglementation municipale sur l'énergie. Grâce à un système employé pour la première fois à l'intérieur de l'auditorium de la Cité de la Musique et déjà vu dans le projet Bandai, Portzamparc a créé une sorte de canal de lumière de près de cent mètres de haut qui, la nuit, balaie la façade d'un halo changeant vert, rouge, bleu et or.

De conception à l'évidence très sophistiquée, ce qui répond

Christian de Portzamparc, LVMH Tower, New York, New York, 1995–98. The final design for the facade takes into account neighboring architecture as well as the particularly restrictive zoning codes of New York City.

Christian de Portzamparc, LVMH Tower, New York, New York, 1995–98. Das endgültige Design der Fassade berücksichtigt nicht nur die umliegende Architektur, sondern auch die strengen Bebauungsvorschriften der Stadt New York.

Christian de Portzamparc, Tour LVMH, New York, New York, 1995–98. Le projet final pour la façade prend en compte l'architecture avoisinante et la réglementation de zoning particulièrement contraignante de la ville de New York.

glass at night with gradually changing tones of green, red, blue and gold.

Obviously a very sophisticated design, as might be appropriate for the Louis Vuitton Moët Hennessy group, Portzamparc's tower has won the praise of New York's most astute architectural critic, Herbert Muschamp, who wrote that "the building is important not only to the identity of 57th Street, but to that of the entire city. With a facade of clear and opalescent glass, it is a teasing, seductive building, and it should radically enlarge the creative scope of American skyscraper design."[12] Obviously quite favorable to Portzamparc, Muschamp concludes, "He belongs to no stylistic school and is perhaps best described as a perpetual student of the city, its past, its texture, its craving for novelty as well as continuity."

It may be that the current period is closer than the preceding one to having a dominant trend, in the form of neo-modernism. Yet even architects who apparently appreciate this style, like Wiel Arets, reject it in name at least, preferring to explain their approach in other terms. Since it is apparent that the smooth lines of a minimalist architecture are being laid out at the same time as the dramatically fragmented forms of Coop Himmelb(l)au, Zvi Hecker or Thomas Spiegelhalter, it can be concluded that no real agreement is in sight as to the direction that future architecture should take. To some extent, however, there is evidence of a generation gap. Younger architects like Ben van Berkel (born in 1957), Arets (born in 1955) or Ricciotti (born in 1952) seem to be at odds with others like Hecker (born in 1931) or Coop Himmelb(l)au principals Wolf D. Prix (born in 1942) and Helmut Swiczinsky (born in 1944). The younger designers are clearly more inclined to a minimalist approach than their elders, though this rule is belied by Spiegelhalter (born in 1959). It could be said that both Hecker and Spiegelhalter are experimenters, by definition at the fringe of the architectural profession, interested in art as it applies to the built form in a more profound way than their colleagues. Once into their fifties and beyond, successful architects tend to have well-defined styles, as might be the case of Mario Botta, Sir Norman Foster, or even the pair Reichen &

fen. Die Tatsache, daß wirtschaftliche Gegebenheiten die Architekten dazu zwingen, jedes Detail sorgfältig auszuarbeiten und
darauf zu achten, daß Projekte im Rahmen strikter Budgetgren-
zen erstellt werden, kann ein Grund für den zur Zeit populären,
relativ strengen Baustil sein – aber sie wird ihren Erfindungs-
reichtum nicht unterdrücken können.

Thomas Spiegelhalter wurde 1959 in Freiburg geboren, wo er
heute als »Bildhauer, Architekt und Kommunikationsdesigner«
tätig ist. Er schrieb: »Ich glaube, daß die traditionelle Trennung
von Kunst und Architektur ziemlich überholt ist und die Kommunikation zwischen den verschiedenen Medien im Keim erstickt.«
Sein 1992–93 fertiggestelltes Haus in Breisach beschränkt sich
nicht nur auf die bloße Assoziation einer Verbindung von Kunst
und Architektur. Die 613 m² großen, gemischten Wohn- und Arbeitsbereiche sind auf 16 verschiedene Ebenen verteilt, die sich
in drei Hauptgruppen spiralförmig um ein zentrales, verglastes
Treppenhaus gruppieren. Spiegelhalters Gebäude wurde für eine
Familie mit Kindern entworfen, die Wert auf ein »umweltbewuß-
tes« Haus zum Wohnen und Arbeiten legte, das sowohl genügend Platz für die ganze Familie bietet als auch die Möglichkeit,
gelegentliche Konzerte und kleinere Ausstellungen zu organisie-
ren. Eine 54 m² große solare Photovoltaikfläche zur Stromgewin-
nung sowie 13 m² große röhrenförmige Vakuumkollektoren zur
Warmwassererzeugung auf dem Dach versorgen das Haus mit
Energie, wobei eine Erdgasanlage die Energieversorgung bei längerem Sonnenscheinausfall ausgleichen kann. Spiegelhalters
Interesse an Kunst und Bildhauerei kommt nicht nur in der
ungewöhnlichen Form dieses Hauses zum Ausdruck, sondern
auch in den von ihm bevorzugten Materialien, die er in und um
die örtlichen Kiesgruben entdeckte: Industriell vorgefertigte Bau-
elemente gesellen sich zu grobem, unbehandeltem Holz.

Das stark fragmentarische Erscheinungsbild dieses Hauses
scheint dem ästhetischen Ansatz von Coop Himmelb(l)au und
Zvi Hecker näherzustehen als dem von Josef Paul Kleihues, obwohl diese Architekten alle in den letzten Jahren in Deutschland
und Österreich tätig waren. Aber allen gemeinsam ist der Entwurf kraftvoller, ausdrucksstarker, architektonischer Formen –

aux attentes d'un groupe comme LVMH, cette tour a séduit le
plus pertinent critique d'architecture new-yorkais, Herbert Muschamp, qui a écrit que «l'immeuble est important, non seulement pour l'identité de la 57th Street, mais pour celle de la ville
entière. Avec sa façade de verre clair opalescent, c'est une tour
séduisante, interpellante, et qui devrait ouvrir des perspectives
créatives radicales à la conception américaine du gratte-ciel.»[12]
Clairement favorable à Portzamparc, Muschamp conclut en no-
tant que l'architecte «n'appartient à aucune école stylistique et
la description qui lui convient le mieux est peut-être celle d'un
éternel étudiant de la ville, de son passé, de son tissu, de sa
quête de nouveauté et en même temps de continuité.»

Il est fort possible que la période actuelle soit plus proche que
la précédente de se trouver un tendance dominante, qui serait
un néo-modernisme. Et pourtant les architectes qui apparemment apprécient ce style, comme Wiel Arets, rejettent ce qualificatif, préférant définir leur approche en d'autres termes. Comme
les lignes épurées de l'architecture minimaliste coexistent sans
problème avec les formes spectaculairement fragmentées de
Coop Himmelb(l)au, Zvi Hecker ou Thomas Spiegelhalter, on
pourrait penser qu'aucun accord n'est en vue sur l'orientation
future de l'architecture. Dans une certaine mesure, cependant,
on peut constater un fossé entre des générations. Des architectes plus jeunes, comme Ben van Berkel (né en 1957), Arets
(né en 1955) ou Ricciotti (né en 1952) semblent à l'opposé de
confrères comme Hecker (né en 1931) ou Wolf D. Prix (1942) et
Helmut Swiczinsky (1944) de Coop Himmelb(l)au. Les plus
jeunes créateurs penchent clairement davantage vers une approche minimaliste que leurs aînés, bien que cette règle
connaisse une exception avec Spiegelhalter (1959). On pourrait
dire que Hecker et Spiegelhalter sont tous deux des expérimen-
tateurs – donc par définition aux franges de la profession architecturale – intéressés par l'art dans ses applications à la forme
construite d'une façon plus approfondie que leurs collègues.
Une fois atteint la cinquantaine et au-delà, les architectes qui ont
réussi tendent à s'arrêter à un style bien défini, comme c'est le
cas de Mario Botta, de Sir Norman Foster, ou même de Reichen

Robert. These styles are influenced by circumstances and current topics such as ecology, but they can be seen as variations on a theme, even for the most talented of architects.

The group of European architects chosen for this book give an idea of the considerable variety of styles that exist at the present time. They also show that despite economic restrictions, Europe continues to be a highly fertile ground for architecture. One clear reason for this is that architecture has once again come into possession of its past, and the European past is far richer than the American one for example. Sensitive both to their own historical environments and to the conquests of the modernist period, which indeed originated in the "old" continent, European architects seem well equipped to deal with the rapidly changing environment of their profession.

1 Van Dyck, Hans: "Conjugal cunning. Recent work by Wiel Arets," *Archis* 4.96.
2 Werner, Frank: *Coop Himmelblau, The Power of the City*. Verlag der Georg Büchner Buchhandlung, Darmstadt, 1988.
3 Interview with Mario Botta, September 3, 1996.
4 Ibid.
5 Feireiss, Kristin (editor): *The Heinz-Galinski-School in Berlin*. Ernst Wasmuth Verlag, Berlin, 1996.
6 Kent, Cheryl: "Kleihues Defies Skepticism to Create Chicago Landmark," *Architectural Record*, August, 1996.
7 Muschamp, Herbert: "A Temple to the Present Leans Heavily on the Past," *The New York Times*, June 30, 1996.
8 Machado, Rodolfo, and Rodolphe El-Khoury: *Monolithic Architecture*. The Heinz Architectural Center, The Carnegie Museum of Art, Prestel Verlag, Munich, 1995.
9 Interview with Ben van Berkel, October 1995.
10 Ibid.
11 Muschamp, Herbert: "A Pair of Skyscrapers, Opposites That Attract," *New York Times*, August 11, 1996.
12 Muschamp, Herbert: "An Elegant Blow Against Kitsch, Vuitton and Chanel Towers Tilt the Balance on 57th Street," *New York Times*, July 23, 1996.

für die sie keine Entschuldigung benötigen. Ihre Kunst zeigt sich eher in räumlichen Begriffen als in ästhetischer Hinsicht – und dies ist ein interessanter Kontrast im Vergleich zu den Arbeiten des französischen Architekten Christian de Portzamparc. Der Gewinner des Pritzker Preises 1994 ist bisher vor allem für seine Cité de la Musique (1984–95) im Nordosten von Paris bekannt; allerdings wird ihn eines seiner aktuellen Projekte wahrscheinlich noch berühmter machen. Der LMVH Tower, den Portzamparc für eine Gruppe der französischen Luxusgüterindustrie entwarf, entsteht auf einem schmalen Gelände an der 57th Street, zwischen Fifth und Madison Avenue und genau gegenüber dem dunklen, massiven IBM Building. Es handelt sich um Portzamparcs dritten Entwurf für einen Turm, nach seinem Tour Crédit Lyonnais (Lille, Frankreich, 1991–95) und dem Bandai Tower (1994), der in Tokio geplant, aber noch nicht errichtet ist. Die »New York Times« schrieb dazu: »Portzamparc besitzt ein ambivalentes Verhältnis zur Moderne. Er verehrt sie als humanistische Ausdrucksform, verurteilt aber ihre entmenschlichenden Auswirkungen. Er würdigt das Neue als ein Zeichen des urbanen Lebens, erkennt aber auch das Bedürfnis nach Kontinuität an.«[11] Kontinuität wird in New York sicherlich etwas anders definiert als in Paris. Dennoch erweist sich Portzamparcs lyrische moderne Architektur in Manhattan als gültige Ausdrucksform in einer Stadt, die zusammen mit Chicago den Wolkenkratzer erfand.

Beim LVMH Tower gelang es ihm komplexe Bebauungsvorschriften zu seinem Vorteil zu nutzen, so daß sein Gebäude den benachbarten (und konkurrierenden) Chanel Tower beträchtlich überragt. Er versah die Fassade mit einer geschwungenen Krümmung, die im weitesten Sinne an die Form einer Blüte erinnert, wobei das siebdruckartige Milchglas Reflexionen des IBM Building vermindern und das Grünglas »den strengen Dämmungswerten« der New Yorker Energiebestimmungen gerecht werden soll. Darüber hinaus plant Christian de Portzamparc die Verwendung eines Lichtkanals von fast 100 m Länge, um das Glas der Fassade nachts in leicht abgestuften Schattierungen von Grün, Rot, Blau und Gold zu beleuchten – ein System, das er zum ersten Mal im Inneren der Konzerthalle der Cité de la Musique

& Robert. Ces styles sont influencés par les circonstances et les tendances du moment, comme l'écologie, mais peuvent aussi être considérés comme des variations sur un même thème, y compris chez les plus talentueux de ces architectes.

La sélection d'architectes européens retenus pour cet ouvrage donne une idée de la variété considérable de styles qui coexistent à l'heure actuelle. Elle montre également que malgré les restrictions économiques, l'Europe constitue toujours un terrain fertile pour l'architecture. La raison en est une fois encore que celle-ci a repris possession de son passé, et que celui de l'Europe est bien plus riche que celui des États-Unis, pour ne prendre qu'un exemple. Sensibles à la fois à leur propre environnement historique et aux conquêtes de la période moderniste, qui a d'ailleurs pris naissance dans ce «vieux» monde, les architectes européens paraissent bien équipés pour faire face à l'évolution rapide de l'environnement de leur profession.

Rudy Ricciotti, Le Stadium, Vitrolles, France, 1994–95. An interior view shows an innovative use of relatively inexpensive materials, which might be likened to the strategies of the Dutch architect Rem Koolhaas.

Rudy Ricciotti, Le Stadium, Vitrolles, Frankreich, 1994–95. Diese Innenansicht zeigt den innovativen Einsatz kostengünstiger Materialien, der an die Strategie des niederländischen Architekten Rem Koolhaas erinnert.

Rudy Ricciotti, Le Stadium, Vitrolles, France, 1994–95. Vue intérieure montrant l'utilisation inventive de matériaux relativement économiques, stratégie qui rappelle celle de l'architecte néerlandais Rem Koolhaas.

und später bei seinem Entwurf für den Bandai Tower einsetzte. Portzamparcs LVMH Tower, dessen sehr kultiviertes Design der Louis Vuitton Moët Hennessy-Gruppe angemessen scheint, erntete das Lob von New Yorks scharfsinnigstem Architekturkritiker, Herbert Muschamp, der schrieb, daß »das Gebäude nicht nur für die Identität der 57th Street, sondern der gesamten Stadt von großer Bedeutung sei. Mit seiner Fassade aus Klar- und Opalglas dürfte dieses provozierende, verführerische Bauwerk das kreative Spektrum des amerikanischen Wolkenkratzerdesigns radikal erweitern.«[12] Der offensichtlich Portzamparc sehr wohlgesonnene Muschamp schreibt weiter: »Er gehört keiner stilistischen Schule an und läßt sich wahrscheinlich am besten beschreiben als ein unermüdlicher Beobachter der Stadt, ihrer Vergangenheit, ihrer Struktur und ihrer Sehnsucht nach sowohl Neuem als auch nach Kontinuität.«

Wahrscheinlich ist die aktuelle Periode einem dominanten Trend näher ist als die vorhergehende, und zwar in Form der Neo-Moderne. Dennoch lehnen selbst Architekten wie Wiel Arets, der diesen Stil offensichtlich schätzt, eine solche Einordnung zumindest dem Namen nach ab und erläutern ihren Ansatz lieber mit Hilfe anderer Begriffe. Da die sanften Formen minimalistischer Architektur zeitgleich mit den dramatischen, gebrochenen Formen von Coop Himmelb(l)au, Zvi Hecker oder Thomas Spiegelhalter entstehen können, darf man davon ausgehen, daß in der Frage, welchen Weg die Architektur der Zukunft einschlagen soll, noch keine Einigung in Sicht ist. Allerdings gibt es Hinweise auf eine Kluft zwischen den Generationen: Jüngere Architekten wie Ben van Berkel (1957 geboren), Arets (1955 geboren) oder Ricciotti (1952 geboren) scheinen mit anderen wie Hecker (1931 geboren) oder den Leitern von Coop Himmelb(l)au, Wolf D. Prix (1942 geboren) und Helmut Swiczinsky (1944 geboren) uneins zu sein. Die Jüngeren sind einem minimalistischen Ansatz deutlich stärker zugeneigt als ihre älteren Kollegen – wobei Spiegelhalter (1959 geboren) die Ausnahme von dieser Regel darstellt. Man könnte behaupten, daß sowohl Hecker als auch Spiegelhalter experimentelle Architekten sind, laut Definition am äußersten Rand des Berufbildes des Architekten stehen und an

der Kunst und ihrer Anwendbarkeit für die gebaute Form stärkeres Interesse zeigen als ihre Kollegen. Dagegen neigen erfolgreiche Architekten, die die Fünfzig überschritten haben, eher zu einem klar definierten, persönlichen Stil, wie im Falle von Mario Botta, Sir Norman Foster und sogar dem Team Reichen & Robert. Auch wenn ihre Stile von verschiedenen Umständen und aktuellen Fragen wie der Ökologie beeinflußt werden, kann man sie als Variation eines Themas sehen – und dies trifft auch für die talentiertesten unter ihnen zu.

Die für dieses Buch ausgewählte Gruppe europäischer Architekten vermittelt einen Eindruck von der bemerkenswerten stilistischen Bandbreite, die zur Zeit existiert. Darüber hinaus zeigt sie uns, daß Europa, trotz wirtschaftlicher Einschränkungen, nach wie vor ein fruchtbarer Nährboden für Architektur ist. Einer der Gründe dafür ist, daß die Architektur sich wieder einmal ihrer Vergangenheit besonnen hat – und die europäische Vergangenheit ist bei weitem reicher als beispielsweise die amerikanische. Sowohl ihrer eigenen historischen Umgebung als auch den Eroberungen der Moderne bewußt – die bekanntlich im »alten« Kontinent ihren Siegeszug begann –, scheinen die europäischen Architekt gut darauf vorbereitet, mit der sich ständig verändernden Umwelt ihres Berufsstandes Schritt zu halten.

Jean Nouvel, Galeries Lafayette, Berlin, Germany, 1993–96. An interior view showing the cone-shaped voids that penetrate the building and make it more transparent.

Jean Nouvel, Galeries Lafayette, Berlin, Deutschland, 1993–96. Die kegelförmigen Hohlräume durchbrechen das Gebäude und lassen es transparenter erscheinen.

Jean Nouvel, Galeries Lafayette, Berlin, Allemagne, 1993–96. Vue intérieure sur les vastes espaces en forme de cônes inversés qui pénètrent le bâtiment et le rendent encore plus transparent.

Wiel Arets

Born in Heerlen, The Netherlands, in 1955, Wiel Arets established his own office there in 1984. He graduated from the Technical University in Eindhoven the year before. A Diploma Unit Master at the Architectural Association, London from 1988 to 1992, he traveled in Russia, Japan, America and Europe from 1984 to 1989. It may be this experience that has led him to objecting to being called a "Dutch" architect. As he has said, "I believe we are sooner a child of our times than born in a certain place. We travel around, teach, and are influenced by things that happen all over the world." Author of the 1990 Academy of Art and Architecture in nearby Maastricht, Arets is known for a strong modern style, which has been compared to that of Tadao Ando. A former visiting Professor at Columbia University in New York (1991–92), Dean of the Berlage Institute, Postgraduate Laboratory of Architecture in Amsterdam (1995–98), Wiel Arets is currently completing 104 apartments, located on the Jacobsplaats in Rotterdam (1995–97).

Wiel Arets wurde 1955 in Heerlen (Niederlande) geboren und gründete dort 1984 sein eigenes Architekturbüro, nachdem er ein Jahr zuvor sein Studium an der Technischen Hochschule Eindhoven abgeschlossen hatte. Von 1984 bis 1989 bereiste Arets Rußland, Japan, Amerika und Europa; daneben war er 1988–92 als Diploma Unit Master an der Architectural Association in London beschäftigt. Wahrscheinlich sind es diese Auslandserfahrungen, die ihn gegen die Bezeichnung »Niederländischer Architekt« Einspruch erheben lassen: »Ich glaube, daß wir eher Kinder unserer Zeit als von einem bestimmten Geburtsort abhängig sind. Wir reisen, lehren, und werden von Dingen beeinflußt, die überall auf der Welt geschehen.« Arets, der Gründer der 1990 entstandenen Akademie für Kunst und Architektur im nahegelegenen Maastricht, ist bekannt für seinen kraftvollen modernen Stil, der mit dem von Tadao Ando verglichen wurde. Zur Zeit stellt der ehemalige Gastprofessor an der Columbia University, New York (1991–92) und Dekan am Berlage Postgraduierteninstitut für Architektur in Amsterdam (1995–98) den Bau von 104 Apartments am Jacobsplaats in Rotterdam fertig (1995–97).

Né à Heerlen, Pays-Bas, en 1955, Wiel Arets y ouvre son agence en 1984, après avoir passé son diplôme de l'Université technique d'Eindhoven l'année précédente. Enseignant du programme de diplôme de l'Architectural Association de Londres, de 1988 à 1992, il voyage en Russie, au Japon, en Amérique et en Europe de 1984 à 1989. C'est peut-être cette expérience internationale qui lui fait refuser le qualificatif d'architecte «néerlandais». Il déclare ainsi: «Je pense que nous sommes davantage les enfants de notre époque que déterminés par notre naissance dans un lieu précis. Nous voyageons, nous enseignons et sommes influencés par tout ce qui se passe dans le monde.» Auteur, en 1990 de l'Académie d'art et d'architecture de la ville voisine de Maastricht, Arets est connu pour un style moderne et puissant qui a été comparé à celui de Tadao Ando. Professeur invité à Columbia University, New York (1991–92), doyen de l'Institut Berlage, laboratoire post-universitaire d'études architecturales d'Amsterdam (1995–98), il achève actuellement un programme de 104 appartements sur Jacobsplaats à Rotterdam (1995–97).

Wiel Arets, AZL Headquarters, Heerlen, The Netherlands, 1991–95.

Wiel Arets, AZL Hauptgebäude, Heerlen, Niederlande, 1991–95.

Wiel Arets, siège social d'AZL, Heerlen, Pays-Bas, 1991–95.

AZL Headquarters

Heerlen, The Netherlands, 1991–1995

This 5,400 square meters administration building for about 220 persons was built for the former Limburg mineworkers pension fund, which has branched out into dealing with major corporation and government pensions. It is located near the center of the small, modern city of Heerlen, close to the pedestrian zone and directly adjoining the elegant 1941 brick structure that had served as the AZL headquarters until now. With its crisp, unexpected concrete forms in sharp contrast with the immediate residential and shopping neighborhood, the AZL building has a parking lot and entrance to one side, cut deeply into the ground. This sculptural parking area, also made of concrete, connects the two parallel roads between which the original headquarters was lodged, Akenstraat, where there are numerous shops and a smaller residential street to the rear where the cars enter. Built at a cost of 12 million florins, it brings to mind the work of Tadao Ando more than the strict neo-modernism so popular in The Netherlands at the moment.

The entrance to the new building is recessed below ground level, creating a gently curved space used as a parking lot. The plan shows the location of the building, with Akenstraat to the right. The darker volumes are the older buildings.

Der Eingang zum neuen Gebäude wurde unter Planum gelegt. Die Fläche davor dient als Parkplatz. Die Karte zeigt den Standort des Gebäudes; die Akenstraat verläuft auf der rechten Seite. Die dunkleren Baukörper sind die älteren Gebäude.

L'entrée du nouveau bâtiment est en dessous du niveau du sol, créant un espace doucement incurvé qui sert de parking. Le plan montre l'implantation de l'immeuble et l'Akenstraat, à droite. Les volumes foncés représentent les bâtiments anciens.

Das 5 400 m² große Verwaltungsgebäude für etwa 220 Mitarbeiter wurde für die ehemalige Pensionskasse der Limburger Bergarbeiter errichtet, die im Laufe der Zeit auch die Pensionsverwaltung anderer Aktiengesellschaften und Regierungsstellen übernahm. Das Bauwerk liegt im Zentrum der kleinen, modernen Stadt Heerlen in unmittelbarer Nähe der Fußgängerzone und grenzt an einen eleganten Ziegelsteinbau aus dem Jahre 1941, der bis vor kurzem als Hauptgebäude der Pensionskasse diente. Die strengen, ungewöhnlichen Betonformen des AZL-Entwurfs, die in starkem Kontrast zu den benachbarten Wohn- und Einkaufsvierteln stehen, erstrecken sich auch auf den Parkplatz und den Eingangsbereich, der auf einer Seite des Gebäudes tief in den Grund eingeschnitten wurde. Die ebenfalls aus Beton erbaute, skulpturale Parkfläche dient als Verbindung zweier parallel verlaufender Straßen, zwischen denen das ursprüngliche Verwaltungsgebäude lag – der Akenstraat mit ihren zahlreichen Geschäften und einer kleineren Wohnstraße auf der Rückseite des Gebäudes, von der aus die Autos auf den Parkplatz einfahren können. Das für eine Summe von 12 Millionen Gulden erbaute Projekt erinnert stärker an die Arbeiten Tadao Andos als an die zur Zeit in den Niederlanden so populäre Neo-Moderne.

Cet immeuble administratif de 5 400 m² conçu pour 220 employés a été construit pour l'ancienne caisse de pension des mineurs du Limbourg, qui gère maintenant les fonds de retraites de grandes entreprises et d'administrations. Situé non loin du centre de la petite ville moderne de Heerlen, il est proche d'une zone piétonnière et adjacent à l'ancien siège social d'AZL, élégante construction de brique (1941). Avec ses formes de béton tendues et suprenantes, contrastant fortement avec le style de ce quartier commercial et résidentiel, l'immeuble AZL est doté d'une entrée et d'un accès de parking profondément encastrés dans le sol. Ce parking sculptural, également en béton, réunit les deux voies parallèles entre lesquelles l'ancien siège était implanté: l'Akenstraat, voie commerçante, et à l'arrière une petite rue résidentielle par laquelle accèdent les véhicules. Construite pour un budget de 12 millions de florins, cette réalisation rappelle plus l'œuvre de Tadao Ando que le néomodernisme strict à la mode actuellement aux Pays-Bas.

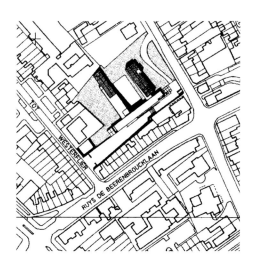

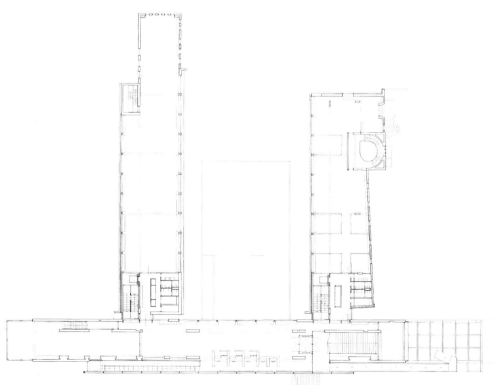

56 Wiel Arets: AZL Headquarters, 1991–95

As the plan to the left shows, the main volume of the addition is in the shape of a bar, at the bottom, "plugging" into the existing brick structures. The slit-shaped opening in the concrete facade faces Akenstraat.

Wie der Grundriß links zeigt, besitzt der Hauptbaukörper des Erweiterungbaus die Form eines Riegels, der den bereits vorhandenen Ziegelsteinbauten »vorgeschoben« wurde. Die schlitzförmige Öffnung in der Betonfassade geht auf die Akenstraat hinaus.

Comme le montre le plan à gauche, le principal volume de l'extension en forme de barre, en bas, se «branche» sur les constructions de brique existantes. La façade de béton à longue ouverture horizontale donne sur l'Akenstraat.

With its strict geometry and controlled views, as well as the use of concrete, the architecture of Wiel Arets here brings to mind the designs of Tadao Ando.

Sowohl in ihrer strengen Geometrie und den kontrollierten Ausblicken als auch in der Verwendung von Beton erinnert Wiel Arets' Architektur an die Entwürfe Tadao Andos.

Avec sa géométrie rigoureuse, ses vues calculées et son recours au béton, l'architecture de Wiel Arets rappelle certaines réalisations de Tadao Ando.

Ben van Berkel

Ben van Berkel, based in Amsterdam, was born in Utrecht in 1957, and was trained at the Architectural Association in London by such figures as Rem Koolhaas and Zaha Hadid. He insists that he is of a different generation, implicitly criticizing his elders for designing buildings to suit their own theories. "If there is a theory," he says, "I would apply it in a more tactile, a more physical way, in the sense that one can rethink typologies of organization or the use of materials." Van Berkel has summed up his approach with the term "mobile forces," or the multitude of public, urban, structural and architectural considerations that give form to a project. Fascinated by 1950s engineer/architects like Nervi or Candela, van Berkel worked briefly with Calatrava in the late 1980s. "I like to believe that you can invent as an architect, like a scientist does," says Ben van Berkel. "I like to transgress ideas to redefine them." Most recently, he has become quite well known in The Netherlands for having designed the new Erasmus Bridge in Rotterdam.

Der in Amsterdam ansässige Ben van Berkel wurde 1957 in Utrecht geboren und erhielt seine Ausbildung an der Architectural Association in London unter Rem Koolhaas und Zaha Hadid. Aber van Berkel betont, daß er einer anderen Generation angehört und wirft seinen Dozenten implizit vor, Bauten nur mit dem Ziel errichtet zu haben, den eigenen Theorien zu genügen. »Wenn überhaupt eine Architekturtheorie existiert«, sagt van Berkel, »würde ich sie auf eine greifbare, physische Art und Weise umsetzen, wobei die Typologien der räumlichen Organisation oder die Verwendung der Materialien neu überdacht werden könnten.« Van Berkel faßt seinen architektonischen Ansatz unter dem Begriff »Mobile Forces« zusammen, worunter er die Vielfalt öffentlicher, urbaner, bautechnischer und architektonischer Erwägungen versteht, die einem Projekt seine bestimmte Form verleihen. Der von den Ingenieuren/Architekten der 50er Jahre wie Nervi oder Candela faszinierte van Berkel arbeitete Ende der 80er Jahre kurz mit Calatrava zusammen. »Ich gebe mich gern der Illusion hin, daß man als Architekt ebenso wie ein Wissenschaftler etwas erfinden kann«, sagt er. »Ich liebe es, Vorstellungen zu durchbrechen, um sie danach wieder neu zu definieren.« Durch den kürzlich fertiggestellten Bau der Erasmusbrücke in Rotterdam wurde van Berkel vor allem in den Niederlanden einer breiteren Öffentlichkeit bekannt.

Installé à Amsterdam, Ben van Berkel est né à Utrecht en 1957, et a fait ses études à l'Architectural Association de Londres sous la direction d'enseignants comme Rem Koolhaas et Zaha Hadid. Il insiste sur la différence de générations qui le sépare de ceux-ci, les critiquant de concevoir des immeubles qui cherchent essentiellement à confirmer leurs théories. «S'il existe une théorie,» dit-il, «je l'appliquerais d'une manière plus tactile, plus physique, dans le sens où l'on pourrait repenser les typologies d'organisation ou d'utilisation des matériaux.» Il a résumé son approche dans l'expression de «force mobiles,» c'est-à-dire la multitude des contraintes publiques, urbaines, structurelles et architecturales qui donnent forme à un projet. Fasciné par les architectes-ingénieurs des années 50, tels Nervi ou Candela, van Berkel a brièvement travaillé auprès de Calatrava à la fin des années 80. «J'aime à croire que l'on peut inventer avec l'architecture, comme un savant peut le faire. J'aime transgresser les idées reçues pour les redéfinir,» ajoute-t-il. Récemment, son projet du pont Érasme, à Rotterdam, lui a apporté une certaine célébrité dans son pays.

Ben van Berkel, Wilbrink House, Amersfoort, The Netherlands, 1992–94.

Ben van Berkel, Wilbrink-Haus, Amersfoort, Niederlande, 1992–94.

Ben van Berkel, villa Wilbrink, Amersfoort, Pays-Bas, 1992–94.

Wilbrink House

Amersfoort, The Netherlands, 1992–1994

Visitors to the Wilbrink house in Amersfoort are greeted not by the traditional, immaculately kept Dutch garden, but by two gently inclined planes covered with colored railway gravel. A passage between the two planes suggests an opening, but this may be one of the more unusual facades in contemporary architecture, especially if one takes into account the traditional or even "kitsch" nature of the neighboring houses. The Wilbrinks apparently do not like gardening, and if that is indeed the case, they certainly got their money's worth. Despite its unusual appearance, this house has been designed to admit a maximum amount of daylight, and does have a garden of sorts at the rear with a geometric arrangement of trees. Ben van Berkel, who often uses rather complex architectural language to explain his efforts, here speaks in terms of "delimitation," "transition" and "introversion." All of these words do in fact describe an attempt to redefine some of the most basic aspects of a home.

Die Besucher des Hauses Wilbrink in Amersfoort werden nicht von einem gepflegten Vorgarten empfangen, sondern von zwei schiefen Ebenen, die mit farbigem Schotter bedeckt sind. Ein Durchgang weist auf eine Öffnung hin und vervollständigt eine der ungewöhnlichsten Fassaden der zeitgenössischen Architektur – vor allem, wenn man sie mit dem Erscheinungsbild der benachbarten Häuser vergleicht. Die Familie Wilbrink legt keinen Wert auf Gartenarbeit und hat wirklich etwas für ihr Geld bekommen. Das Haus wurde so entworfen, daß möglichst viel Tageslicht in die Räume einfallen kann; darüber hinaus besitzt es auf der Rückseite eine Art Garten mit einem geometrischen Arrangement von Bäumen. Ben van Berkel, der sich häufig einer recht komplexen architektonischen Terminologie bedient, spricht in diesem Zusammenhang von »Abgrenzung«, »Übergang« und »Introversion« – alles Worte, die im Grunde den Versuch beschreiben, einige Grundlagen des Wohnhausbaus neu zu definieren.

Les visiteurs de la villa Wilbrink à Amersfoort sont accueillis non par le traditionnel jardin impeccable des maisons hollandaises, mais par deux plans doucement inclinés et une allée de gravier coloré. Un passage entre ces deux plans suggère une ouverture. C'est sans doute l'une des plus extraordinaires façades de l'architecture contemporaine, surtout si l'on prend en compte la nature traditionnelle ou même kitsch des villas avoisinantes. Les Wilbrink n'aiment apparemment pas le jardinage, et ont été comblés à cet égard. Malgré son apparence étonnante, cette maison a été conçue pour bénéficier du maximum de lumière naturelle, et possède une sorte de jardin animé de quelques arbres fruitiers. Ben van Berkel parle ici de «délimitation,» de «transition» et «d'introversion,» pour décrire cette tentative de redéfinir quelques-uns des aspects les plus basiques d'une maison.

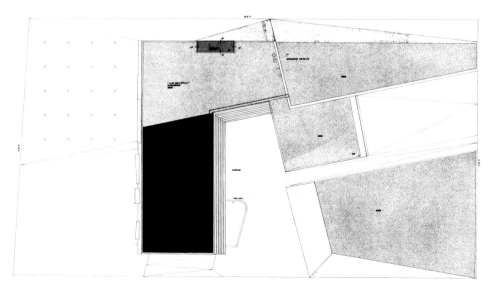

Page 62: The street side "facade" of the house is covered with gravel. These inclined planes are visible on the right-hand section of the plan.
Page 63: The inner areas of the house provide carefully calculated openings for daylight.

Seite 62: Die zur Straße weisende »Fassade« des Hauses wurde mit Schotter bedeckt. Diese ansteigenden Ebenen sind im rechten Teil des Grundrisses zu erkennen.
Seite 63: Die inneren Bereiche des Hauses besitzen sorgfältig berechnete Öffnungen, durch die Tageslicht in die Räume einfallen kann.

Page 62: La «façade» côté rue est recouverte de gravier. Ces plans inclinés sont visibles sur le plan, à droite.
Page 63: Les espaces intérieurs offrent des ouvertures soigneusement calculées pour capter la lumière naturelle.

64 Ben van Berkel: Wilbrink House, 1992–94

At the rear of the house, a small orchard provides the only direct intervention of nature. The skewed angles of the exterior are carried through to the very hospitable interior. The west elevation of the house shows the angular form of the whole structure.

Der kleine Obstgarten hinter dem Haus ist die einzige Präsenz von Natur. Die schiefen Ebenen des Äußeren werden auch im gastlichen Hausinneren aufrechterhalten. Eine Ansicht von Westen zeigt die winklige Form des gesamten Gebäudes.

À l'arrière, un petit verger est la seule présence directe de la nature. Les angles aigus de l'extérieur se traduisent en réalité par un plan intérieur très hospitalier. L'élévation ouest montre la forme anguleuse de la construction.

Ben van Berkel: Wilbrink House, 1992–94 **65**

Mario Botta

A number of Swiss cities like Lugano have been marked by the architecture of Mario Botta. Basel in the north has recently become the home not only of the new Tinguely Museum, but also of a headquarters building for the UBS on the Aeschenplatz, a large cylindrical form with a cladding of dark and light alternating bands of gray granite. Cylinders are in fact a preferred form for this architect, born in Mendrisio, Switzerland, near the Italian border, in 1943. Mario Botta designed his first house at the age of 16. Brief contacts with Le Corbusier in Paris in 1965 and with Louis Kahn in Venice in 1968 seem to have influenced him, but by the 1970s he had developed a strong personal style most clearly expressed in the private houses built in Cadenazzo (1970–71), Riva San Vitale (1971–73), or Ligornetto (1975–76), all in Switzerland. In the 1980s, Botta continued to create powerful geometric designs for houses, often built with brick, but he also began larger-scale work, such as his Médiathèque in Villeurbanne, France (1984–88) or his cultural center in Chambéry, France (1982–87). His Évry Cathedral and San Francisco Museum of Modern Art buildings placed him in the international elite of contemporary architecture.

Mario Botta hat mit seiner Architektur eine Reihe von Schweizer Städten geprägt. Dazu zählt neben Lugano auch Basel, wo vor kurzem nicht nur das neue Tinguely-Museum entstand, sondern auch das Hauptgebäude des Schweizerischen Bankvereins am Aeschenplatz – eine große, zylindrische Form, verkleidet mit Bändern aus abwechselnd hell- und dunkelgrauem Granit. Zylinder sind in der Tat eine der bevorzugten Bauformen dieses 1943 in Mendrisio, in der Nähe der italienischen Grenze geborenen Architekten. Mario Botta entwarf sein erstes Haus im Alter von 16 Jahren. Die kurze Zusammenarbeit mit Le Corbusier in Paris (1965) und Louis Kahn in Venedig (1968) schien ihn zunächst stark zu beeinflussen, aber bereits Anfang der 70er Jahre hatte er einen ausgeprägten persönlichen Stil entwickelt, der in den Privathäusern in der Schweiz in Cadenazzo (1970–71), Riva San Vitale (1971–73) und Ligornetto (1975–76) deutlich zum Ausdruck kommt. In den 80er Jahren entwarf Botta weiterhin expressive, geometrische Gebäude, die häufig als Ziegelbauten entstanden, aber er widmete sich auch größeren Projekten wie etwa der Médiathèque in Villeurbanne, Frankreich (1984–88) oder dem Kulturzentrum in Chambéry, Frankreich (1982–87). Mit seiner Cathédrale d'Évry und dem San Francisco Museum of Modern Art sicherte sich Botta endgültig einen Platz in der internationalen Elite zeitgenössischer Architekten.

Un certain nombre de villes suisses, comme Lugano, sont marquées par l'architecture de Mario Botta. Au nord, Bâle s'est récemment enrichie non seulement du nouveau musée Tinguely, mais du siège de l'Union des Banques Suisses, Aeschenplatz, vaste construction cylindrique recouverte de bandeaux alternés de granit sombre et clair. Le cylindre est une des formes préférées de cet architecte suisse né à Mendrisio, près de la frontière italienne, en 1943. Mario Botta a dessiné sa première maison à 16 ans. De brefs contacts avec Le Corbusier à Paris en 1965 et Louis Kahn à Venise, en 1968, semblent l'avoir influencé, mais à partir des années 70, il a développé un style personnel et puissant qui s'est d'abord exprimé dans des résidences privées construites à Cadenazzo (1970–71), Riva San Vitale (1971–73) ou Ligornetto (1975–76). Dans les années 80, il continue à créer des formes à la géométrie affirmée souvent en briques, mais aussi des projets plus importants comme la Médiathèque de Villeurbanne (1984–88), ou le centre culturel de Chambéry (1982–87). Sa cathédrale pour Évry et le San Francisco Museum of Modern Art ont fait de lui un membre à part entière de l'élite architecturale internationale.

Mario Botta, Tamaro Chapel, Ticino, Switzerland, 1990–96.

Mario Botta, Tamaro-Kapelle, Tessin, Schweiz, 1990–96.

Mario Botta, chapelle au Monte Tamaro, Tessin, Suisse, 1990–96.

Tamaro Chapel

Ticino, Switzerland, 1990–1996

This chapel is located at an altitude of almost 2,000 meters above the highway that links Bellinzona to Lugano. It has an uninterrupted view over the valley of Lugano, and is indeed one of the most spectacular works of contemporary European architecture. Its rugged power is defined not only by its strong forms, but also by its unusual cladding of rusticated porphyry. The whole is completed by a group of frescoes by the Italian painter Enzo Cucchi, who seems to have been very much in tune with the spiritual nature of the architect's scheme. Both the chapel itself and its decor are indisputably modern, and yet they also appear to have roots in ancient architecture. In no case are they incompatible either with their setting, or with their intended function, which is in itself a substantive commentary on the positive evolution of contemporary architecture.

Die Kapelle liegt auf einer Höhe von etwa 2 000 m, über der Autobahn, die Bellinzona mit Lugano verbindet. Das Bauwerk – von dem aus sich dem Besucher ein völlig freier Blick über das Tal von Lugano bietet – zählt zu den eindrucksvollsten Arbeiten der zeitgenössischen europäischen Architektur. Der Gesamteindruck roher Kraft entsteht nicht nur aufgrund der massigen Gebäudeformen, sondern auch durch die ungewöhnliche Bossenwerkverkleidung aus Porphyr. Vervollständigt wird das Projekt durch eine Freskengruppe des italienischen Künstlers Enzo Cucchi, dessen Arbeiten die spirituelle Natur des Gebäudeentwurfs widerzuspiegeln scheinen. Kapelle und Dekoration wirken unzweifelhaft modern, verweisen aber gleichzeitig auf ihre Ursprünge in der Architektur der Antike. Damit stehen sie nicht nur im Einklang mit ihrer direkten Umgebung, sondern werden auch ihrer beabsichtigten Funktion gerecht – einem eigenständigen Kommentar zur positiven Entwicklung der zeitgenössischen Architektur.

Située à près de 2 000 m d'altitude, cette chapelle domine l'autoroute qui relie Bellinzona à Lugano. Bénéficiant d'une vue presque illimitée sur la vallée de Lugano, elle constitue l'une des œuvres les plus spectaculaires de l'architecture européenne contemporaine. Sa force brute se définit non seulement par ses formes puissantes, mais également par son parement inhabituel de porphyre rustiqué. L'ensemble est complété par une suite de fresques du peintre italien Enzo Cucchi, qui semble être entré en phase avec la nature spirituelle du projet de l'architecte. La chapelle elle-même et son décor, indiscutablement modernes, n'en donnent pas moins l'impression de prendre leurs racines dans une architecture plus ancienne. Tous deux sont en parfait accord avec leur cadre et leur fonction, ce qui en soit est un aspect positif de l'évolution de l'architecture contemporaine.

A drawing by Mario Botta shows the relation of the chapel to the ski-lift structure and restaurant, with the Monte Tamaro itself to the rear. Blending in with the topography of the site, the Chapel dominates the valley of Bellinzona.

Diese Zeichnung Mario Bottas verdeutlicht die Dimensionen der Kapelle im Vergleich zum Skilift und zum Restaurant; im Hintergrund erkennt man den Monte Tamaro. Obwohl sich die Kapelle in die topographische Beschaffenheit der Umgebung einfügt, beherrscht sie das Tal von Bellinzona.

Ce dessin de Mario Botta montre la relation entre la chapelle, le terminal et le restaurant de la remontée mécanique, et le Monte Tamaro lui-même, en arrière-plan. Intégrée à la topographie, la chapelle domine la vallée de Bellinzona.

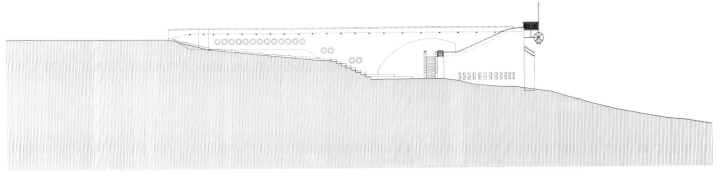

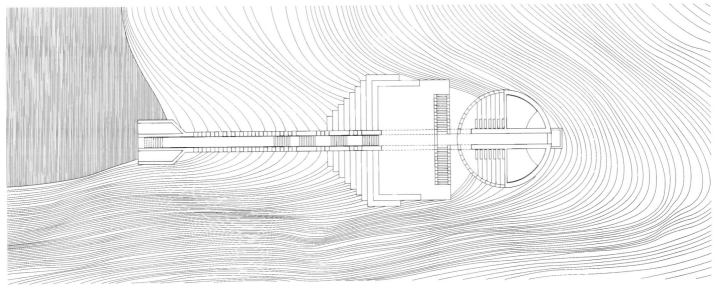

Mario Botta: Tamaro Chapel, 1990–96 **69**

Page 70: *An upper walkway leads to an observation point.*
Page 71: *The frescoes of the painter Enzo Cucchi begin outside and continue into the chapel itself, with the representation of two cupped hands behind the altar.*

Seite 70: *Ein Laufgang führt zu einem Aussichtspunkt.*
Seite 71: *Die Fresken des Malers Enzo Cucchi beginnen auf der Außenseite des Bauwerks und setzen sich im Inneren der Kapelle fort; direkt hinter dem Altar erkennt man die Darstellung zweier geöffneter Hände.*

Page 70: *Une passerelle-promenoir en partie supérieure mène à un belvédère.*
Page 71: *Les fresques du peintre Enzo Cucchi commencent à l'extérieur et se poursuivent dans la chapelle elle-même, s'achevant derrière l'autel par deux mains jointes en geste d'offrande.*

Pages 72–73: *In this night view, the "sacred heart" shape of the chapel is visible with the arched flyover leading to the observation platform. The use of porphyry for the cladding gives a rugged, almost medieval aspect to the whole.*

Seite 72–73: *Auf der Nachtansicht erkennt man die »Herz-Jesu«-Form der Kapelle und die zweiläufige Treppe, die zur Aussichtsplattform führt. Die Verwendung von Porphyr verleiht dem Bauwerk ein rauhes, mittelalterlich anmutendes Äußeres.*

Pages 72–73: *Dans cette vue nocturne, la forme de «cœur sacré» de la chapelle se dessine sous la passerelle menant à la plate-forme d'observation. Le porphyre des murs donne un aspect brut, presque médiéval, à l'ensemble.*

Mario Botta: Tamaro Chapel, 1990–96 **71**

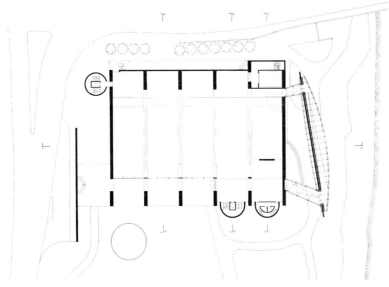

74 Mario Botta: Tinguely Museum, 1993–96

Tinguely Museum
Basel, Switzerland, 1993–1996

With 2,866 square meters of exhibition space and a total area of 6,057 square meters, the new Tinguely Museum was built through the generosity of the pharmaceuticals giant F. Hoffmann-La Roche AG and the widow of the artist Niki de Saint Phalle, and was erected on the premises of the corporation, on the banks of the Rhine, opposite the old city of Basel. The site, although in many respects quite attractive, posed numerous architectural problems, not the least of which was the highway and rail link that passes directly next to the building. Built for a budget of 30 million Swiss francs, the structure is clad in a pink Alsace sandstone (Rosé de Champenay), which immediately differentiates it from Botta's more frequent use of brick. The materials used inside, such as gray-tinted oak floors or Venetian black stucco (Stucco lucido veneziano), were chosen by the architect in intentional contrast to the ephemeral, largely metallic creations of the sculptor Jean Tinguely. The most spectacular architectural gesture seen in the museum is what Botta calls "La Barca," a long sloping gallery leading visitors into the museum as it offers them a view of the Rhine.

Das neue Tinguely-Museum, das bei 6 057 m² Gesamtfläche 2 866 m² an Ausstellungs-flächen bietet und aufgrund der Großzügigkeit des Pharma-Giganten Hoffmann-La Roche und der Witwe des Künstlers, Niki de Saint Phalle, erbaut werden konnte, entstand auf einem Grundstück der Firma am Ufer des Rheins, direkt gegenüber der Altstadt von Basel. Obwohl das Baugelände in vieler Hinsicht äußerst attraktiv war, warf es dennoch eine Reihe architektonischer Probleme auf, zu denen auch die Autobahn und eine Eisenbahn-verbindung beitrugen, die in unmittelbarer Nähe an den Gebäuden vorüberführen. Das mit einem Etat von 30 Millionen Schweizer Franken erbaute Museum ist mit rosa Sand-stein aus dem Elsaß (Rosé de Champenay) verkleidet und unterscheidet sich dadurch bereits auf den ersten Blick von den für Botta so typischen Ziegelbauten. Die im Inneren verwendeten Materialien wie grau gefärbte Eichenböden und venezianischer schwarzer Stuck (Stucco lucido veneziano) wurden vom Architekten im bewußten Kontrast zu den fili-granen, meist metallischen Kreationen des Bildhauers Jean Tinguely ausgewählt. Das im-posanteste architektonische Element dieses Bauwerks ist eine lange ansteigende Galerie, die Botta als »La Barca« bezeichnet und die den Besuchern beim Betreten des Museums einen Blick auf den Rhein bietet.

Avec ses 2 866 m² d'espaces d'exposition et une surface totale de 6 057 m² ce nouveau mu-sée a été construit grâce à la générosité du géant de l'industrie pharmaceutique, Hoff-mann-La Roche et de la veuve de l'artiste, Niki de Saint Phalle. Il a été édifié sur des terrains appartenant à l'entreprise en bordure du Rhin, face à la vieille ville de Bâle. Le site, bien que très séduisant à de nombreux égards, a posé de nombreux problèmes d'ordre architectural, les moindres n'étant pas les liaisons ferrées et autoroutières qui passent directement à proxi-mité. Construit pour un budget de 30 millions de francs suisses, le bâtiment est recouvert de calcaire rosé d'Alsace (Rosé de Champenay), inhabituel chez un Botta habitué à la brique. Les matériaux intérieurs, comme les sols en chêne teinté gris et le stuc noir (stucco lucido veneziano) ont été volontairement choisis par l'architecte pour contraster avec les créations essentiellement métalliques du sculpteur Jean Tinguely. Le geste architectural le plus specta-culaire est ce que Botta appelle «la barca», une longue galerie en pente, le long du Rhin, qui conduit les visiteurs vers le bâtiment.

A street-side facade with the enlarged signature of Jean Tinguely. On the plan, the Rhine is located to the right, and the Basel-Berne highway above.

Ansicht der Straßenfassade mit einer vergrößerten Signatur von Jean Tinguely. Auf dem Grundriß erkennt man rechts den Rhein und oben die Autobahn Basel-Bern.

Façade sur la rue avec la signature de Jean Tinguely. Sur le plan, le Rhin se trouve à droite, et l'autoroute Bâle-Berne en haut.

Left: The entrance area of the museum with a fountain by Jean Tinguely.
Below: Interior and exterior views of the "barca" entrance ramp, with its view out onto the Rhine and the old city of Basel.

Links: Der Eingangsbereich des Museums mit einem Brunnen von Jean Tinguely.
Unten: Innen- und Außenansicht der als »Barca« bezeichneten Eingangsrampe, die einen Blick über den Rhein und die Altstadt von Basel ermöglicht.

À gauche: La zone d'entrée du musée, avec une fontaine de Jean Tinguely.
Ci-dessous: Vues intérieures et extérieures de la «barca», la rampe d'accès de l'entrée qui donne sur le Rhin et le vieux Bâle.

Mario Botta: Tinguely Museum, 1993–96 **77**

The main exhibition area on the ground floor, with a view onto the neighboring park. The mezzanine, which is the first space the visitor sees inside, looks out onto this main exhibition floor. Cross-sections show the building from each angle. The entrance area is visible on the bottom drawing.

Die größte Ausstellungsfläche liegt im Erdgeschoß und bietet Ausblick auf den benachbarten Park. Vom Zwischengeschoß aus, durch das der Besucher das Museum betritt, führt der Blick auf die darunter liegende Ausstellungsfläche. Die Querschnitte zeigen das Gebäude aus jedem Winkel; ganz unten der Eingangsbereich.

La principale galerie d'exposition du rez-de-chaussée, qui donne sur le parc. La mezzanine, première salle parcourue par les visiteurs en entrant, domine le grand espace d'exposition. Les coupes montrent le bâtiment sous divers angles, l'entrée figure sur la dernière.

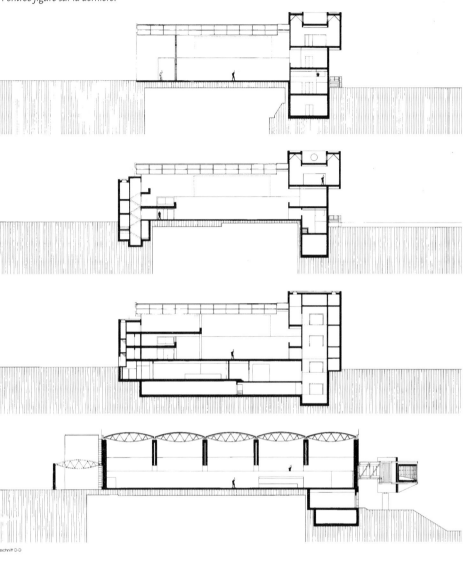

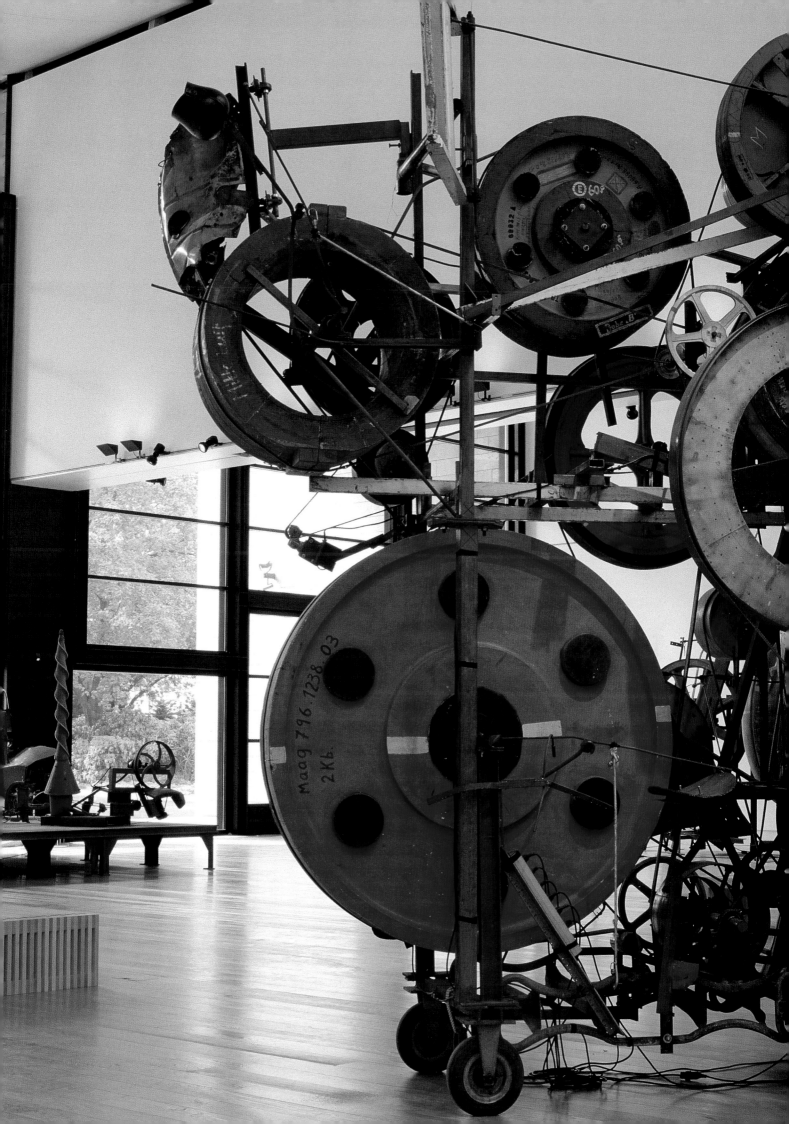

Coop Himmelb(l)au

Wolf D. Prix *Helmut Swiczinsky*

Coop Himmelb(l)au was founded in 1968 in Vienna, Austria by Wolf D. Prix and Helmut Swiczinsky. They form an unusual team in that their background is very international. Wolf Prix was born in 1942 in Vienna. He was educated at the Technische Universität, Vienna, the Southern California Institute of Architecture (SCI-Arc), and the Architectural Association (AA) in London. Helmut Swiczinsky was born in 1944 in Poznan, Poland. Raised in Vienna, he was also educated at the Technische Universität, Vienna and at the AA in London. Partly through their connection to such prestigious teaching institutions as the AA and SCI-Arc, Coop Himmelb(l)au have already long been members of the international elite of architecture, despite the fact that their body of built work is limited. Since their participation in the landmark exhibition at New York's Museum of Modern Art on "Deconstructivism," they have been considered leading members of that movement.

Coop Himmelb(l)au wurde 1968 in Wien von Wolf D. Prix und Helmut Swiczinsky gegründet. Die beiden Männer bilden eine ungewöhnliche Architektengemeinschaft mit einem sehr internationalen Hintergrund: Wolf Prix wurde 1942 in Wien geboren und studierte an der Technischen Universität Wien, am Southern California Institute of Architecture (SCI-Arc) und an der Architectural Association (AA) in London. Helmut Swiczinsky kam 1944 in Poznan (Polen) zur Welt, wuchs in Wien auf und erhielt seine Ausbildung an der Technischen Universität Wien und an der AA in London. Obwohl die Anzahl ihrer realisierten Entwürfe relativ klein ist, zählen Coop Himmelb(l)au – nicht zuletzt aufgrund ihrer Verbindung zu so berühmten Lehrinstituten wie der AA und dem SCI-Arc – schon seit längerem zur internationalen Architekturelite. Seit ihrer Teilnahme an der bahnbrechenden Dekonstruktivismus-Ausstellung im New Yorker Museum of Modern Art gelten sie als führende Mitglieder dieser Bewegung.

Coop Himmelb(l)au a été fondé en 1968 à Vienne, Autriche, par Wolf D. Prix et Helmut Swiczinsky. Cette curieuse équipe est de formation très internationale. Wolf Prix est né en 1942 à Vienne, et a étudié à la Technische Universität, Vienne, au Southern California Institute of Architecture (SCI-Arc), Los Angeles, et à l'Architectural Association (AA) à Londres. Helmut Swiczinsky est né en 1944 à Poznan, Pologne. Élevé à Vienne, il a également étudié à la Technische Universität de Vienne et à l'AA de Londres. C'est en partie grâce à leurs contacts à travers ces prestigieuses institutions que sont l'AA et le SCI-Arc que Coop Himmelb(l)au fait partie depuis longtemps de l'élite de l'architecture internationale, bien que le nombre de leurs réalisations soit limité. Depuis leur participation à l'exposition historique sur le déconstructivisme du Museum of Modern Art de New York, ils figurent parmi les représentants les plus éminents de ce mouvement.

Coop Himmelb(l)au, Research Center, Seibersdorf, Austria, 1993–95.

Coop Himmelb(l)au, Forschungszentrum, Seibersdorf, Österreich, 1993–95.

Coop Himmelb(l)au, Centre de recherches, Seibersdorf, Autriche, 1993–95.

Research Center

Seibersdorf, Austria, 1993–1995

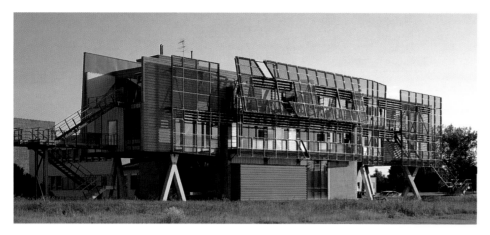

This project for the Austrian Research Center is an exploration of the theme of the connection between the old and the new, between existing architectural forms and added ones. Here an existing warehouse was remodeled and added onto in order to create an office building. The "simultaneity" of the different structural systems became an organizational guideline for the architects, much as they noted that the work planned for the users of the building was also to be differentiated into such tasks as systems analysis, mathematics and environmental engineering. Although some might consider that the skewed or fractured forms of this design correspond to a style that was in vogue, intellectually speaking, in the 1980s, few projects actually incorporating such radical concepts have in fact been built. It is entirely possible that the visual strengths of the architecture itself will engender other such compositions, but it can be asked if the powerful ideas of Coop Himmelb(l)au can really give rise to anything but formal exercises that do not, and cannot, address the original concepts in a meaningful way.

Dieses Projekt eines österreichischen Forschungszentrums stellt eine Auseinandersetzung mit dem Thema der Beziehungen zwischen Alt und Neu, zwischen bereits existierenden und neu erschaffenen architektonischen Formen dar. Für dieses Zentrum wurde ein altes Lagerhaus umgebaut, erweitert und in ein Bürogebäude umgestaltet. Die »Gleichzeitigkeit« der unterschiedlichen Konstruktionssysteme entwickelte sich für die Architekten zu einer organisatorischen Richtlinie; daneben legten sie Wert darauf, daß die Arbeitsbereiche für die zukünftigen Benutzer des Gebäudes in unterschiedliche Aufgabenbereiche wie Systemanalyse, Mathematik und Umwelttechnik unterteilt wurden. Obwohl man argumentieren könnte, daß die schiefwinkligen, durchbrochenen Formen des Entwurfs intellektuell gesehen in den 8oer Jahren in Mode waren, sind nur wenige Projekte mit einem solch radikalen Grundkonzept tatsächlich realisiert worden. Es ist durchaus denkbar, daß die visuelle Kraft dieser Architektur zahlreiche ähnliche Kompositionen nach sich ziehen wird; dennoch stellt sich die Frage, ob die eindrucksvollen Ideen von Coop Himmelb(l)au wirklich zu etwas anderem als zum Entwurf formaler Übungen führen, die das ursprüngliche Konzept weder mit neuer Bedeutung füllen wollen noch können.

Ce projet pour le Centre autrichien de recherche explore les rapports entre l'ancien et le nouveau, entre la juxtaposition de formes architecturales existantes et nouvelles. Ici, un ancien entrepôt a été remodelé et agrandi pour créer un immeuble de bureaux. La «simultanéité» des différents systèmes structurels est devenu un principe d'organisation pour Coop Himmelblau, d'autant plus que les deux architectes devaient prendre en compte le travail très différencié des divers utilisateurs de l'immeuble: analyse de systèmes, ingénierie mathématique et de l'environnement. Si l'on peut considérer que ces formes allongées et fracturées correspondent à un style à la mode – intellectuellement parlant – dans les années 80, peu de projets reposant sur des concepts aussi radicaux ont en fait été menés à bien. Il est tout à fait possible que la force visuelle de cette architecture génère d'autres propositions du même style, mais les idées affirmées de Coop Himmelb(l)au peuvent-elles déboucher sur autre chose que des exercices formels qui ne répondent pas et ne peuvent pas répondre de façon significative aux concepts originaux?

A linking and a confrontation of two forms, one older and one entirely designed by the architects, makes for a richly articulated plan and a very changeable appearance according to the angle of view.

Die Verbindung und gleichzeitige Konfrontation älterer und von den Architekten völlig neu erschaffener Formen ergibt einen vielfältig gegliederten Grundriß sowie ein – je nach Blickwinkel – immer wieder variierendes Erscheinungsbild.

La liaison et la confrontation de deux formes, l'une ancienne, l'autre entièrement conçue par les architectes, génère un plan aux articulations complexes et d'apparence changeante selon l'angle de vue.

The use of inclined pilotis and elevated walkways
highlights the rather ephemeral appearance of the
center and even gives an impression that the whole
must somehow be able to move forward.

Schräge Stützen und erhöhte Laufgänge unterstreichen
das ephemere Erscheinungsbild des Zentrums und
erwecken den Eindruck, als ob sich das Gebäude vor-
wärtsbewegen könnte.

Les pilotis inclinés et les passerelles surélevées soulignent
l'aspect presque éphémère de ce centre et donnent
l'impression qu'il pourrait se mettre en marche.

84 Coop Himmelb(l)au: Research Center, 1993–95

The style of the architects makes heavy use of skewed angles and planes, which are often apparently detached from their immediate structural background. The challenge of course is to make a harmonious working environment with such a spatially complex design.

Typisch für den Stil der Architekten ist die Verwendung schräger Winkel und schiefer Ebenen, die häufig wie losgelöst von ihrer unmittelbaren baulichen Umgebung erscheinen. Dabei besteht die größte Herausforderung darin, aus einem räumlich derart komplexen Design eine harmonisch ineinandergreifende Arbeitsumgebung zu schaffen.

Le style des architectes fait largement appel aux angles aigus et à des plans découpés qui semblent souvent détachés de la partie du bâtiment qu'ils recouvrent. L'objectif de cette complexité spatiale est d'offrir un environnement de travail harmonieux.

Sir Norman Foster

Sir Norman Foster is currently one of the most successful architects in the world. His office, based in the purpose-built Riverside Three building near Battersea Bridge in London, employs over 400 people worldwide. Current large projects include the new Hong Kong Airport, the refurbishment of the Reichstag in Berlin and the British Museum in London, and construction of the world's longest land bridge, the 2.5 kilometer long Millau Viaduct in France. Foster's method consists in first analyzing the requirements of a given job, and then seeking to meet those aims in the most efficient way possible. This has resulted in numerous technical breakthroughs, such as his extremely thin Telecommunications Tower in Barcelona (Torre de Collserola, 1990–92) or his luminous, simple design for London's Third Airport (Stansted, 1987–91), which was built at a cost some 15% less than previous UK terminal buildings. A current area of intense interest in Foster's office is the design of environmentally friendly buildings, surprisingly including some very tall ones.

Sir Norman Foster zählt zu den erfolgreichsten Architekten der heutigen Zeit. Sein Büro, dessen Hauptsitz sich im speziell zu diesem Zweck entworfenen Riverside Three Building in der Nähe der Londoner Battersea Bridge befindet, beschäftigt weltweit über 400 Mitarbeiter. Zu den momentanen Großprojekten von Foster and Partners zählen der neue Flughafen von Hongkong, die Umgestaltung des Reichstags in Berlin und des British Museum in London sowie die Konstruktion der längsten Landbrücke der Welt, des 2,5 km langen Millau Viaduct in Frankreich. Fosters Methode besteht darin, zunächst die Anforderungen eines bestimmten Projekts genau zu analysieren und danach diese Ziele so effektiv wie möglich umzusetzen. Dies führte zu einer ganzen Reihe technischer Meisterleistungen, wie Fosters extrem dünnem Torre de Collserola, einem Telekommunikationsmast in Barcelona (1990–92), oder seinem brillianten, schlichten Entwurf für den Stansted Airport in London (1987–91), dessen Baukosten etwa 15 % unter denen früherer englischer Flughafenterminals lagen. Im Augenblick beschäftigt sich Fosters Büro besonders intensiv mit dem Entwurf umweltfreundlicher Gebäude, zu denen überraschenderweise auch einige besonders hohe Bauten zählen.

Sir Norman Foster est actuellement l'un des architectes qui remporte le plus de succès professionnels de par le monde. Installée dans l'immeuble Riverside Three construit pour elle près du pont de Battersea à Londres, son agence emploie plus de 400 personnes. Parmi ses grands projets actuels figurent le nouvel aéroport de Hongkong, l'aménagement du Reichstag à Berlin et du British Museum à Londres, ainsi que la construction du plus long viaduc du monde – 2,5 km de long – à Millau (France). La méthode fostérienne consiste en une analyse approfondie du cahier des charges et des contraintes d'un projet, et à la recherche des solutions les plus efficaces. Elle a abouti à des avancées technologies spectaculaires, comme pour la tour de télécommunications de Barcelone à l'impressionnante finesse (Torre de Collserola, 1990–92), ou le projet d'une lumineuse simplicité du troisième aéroport de Londres (Stansted, 1987–91), construit pour un budget de 15% inférieur au coût des autres terminaux britanniques. L'agence de Foster s'intéresse aujourd'hui particulièrement à la conception d'immeubles plus écologiques, dont – curieusement – certains projets de tours de grande hauteur.

Norman Foster, Faculty of Law, University of Cambridge, Cambridge, Great Britain, 1993–95.

Norman Foster, Faculty of Law, University of Cambridge, Cambridge, Großbritannien, 1993–95.

Norman Foster, Faculté de droit, Université de Cambridge, Cambridge, Grande-Bretagne, 1993–95.

Faculty of Law, University of Cambridge

Cambridge, Great Britain, 1993–1995

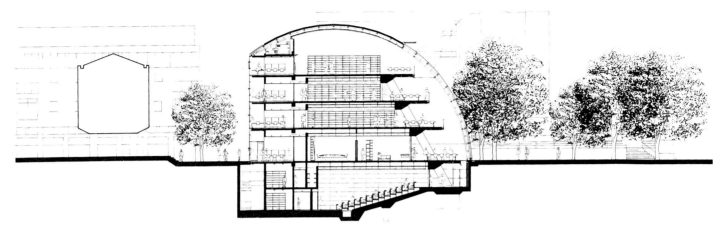

Located on the modern Sidgwick Avenue Campus, directly next to James Stirling's 1967 History Faculty Library, Norman Foster's Faculty of Law is a skillful blend of modern design and respect for an existing environment. Taking into account mature trees, and modifying the ground levels near the building to unify it more closely with its neighbors, Norman Foster has rendered the immediate environment of the Law Faculty more harmonious. Contractually designed for a minimum life span of fifty years, the building contains the Squire Law Library, five auditoria, seminar rooms and administrative offices. The outstanding feature of the 8,360 square meters building is its sweeping, curved glass facade, facing north, away from Hugh Casson's Medieval Languages Faculty and Library. With the glass panels bonded onto subframes off the site, it was possible to create a particularly smooth skin. Particular attention has been taken to making the building energy efficient, with only the underground lecture rooms being air conditioned. Careful calculations of sun angles and use of the concrete mass to cool the building result in a pleasant interior temperature, even during hot spells.

Norman Fosters Faculty of Law, die auf dem modernen Sidgwick Avenue Campus in unmittelbarer Nähe von James Stirlings 1967 erbauter History Faculty Library entstand, stellt eine geschickte Mischung aus modernem Design und Respekt vor der bestehenden Bebauung dar. Durch die Integration von Bäumen und die Anpassung der unterschiedlichen Bodenniveaus gelang es Foster, das Bauwerk enger mit den benachbarten Gebäuden zu verbinden und sogar das direkte Umfeld der juristischen Fakultät zu verbessern. Das für eine minimale Lebensdauer von 50 Jahren geplante Bauwerk umfaßt die Squire Law Library, fünf Hörsäle, Seminarräume und Verwaltungsbüros. Ein herausragendes Merkmal des 8 360 m² großen Gebäudes bildet die schwungvolle, gewölbte Glasfassade, die nach Norden und damit weg von Hugh Cassons Medieval Languages Faculty and Library weist. Durch die vorab erfolgte Montage der Glasscheiben auf Unterrahmen gelang Foster eine besonders glatte Fassade. Darüber hinaus legte er großen Wert auf eine energiesparende Bauweise, wobei nur die unterirdischen Hörsäle mit einer Klimaanlage ausgestattet werden mußten. Aufgrund genauer Berechnungen der Sonneneinstrahlung und der Nutzung der Baumasse zur Kühlung der Konstruktion herrscht in diesem Bauwerk selbst an heißen Tagen eine angenehme Temperatur.

Située sur le campus moderne de Sidgwick Avenue, juste à côté de la bibliothèque de la faculté d'histoire de James Stirling (1967), cette nouvelle faculté de droit est un mélange habile de conception moderne et de respect de l'environnement existant. Destiné, par contrat, à durer plus de cinquante ans, le bâtiment contient la Squire Law Library, cinq auditoriums, des salles de séminaires, et des bureaux administratifs. L'élément le plus remarquable de cet immeuble de 8 360 m², est sa façade de verre en courbe, face au nord, non loin de la faculté et de la bibliothèque des langues médiévales de Hugh Casson. Grâce à un montage à fleur des panneaux transparents, cette peau de verre paraît extrêmement lisse. Des efforts particuliers ont permis de rendre cette construction plus économique en termes de consommation énergétique, et seules les salles de conférences souterraines ont besoin d'un conditionnement de l'air. Des calculs précis sur l'angle des rayons du soleil et des murs en béton permettent de conserver à l'intérieur une température agréable, même pendant les périodes les plus chaudes.

The long curved glass facade of the Faculty of Law faces a pleasant green area to the north, minimizing heat gain. The Hugh Casson Medieval Languages Faculty is to the right of the stone facade visible on the drawing to the right.

Die langgestreckte, geschwungene Glasfassade der Faculty of Law bietet einen angenehmen Ausblick auf eine Grünanlage im Norden des Gebäudes; durch diese Ausrichtung konnte eine übermäßige Aufheizung verhindert werden. Auf der Zeichnung erkennt man rechts neben der Steinfassade die Hugh Casson Medieval Languages Faculty.

Au nord, la longue façade transparente incurvée de la faculté de droit fait face à un agréable espace vert qui compense l'élévation de température générée par le verre. La faculté des langues médiévales d'Hugh Casson se trouve à droite de la façade de pierre (sur la droite du dessin).

green weave

phase 2   phase 1

← entrance   entrance →   ← entrance

entrance →

←--- link below ground ---→

The existing trees are important - they inform massing & phasing - a foil to the transparency beyond

3 NF may 90

Pages 94–95: The north facade seen at night offers views into the building from the park side. James Stirling's History Faculty Library can be seen behind the trees to the right.

Seite 94–95: Die Nordseite bietet bei Nacht vom Park aus Einblick in das Gebäude. Rechts hinter den Bäumen erkennt man James Stirlings History Faculty Library.

Pages 94–95: La nuit, la façade nord laisse voir l'intérieur du bâtiment, côté parc, tandis que la bibliothèque de la faculté d'histoire de James Stirling se distingue derrière les arbres.

Page 92: A long, slender non-supporting column marks the entrance to the Faculty building.
Page 93: An early drawing (top) by Norman Foster shows the relationship of the structure to an intended second phase. A ground-floor plan (bottom) shows the entrance to the lower left with its rather modest revolving door.

Seite 92: Eine lange, schlanke, nichttragende Säule markiert den Eingang zum Fakultätsgebäude.
Seite 93: Eine frühe Skizze von Norman Foster (oben) verdeutlicht die Beziehung dieses Bauwerks zu einem geplanten zweiten Gebäude. Auf dem Grundriß (unten) erkennt man links unten den Eingang mit der relativ bescheidenen Drehtür.

Page 92: Une haute colonne non porteuse marque l'entrée de la faculté.
Page 93: Un des premiers dessins de Foster (en haut) montre la relation entre l'immeuble et une seconde phase qui reste à construire. Le plan de masse (en bas) montre l'entrée à gauche, et sa porte à tambour de taille relativement modeste.

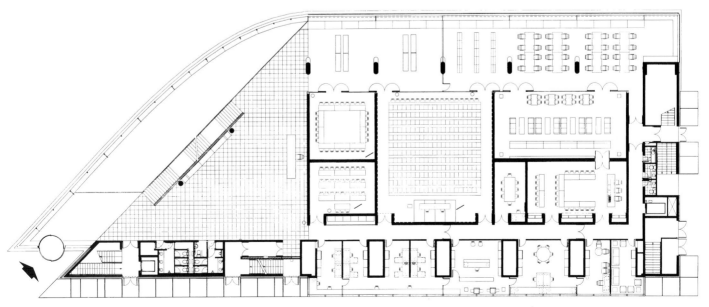

London Millennium Tower

London, Great Britain, 1996

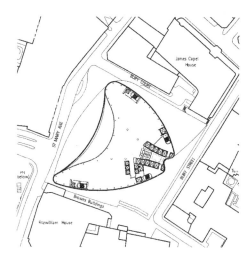

Already the author of the highest office tower in Europe (Commerzbank, Frankfurt am Main, 1994–97), Norman Foster plans to break his own record on the site of the Baltic Exchange, a structure in London's City damaged by an IRA bomb in 1992. The scheme calls for a ninety-five-story office building to go up in the same quadrant as Lloyd's Headquarters, the Bank of England and Broadgate. Its height of 400 meters, or 435 meters to the top of the mast, would make it about 20 meters smaller than the tallest building in the world, currently the Petronas Twin Towers in Kuala Lumpur (Cesar Pelli). From level seventy-three upwards, there will be twelve stories of apartments in the north section, and seven in the south. Since the Baltic Exchange is a Grade II listed building the project requires the agreement of English Heritage, but it is one of the few sites in the City that is not inhibited by height-limiting factors such as the sight lines toward St. Paul's Cathedral. A public viewing platform would be situated at precisely 1000 feet, symbolizing the Millennium for which the project is named.

Obwohl er bereits der Schöpfer des höchsten Bürogebäudes Europas ist (der Commerzbank in Frankfurt am Main, 1994–97), plant Norman Foster einen noch höheren Turm auf dem Gelände der Baltic Exchange – eines Gebäudes in der Londoner City, das 1992 durch einen Bombenanschlag der IRA beschädigt wurde. Sein Entwurf sieht ein Bürogebäude mit 95 Geschossen vor, das im gleichen Viertel entstehen soll, in dem sich auch die Hauptverwaltung von Lloyd's, die Bank of England und Broadgate befinden. Mit einer Höhe von 400 m (bzw. 435 m bis zur Mastspitze) ist Fosters Bauvorhaben nur knapp 20 m kleiner als das derzeit höchste Gebäude der Welt, die Zwillingstürme der Petronas Towers in Kuala Lumpur (Cesar Pelli). Ab der 73. Etage sollen im nördlichen Bereich zwölf und im südlichen Bereich sieben Wohngeschosse folgen. Da die Baltic Exchange auf der Liste der besonders erhaltenswerten Bauwerke steht, benötigt das Projekt die Zustimmung des English Heritage. Aber der Baugrund zählt zu den wenigen in der Londoner City, für den keine besonderen Bauhöhenbestimmungen bestehen, wie es etwa für die Sichtachsen zur St. Paul's Cathedral der Fall wäre. In einer Höhe von genau 1000 Fuß ist eine öffentliche Aussichtsplattform geplant, die die Jahrtausendfeier symbolisiert, nach der das Projekt seinen Namen erhält.

Déjà auteur de la plus haute tour de bureaux d'Europe (Commerzbank, Francfort-sur-le-Main, 1994–97), Norman Foster se prépare à battre ce record sur le site de l'ancien Baltic Exchange, bâtiment gravement endommagé par une bombe de l'IRA en 1992. Le projet consiste en un immeuble de 95 étages au voisinage du siège des Lloyd's et de la Banque d'Angleterre. Sa hauteur de 400 m – 435 m au sommet du mât – est de 20 m inférieure seulement à celle des Tour Petronas jumelles de Kuala Lumpur (Cesar Pelli). Les 12 derniers étages de la partie sud et les 7 de la partie nord seront réservés à des appartements. Comme le Baltic Exchange est un monument classé, le projet requiert des autorisations particulières, bien que son site soit l'un des rares de la City a ne pas être soumis à des limitations de hauteur, pour protéger les vues de la cathédrale Saint-Paul par exemple. Un belvédère ouvert au public sera créé à la hauteur de 1000 pieds pour symboliser le millénaire auquel le projet doit son nom.

Model views and a site plan emphasize the unusual form of the London Millennium Tower with its curved facade and bi-partite design. The upper levels of both sections are to be occupied by apartments.

Modellansichten und ein Lageplan verdeutlichen die ungewöhnliche Formgebung des London Millennium Tower mit seinen geschwungenen Fassaden und seinem zweiflügligen Design. Die obersten Geschosse der beiden Flügel sollen für Wohnungen reserviert werden.

Les maquettes et le plan du site montrent la forme très inhabituelle de cette Millennium Tower à la façade incurvée en deux parties. Les niveaux supérieurs des deux sections devraient être occupés par des appartements.

Sir Norman Foster: London Millennium Tower, 1996 **97**

von Gerkan, Marg und Partner

Meinhard von Gerkan   *Volkwin Marg*

Both principals of the firm von Gerkan, Marg und Partner, Meinhard von Gerkan who was born in 1935 in Riga, Latvia, and Volkwin Marg who was born in 1936 in Königsberg studied architecture in Berlin and Braunschweig. They have been working together since 1965, and they currently employ approximately 200 people. Aside from the Leipzig Fair buildings published here, their completed work includes the Music and Congress Hall in Lübeck (1990), the Saar-Galerie in Saarbrücken (1991), 747 Servicing Facilities and a workshop for Lufthansa in Hamburg (1992), Zürich-Haus in Hamburg (1993), Deutsche Revision AG in Frankfurt (1994), and the Galeria Duisburg in Duisburg (1994), all in Germany. Their major projects include the Lehrter Bahnhof in Berlin. Participating like Ungers, Kleihues and Böhm in a renewal of post-War German architecture, von Gerkan and Marg have made efficient use of modern forms while admitting a certain degree of historical reference to their work, as is certainly the case for the Leipzig building published here.

Beide Gründer der Firma von Gerkan, Marg und Partner – der 1935 in Riga, Lettland, geborene Meinhard von Gerkan und der 1936 in Königsberg geborene Volkwin Marg – studierten in Berlin und Braunschweig Architektur. Seit 1965 arbeiten sie zusammen, und ihr Büro beschäftigt zur Zeit etwa 200 Mitarbeiter. Neben den hier vorgestellten Gebäuden der Neuen Messe Leipzig zählen zu den von ihnen realisierten Bauten u.a. die Musik- und Kongreßhalle in Lübeck (1990), die Saar-Galerie in Saarbrücken (1991), ein 747-Instandhaltungsgebäude und eine Werkshalle für die Lufthansa in Hamburg (1992), das Zürich-Haus in Hamburg (1993), die Deutsche Revision AG in Frankfurt (1994) und die Galeria Duisburg in Duisburg (1994). Zu den momentanen Großprojekten des Büros gehört der Bau des Lehrter Bahnhofs in Berlin. Von Gerkan und Marg, die ebenso wie Ungers, Kleihues und Böhm für eine Erneuerung der deutschen Nachkriegsarchitektur stehen, nutzen in ihren Arbeiten wirkungsvoll moderne Formen, während sie gleichzeitig auch historische Bezüge zulassen – ein Eindruck, der in ihrem Leipziger Entwurf deutlich bestätigt wird.

Les deux associés de l'agence von Gerkan, Marg und Partner, Meinhard von Gerkan, né en 1935 à Riga (Lituanie) et Volkwin Marg, né en 1936 à Königsberg ont étudié l'architecture à Berlin et Brunswick. Ils collaborent depuis 1965 et emploient actuellement 200 personnes environ. En dehors des nouveaux bâtiments de la Foire de Leipzig illustrés ici, ils ont réalisé, entre autres, l'auditorium de Lübeck (1990), la Saar-Galerie de Sarrebruck (1991), les ateliers d'entretien des 747 et un atelier pour Lufthansa à Hambourg (1992), la Zürich-Haus à Hambourg (1993), le siège de la Deutsche Revision AG, Francfort (1994), la Galeria Duisburg à Duisburg (1994), et, plus important encore, la gare centrale de Lehrter à Berlin. Acteurs du renouveau de l'architecture allemande de l'après-guerre avec Ungers, Kleihues et Böhm, von Gerkan et Marg utilisent un vocabulaire moderne efficace tout en admettant un certain degré de références historiques, comme dans le cas de la Foire de Leipzig.

von Gerkan, Marg und Partner, New Leipzig Fair, Leipzig, Germany, 1993–96.

von Gerkan, Marg und Partner, Neue Messe Leipzig, Deutschland, 1993–96.

von Gerkan, Marg und Partner, Nouvelle Foire de Leipzig, Leipzig, Allemagne, 1993–96.

New Leipzig Fair

Leipzig, Germany, 1993–96

The architects make specific reference to the 1889 Galerie des Machines in Paris in describing their intentions in this very large exhibition complex. Although the 243 meter long main hall does not really compare to the size of the 420 meter length of the original, the newer complex does bring together an impressive list of vital statistics. Covering a total area of 986,000 square meters for a built area of 272,300 square meters and an indoor exhibition space of 102,500 square meters, the group of structures includes five standard halls with 20,500 square meters each and an unobstructed height of 8 meters. The construction cost, including interior furnishings and equipment, outdoor utilities and landscaping, was 1.335 billion D-marks. Von Gerkan, Marg und Partner, teamed with the landscape architects Wehberg, Eppinger, Schmidtke, defeated fourteen other invited architects' teams in 1991 to win this prestigious commission. Although the large glass-covered hall has remained popular both for exhibition purposes and for railway stations, von Gerkan, Marg und Partner prove here that the genre still retains much of its original vitality, and is capable of being adapted to the requirements of modern construction and function.

Bei der Beschreibung ihrer Zielsetzungen für diesen sehr großen Ausstellungskomplex bezogen sich die Architekten ganz bewußt auf die 1889 in Paris erbaute Galerie des Machines. Obwohl die 243 m lange zentrale Glashalle sich nur schwer mit den Maßstäben des 420 m langen Originals messen läßt, kann auch der neuere Komplex eine eindrucksvolle Liste von Zahlen und Statistiken vorweisen. Auf einer Gesamtfläche von 986 000 m² und einer bebauten Fläche von 272 300 m² entstanden 102 500 m² an Ausstellungsflächen, aufgeteilt auf fünf Messehallen von je 20 500 m² Fläche und einer lichten Höhe von 8 m. Die Baukosten – einschließlich Inneneinrichtung und Ausstattung, Außengestaltung und Landschaftsarchitektur – beliefen sich auf 1,335 Milliarden DM. Bei der Ausschreibung für dieses prestigeträchtige Projekt konnten sich von Gerkan, Marg und Partner (in Zusammenarbeit mit den Landschaftsarchitekten Wehberg, Eppinger und Schmidtke) gegen 14 andere Mitbewerber durchsetzen. Obwohl große, verglaste Hallenkonstruktionen sich sowohl zu Ausstellungszwecken als auch als Bahnhofshallen ungebrochener Beliebtheit erfreuen, beweisen von Gerkan, Marg und Partner mit diesem Projekt, daß das Genre kaum etwas von seiner ursprünglichen Vitalität eingebüßt hat und in der Lage ist, sich den Anforderungen moderner Konstruktion und Funktion anzupassen.

Les architectes font ici une référence explicite à la Galerie des Machines de Paris (1889) lorsqu'ils décrivent leurs intentions pour ce très vaste ensemble de foires et expositions. Bien que le hall principal de 243 m de long ne puisse se comparer aux 420 m de l'original, ce nouvel ensemble n'en additionne pas moins des chiffres impressionnants. En couvrant une surface totale de 986 000 m² pour une surface construite de 272 300 m² et un espace d'exposition de 102 500 m², l'ensemble comprend cinq grands halls de 20 500 m² chacun et d'une hauteur de huit mètres. Le coût de construction, y compris les aménagements intérieurs, le mobilier, les équipements extérieurs et les espaces verts s'est élevé à 1,335 milliards de DM. Von Gerkan, Marg und Partner, en équipe avec les architectes paysagers Wehberg, Eppinger, Schmidtke, sont arrivés vainqueurs devant 14 autres équipes lors du concours organisé en 1991 pour ce prestigieux contrat. Les deux architectes ont prouvé ici que le principe des grands halls à verrière si populaires pour les gares et les salons et expositions a gardé toute sa vitalité originale, et peut s'adapter aux exigences d'une construction et de fonctions modernes.

Located outside of the city center, the new fair grounds are articulated around the 243 meter long central glass hall, whose interior is visible on page 101 top. Several contemporary artists participated in the project, including the American Sol Lewitt (page 101 bottom).

Die außerhalb der Stadt gelegene Neue Messe Leipzig gruppiert sich um die 243 m lange zentrale Glashalle, deren Innenansicht auf Seite 101 oben zu sehen ist. An diesem Projekt waren mehrere zeitgenössische Künstler beteiligt, darunter auch der Amerikaner Sol Lewitt (Seite 101 unten).

Situés hors du centre ville, les nouvelles installations de la foire s'articulent autour d'un hall central en verre et métal, de 243 m de long, dont l'intérieur est représenté sur la page 101 en haut. Plusieurs artistes ont participé à ce projet, dont l'Américain Sol Lewitt (page 101 en bas).

The Leipzig project is in fact a sophisticated blend of the influence of 19th century glass and iron architecture as epitomized in the Crystal Palace or the Galerie des Machines, and a much more up-to-date technologically oriented mastery of glass and steel.

Die Leipziger Halle entstand als kunstvolle Mischung – beeinflußt von der Stahl-Glas-Architektur des 19. Jahrhunderts, als deren Inbegriff der Crystal Palace oder die Galerie des Machines gelten, und einem modernen technologisch orientierten Umgang mit Glas und Stahl.

Le projet de Leipzig est un mariage sophistiqué entre l'influence de l'architecture de verre et de fer du XIXe siècle – symbolisée par le Crystal Palace ou la Galerie des machines – et la maîtrise technologique contemporaine du verre et de l'acier.

von Gerkan, Marg und Partner: New Leipzig Fair, 1993–96 **103**

The New Leipzig Fair represents an effort to reconquer some of the prestige that this East German city lost to its western counterparts such as Hanover, or Düsseldorf after the War.

Die Neue Messe Leipzig verkörpert den Versuch, ein wenig vom Prestige dieser ostdeutschen Stadt zurückzugewinnen, das sie nach dem Krieg an ihre westlichen Konkurrenten Hannover oder Düsseldorf verloren hatte.

Pour Leipzig, cette nouvelle Foire représente une tentative de reconquérir un prestige perdu après guerre au profit de cités comme Hanovre ou Düsseldorf.

104 von Gerkan, Marg und Partner: New Leipzig Fair, 1993–96

Zvi Hecker

"Our growing perception of the complexity of man's environment," writes Zvi Hecker, "excludes the narrow view of architecture as a mere sum of programmatic requirements, even if such requirements can be arranged in orderly functionalistic patterns. Architectural form cannot be derived from function alone, but must unfold within the confines of an artist's consciousness." Born in Cracow, Poland in 1931, Zvi Hecker emigrated to Israel in 1950. As well as studying architecture, he also studied painting at Avni Academy of Art in Tel Aviv (1955–57). Hecker's crystalline buildings (Aeronautic Laboratory, Technion Campus, Haifa, Israel, 1963–66), like others that are closely related to the form of the sunflower, emphasize his interest in the vocabulary of the natural world, and set him apart from most of his contemporaries. Although his fractured forms do bring to mind the shapes of deconstructivism, he used such patterns long before the ideas of Jacques Derrida came into vogue in Europe and America.

»Unsere zunehmende Erkenntnis der Komplexität der menschlichen Umgebung«, schreibt Zvi Hecker, »schließt eine eindimensionale Auffassung von Architektur als reiner Summe programmatischer Anforderungen aus, selbst wenn diese Anforderungen in geordneten funktionalistischen Mustern gruppiert werden können. Die architektonische Form kann nicht allein aus ihrer Funktion abgeleitet werden, sondern muß sich im Rahmen der Beschränkungen eines künstlerischen Bewußtseins entfalten.« Der 1931 in Krakau (Polen) geborene Zvi Hecker emigrierte 1950 nach Israel. Nach seinem Architekturstudium studierte er Malerei an der Avni Academy of Art in Tel Aviv (1955–57). Neben anderen Bauten, die eng an die Form einer Sonnenblume angelehnt sind, zeigen auch Heckers kristalline Gebäude (Aeronautic Laboratory, Technion Campus, Haifa, Israel, 1963–66) sein großes Interesse für die Formensprache der Natur – was ihn von einem Großteil seiner Zeitgenossen unterscheidet. Obwohl seine gebrochenen Formen an den Dekonstruktivismus erinnern, benutzte Hecker solche Muster, lange bevor die Gedanken eines Jacques Derrida in Europa und Amerika populär wurden.

«Notre perception grandissante de la complexité de l'environnement de l'homme,» écrit Zvi Hecker, «exclut la vision étroite d'une architecture qui serait tout au plus l'addition de contraintes programmatiques, même si celles-ci peuvent être traitées et organisées de façon fonctionnelle. La forme architecturale ne peut dériver de la seule fonction, mais doit se déployer aux confins de la conscience artistique.» Né à Cracovie, Pologne en 1931, Zvi Hecker émigre en Israël en 1950. Tout en étudiant l'architecture, il apprend également la peinture à l'Académie d'art Avny de Tel Aviv (1955–57). Ses immeubles cristallins (comme le Laboratoire d'aéronautique, Campus Technion, Haïfa, Israël, 1963–66), ou d'autres formellement inspirés du tournesol traduisent son intérêt pour la nature, et lui confèrent une position à part parmi ses contemporains. Même si ses formes fracturées évoquent celles du déconstructivisme, il les pratique depuis bien avant que les idées de Jacques Derrida ne deviennent à la mode en Europe et en Amérique.

Zvi Hecker, Heinz-Galinski-School, Berlin, Germany, 1992–95.

Zvi Hecker, Heinz-Galinski-Schule, Berlin, Deutschland, 1992–95.

Zvi Hecker, école Heinz-Galinski, Berlin, Allemagne, 1992–95.

Heinz-Galinski-School

Berlin, Germany, 1992–1995

The formal complexity of the Heinz-Galinski-School is expressed not only in its volumes but in the variety of materials used. It is in this accumulation of shapes and surfaces that the structure can be assimilated to a cityscape in itself.

Die formale Komplexität der Heinz-Galinski-Schule kommt nicht nur in ihren Baukörpern, sondern auch in der Vielfalt der verwendeten Materialien zum Ausdruck. Diese Anhäufung von Formen und Oberflächen läßt den Entwurf wie eine in sich geschlossene Stadtland-schaft erscheinen.

La complexité formelle de l'école Heinz-Galinski ne s'exprime pas seulement dans ses volumes, mais aussi dans la diversité de ses matériaux. Cette accumulation de formes et de surfaces crée un véritable paysage urbain.

Although the fractured form of the new Heinz-Galinski-School seems to be directly related to the cataclysmic events of World War II, it should be pointed out that Zvi Hecker has experimented with such forms in other contexts, such as the "Sunflower" commercial and residential center in Ramat Hasharon, Israel (1964–90) or the Spiral Apartment building he completed in Ramat Gan, Israel in 1990. Located in the west of Berlin, this Jewish primary school, named in honor of the long-time Chairman of the Berlin Jewish community, was built by Zvi Hecker after a July 1990 competition that resulted in five equal prizes out of 83 entries. The final selection was made in March, 1991. As he has made clear in his own comments, the architect considers the design to be a metaphor for the city.

Obwohl die gebrochenen Formen der neuen Heinz-Galinski-Schule in direkter Verbindung zu den apokalyptischen Ereignissen des Zwei-ten Weltkriegs zu stehen scheinen, sollte deut-lich werden, daß Hecker bereits in anderen Zusammenhängen mit ähnlichen Formen experimentierte, etwa im Falle des »Sunflower« Wohn- und Geschäftszentrums in Ramat Hasharon, Israel (1964–90) oder dem Spiral-Apartmenthaus, das er 1990 in Ramat Gan, Israel, fertigstellte. Hecker erhielt den Auftrag für diese im Westen Berlins gelegene jüdische Grundschule, die nach dem langjährigen Vor-sitzenden der Jüdischen Gemeinde Berlins benannt wurde, nach einer Ausschreibung im Juli 1990, bei der aus 83 Beiträgen fünf erste Preise ausgewählt wurden. Die endgültige Ent-scheidung fand im März 1991 statt. Hecker beschreibt seinen Entwurf als eine Metapher auf die Stadt.

Si les formes fracturées de la nouvelle école Heinz-Galinski semblent directement inspi-rées du cataclysme de la Seconde Guerre mondiale, Zvi Hecker avait déjà travaillé dans ce sens dans des contextes tout différents, comme le centre commercial et résidentiel «Tournesol» de Ramat Hasharon, Israël (1964–90), ou l'immeuble d'appartements «Spiral» achevé en 1990 à Ramat Gan, Israël. Située dans l'ex-Berlin-Ouest, cette école pri-maire juive, dont le nom rend hommage à l'ancien président de la communauté juive de Berlin, a été construite par Zvi Hecker à l'issue d'un concours organisé en juillet 1990 et qui vit l'attribution de cinq prix ex-aequo sur 83 participations. La sélection finale fut effectuée en mars 1991. Dans ses écrits, l'architecte explique que ce projet est une métaphore de la ville.

Zvi Hecker: Heinz-Galinski-School, 1992–95 **109**

Although a sunflower pattern may not be the most obvious way to create readily usable school space, the stimulus provided by such an architectural tour-de-force undoubtedly makes up for any difficult-to-reach corners.

Obwohl ein Grundriß in Form einer Sonnenblume bei der Planung leicht zugänglicher Schulräume nicht unbedingt die naheliegendste Wahl darstellt, wiegt der Anreiz einer solchen architektonischen tour de force alle Schwierigkeiten auf, die sich dem Benutzer auf dem Weg in die äußersten Räume in den Weg stellen.

Si le tournesol n'est pas le modèle le plus évident pour créer des espaces d'enseignement, l'effet stimulant de ce tour de force architectural compense la difficulté pratique d'atteindre certains recoins.

The radiating spiral pattern of the design is most evident in drawings such as the one reproduced above, left. Although Zvi Hecker refers to the sunflower, the spiral is a frequent source of artistic and even architectural inspiration.

Das Strahlenmuster des Entwurfs kommt im Grundriß oben links besonders deutlich zum Ausdruck. Auch wenn Zvi Hecker von einer »Sonnenblume« spricht, die Spiralform ist oft Quelle künstlerischer und architektonischer Inspiration.

Le motif en spirale utilisé dans la conception est surtout évident dans les dessins. Si Hecker se réfère au tournesol, le thème de la spirale a souvent été utilisé, en art comme en architecture.

Zvi Hecker: Heinz-Galinski-School, 1992–95 **113**

Herman Hertzberger

Born in Amsterdam in 1932, Herman Hertzberger studied at the Technical University in Delft, graduating in 1958. Influenced by Aldo van Eyck, he has long insisted on the fact that the forms of architecture must evolve from the wishes of their intended users. He has written: "The architect's task is above all to apply more than cut-to-fit, ready-made solutions and as much as possible to free in the users themselves whatever they think they need, by evoking images in them which can lead to their own personally valid solutions." Chairman of the Berlage Institute in Amsterdam from 1990 to 1995, his built work includes eight experimental houses, Gebbenlaan, Delft (1969–70); the Vredenburg Music Center, Utrecht (1973–78); "De Evenaar" kindergarten/primary school, Amsterdam (1984–86); an office building for the Ministry of Social Welfare and Employment, The Hague (1979–90); the Theater Center Spui, The Hague (1986–93), located just opposite Richard Meier's new City Hall; and the Markant Theater, Uden (1993–96), all in The Netherlands.

Herman Hertzberger wurde 1932 in Amsterdam geboren und studierte an der Technischen Hochschule Delft, an der er 1958 sein Diplom erhielt. Aufgrund des starken Einflusses von Aldo van Eyck vertrat er lange die These, daß sich die Form der Architektur aus den Wünschen der zukünftigen Nutzer ergeben muß. Er schrieb dazu: »Die Aufgabe des Architekten besteht vor allem darin, mehr als nur vorgefertigte Lösungen von der Stange zu liefern. Er sollte die Benutzer unbedingt dazu anregen, die eigenen Wünsche und Bedürfnisse zu äußern, indem er Bilder erweckt, die zu ihren persönlichen Werten und Lösungen führen.« Von 1990–95 war Hertzberger Dekan des Berlage Institut für Architektur in Amsterdam. Zu seinen fertiggestellten Bauten zählen acht experimentelle Häuser in den Niederlanden, in Gebbenlaan, Delft (1969–70); das Vredenburg Musikzentrum Utrecht (1973–78); Kindergarten und Grundschule »De Evenaar« in Amsterdam (1984–86); das Verwaltungsgebäude für das niederländische Arbeits- und Sozialministerium in Den Haag (1979–90); das Theaterzentrum Spui in Den Haag (1986–93), genau gegenüber von Richard Meiers neuem Rathaus, sowie das Theater Markant in Uden (1993–96).

Né à Amsterdam en 1932, Herman Hertzberger fait ses études à l'Université technique de Delft, dont il sort diplômé en 1958. Influencé par Aldo van Eyck, il a longtemps défendu l'idée que les formes de l'architecture devaient évoluer à partir des souhaits de leurs utilisateurs. Il a ainsi écrit: «La tâche de l'architecte est par-dessus tout d'arriver à des solutions sur mesure, et autant que possible de libérer les usagers eux-mêmes de leurs préjugés sur leurs besoins, en faisant naître en eux des images qui peuvent conduire à des solutions personnalisées.» Président de l'Institut Berlage à Amsterdam, de 1990 à 1995, ses réalisations comprennent huit maisons expérimentales, Gebbenlaan, Delft (1969–70); le Centre de musique Vredenburg, Utrecht (1973–78), le jardin d'enfants/école primaire «De Evenaar», Amsterdam (1984–86), un immeuble de bureaux pour le ministère des affaires sociales et de l'emploi, La Haye (1979–90), le Theater Center Spui, La Haye (1986–93), situé juste en face de l'hôtel de ville de Richard Meier, et le Markant Theater, Uden (1993–96).

Herman Hertzberger, Chassé Theater, Breda, The Netherlands, 1992–95.

Herman Hertzberger, Chassé Theater, Breda, Niederlande, 1992–95.

Herman Hertzberger, Chassé Theater, Bréda, Pays-Bas, 1992–95.

Chassé Theater

Breda, The Netherlands, 1992–1995

Once again demonstrating his theory that the exterior of a building is a sort of packaging, Herman Hertzberger has covered the new Chassé Theater with a spectacular undulating roof. The complex includes a main auditorium with a seating capacity of 1,286, a central hall that can be used as a 500 seat concert area, two other halls with respective capacities of 730 and 295 persons, and two smaller theaters for film. The cost of the building was 60 million florins. Quite outspoken about the difficulties encountered in this case, Hertzberger writes, "This project presented us with little or no opportunity to test the constituent parts against the whole during construction. The building process proceeded chaotically, with often fundamental changes being made at unexpected moments, leaving the architect and his team with only restricted control over events. Forced to adopt a piecemeal approach, our main concern at all times was to see to it that the major architectural and spatial themes of the design were preserved."

Auch bei diesem Gebäude kommt Herman Hertzbergers Theorie, daß das Äußere eines Bauwerks eine Art Verpackung darstellt, wieder deutlich zum Ausdruck: Sein neues Chassé Theater besitzt eine aufsehenerregende, wellenförmige Dachkonstruktion. Der Komplex umfaßt einen großen Saal mit 1286 Plätzen, eine zentrale Halle (die als Konzerthalle mit 500 Plätzen genutzt werden kann), zwei weitere Hallen für jeweils 730 bzw. 295 Personen sowie zwei kleinere Kinosäle. Die Baukosten beliefen sich auf 60 Millionen Gulden. Über die Schwierigkeiten, vor die Hertzberger und sein Team im Zusammenhang mit diesem Bauvorhaben gestellt wurden, schreibt er freimütig: »Dieses Projekt ließ uns wenig, wenn nicht sogar gar keine Möglichkeit, die einzelnen Komponenten während der Bauzeit auf ihre Verträglichkeit mit dem Komplex als Ganzem zu überprüfen. Die Bauarbeiten verliefen chaotisch, mit häufig fundamentalen Veränderungen im völlig unerwarteten Moment, so daß der Architekt und sein Team den Fortgang der Arbeiten nur im eingeschränkten Maße kontrollieren und beeinflussen konnten. Da uns eine schrittweise Vorgehensweise aufgezwungen wurde, lag unser Hauptaugenmerk während der gesamten Bauzeit darauf, die wichtigsten architektonischen und räumlichen Themen dieses Entwurfs zu erhalten.«

Illustrant une fois de plus sa théorie selon laquelle l'extérieur d'un bâtiment est une sorte de conditionnement, Herman Hertzberger a recouvert son Chassé Theater d'un spectaculaire toit ondulé. Pour un coût de 60 millions de florins, l'ensemble comprend un auditorium principal de 1286 places, un hall central qui peut servir de salle de concert pour 500 personnes, deux autres salles respectivement de 730 et 295 sièges, et deux salle plus petites pour le cinéma. Assez prolixe sur les difficultés rencontrées au cours de la réalisation de cette commande, Hertzberger écrit: «Ce projet ne nous a laissé pratiquement aucune opportunité de tester les différentes composantes par rapport à l'ensemble. La construction a progressé dans le chaos, des modifications fondamentales intervenant même de façon inopinée, ne laissant à l'architecte et à son équipe qu'un contrôle réduit sur les événements. Forcés d'adopter une approche hachée, notre principale préoccupation fut en permanence de vérifier si les thèmes architecturaux et spatiaux majeurs de notre projet étaient néanmoins préservés.»

The architect has observed that the flytowers (large-scale theater towers) threatened to completely dominate the structure and block the view toward the town. His solution was to design a flowing roof to cover the whole.

Der Architekt stellte fest, daß die Bühnentürme den gesamten Komplex vollständig zu beherrschen und den Blick auf die Stadt zu verstellen drohten. Seine Lösung bestand im Entwurf einer fließend geschwungenen Dachkonstruktion.

L'architecte craignant que les tours des cintres ne dominent complètement le bâtiment et ne bloquent la vue vers la cité, a opté pour un toit en forme de vague qui recouvre l'ensemble.

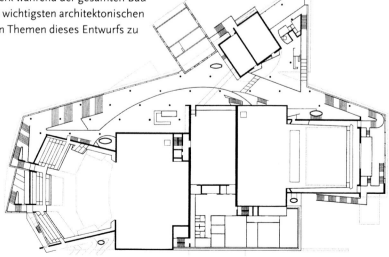

According to the architect, the painted concrete columns that hold up the foyer roof "draw the attention away from an unavoidably amorphous periphery, bind the space together and give it form."

Nach Aussage des Architekten lenken die gestrichenen Betonstützen, die das Foyerdach tragen, »den Blick des Betrachters von der unvermeidlich amorphen Peripherie ab; sie binden den Raum und verleihen ihm Form.«

Selon l'architecte, les colonnes de béton peint qui soutiennent le toit du foyer «détournent l'attention d'un environnement inévitablement amorphe, lient l'espace et lui donnent une forme.»

Josef Paul Kleihues

Born in Westphalia in 1933, Josef Paul Kleihues studied in Stuttgart and Berlin, but also at the École de Beaux-Arts in Paris (1959–60). He worked afterwards with Hans Scharoun. As Planning Director for the 1984 Bauausstellung, Berlin (1979–84), and subsequently as Consultant to the Senate for Housing and Construction in Berlin, Kleihues has exerted a considerable influence on the emerging face of the reunited German capital. Describing himself as a "poetic rationalist" in contrast with the Italian definition of the term, Kleihues seeks what he calls a "dialectic with Alberti, Palladio, Schinkel, and all the saints." Indeed his debt to Schinkel and the Italians seems apparent in his rational concept of space and its hierarchy. As a teacher at the University of Dortmund (1973–94), he initiated the Dortmund Architecture Days (Dortmunder Architekturtage), which served to introduce the post-modern style to Germany. Despite his appetite for historic references, Kleihues has clearly differentiated himself from the post-modern pastiche, seeking rather a new, historically aware version of modernism.

Der 1933 im westfälischen Rheine geborene Josef Paul Kleihues studierte in Stuttgart und Berlin sowie an der École des Beaux-Arts in Paris (1959–60) und arbeitete danach im Büro von Hans Scharoun. Als Planungsdirektor der »Internationalen Bauausstellung Berlin 1984« (1979–84) und späterer Berater des Berliner Senators für Bauen, Wohnen und Verkehr übte er einen beträchtlichen Einfluß auf das neu entstehende Erscheinungsbild der Hauptstadt des wiedervereinigten Deutschlands aus. Kleihues bezeichnet sich selbst als »poetischen Rationalisten« – im Gegensatz zur italienischen Definition des Begriffs – und strebt nach einer »dialektischen Auseinandersetzung mit Alberti, Palladio, Schinkel und allen anderen Heiligen«. Daß er tatsächlich stark von Schinkel und den italienischen Architekten beeinflußt ist, zeigt sich auch in seinem rationalen Konzept von Räumen und deren Hierarchie. Als Professor an der Universität Dortmund (1973–94) rief er die Dortmunder Architekturtage ins Leben, die zur Einführung des postmodernen Stils in Deutschland beitrugen. Ungeachtet seiner Vorliebe für historische Bezüge distanziert sich Kleihues deutlich vom postmodernen Pasticcio und strebt statt dessen nach einer neuen, historisch bewußten Version der Moderne.

Né en Westphalie en 1933, Josef Paul Kleihues a fait ses études à Stuttgart, Berlin et à l'École des Beaux-Arts de Paris (1959–60). Il a collaboré par la suite avec Hans Scharoun. Directeur de la programmation de la Bauausstellung 1984 de Berlin (1979–84), puis consultant du Sénat de la ville pour le logement et la construction, Kleihues a exercé une influence considérable sur le nouveau visage de la capitale allemande réunifiée. Se décrivant comme «un rationaliste poétique» par contraste avec la définition italienne du rationalisme, il cherche ce qu'il appelle une «confrontation dialectique avec Alberti, Palladio, Schinkel, et tous les grands.» Sa dette envers Schinkel et les Italiens transparaît dans son concept rationnel de l'espace et de sa hiérarchisation. Enseignant à l'Université de Dortmund (1973–94), il a lancé les Dortmunder Architekturtage (Journées de l'architecture) qui ont contribué à introduire le style postmoderniste en Allemagne. Malgré son goût pour les références historiques, il s'est clairement différencié du pastiche postmoderne, s'orientant plutôt vers une version du modernisme consciente de ses racines historiques.

Josef Paul Kleihues, Museum of Contemporary Art, Chicago, Illinois, 1992–96.

Museum of Contemporary Art
Chicago, Illinois, USA, 1992–1996

The Chicago Museum of Contemporary Art was founded in 1967. In 1989, the institution arranged to take over the site of the Chicago Avenue Armory where the Illinois National Guard had been located for eighty years, described as one of the most spectacular sites in urban America. Kleihues was selected from a short list of six architects (Emilio Ambasz, Tadao Ando, Fumihiko Maki, Christian de Portzamparc and Thom Mayne of Morphosis) in 1991. For a project cost of $46 million, the new MCA offers about 4,000 square meters of gallery space, allotted almost equally to temporary and permanent exhibitions. For Kleihues, who first visited Chicago in 1981, there are historical references to the Acropolis and Schinkel's Schauspielhaus implicit in the new building, but it is a fortuitous coincidence that the building actually faces Mies van der Rohe Way. The modern classicism of Mies is also apparent in the design of Kleihues, who also refers to Louis Sullivan's Carson, Pirie, Scott store for its simple, geometric interior plan.

Das Chicago Museum of Contemporary Art wurde 1967 gegründet. 1989 gelang dieser Einrichtung die Übernahme des Geländes der Chicago Avenue Armory (auf dem 80 Jahre lang die Illinois National Guard untergebracht war) – eines der spektakulärsten Grundstücke des urbanen Amerika. Kleihues wurde 1991 aus einer engeren Auswahlliste von sechs Architekten (Emilio Ambasz, Tadao Ando, Fumihiko Maki, Christian de Portzamparc und Thom Mayne von Morphosis) ausgewählt. Mit einer Projektsumme in Höhe von 46 Millionen Dollar bietet das neue MCA etwa 4 000 m² Ausstellungsflächen, die jeweils zur Hälfte für Dauer- bzw. Wechselausstellungen dienen. Laut Kleihues, der 1981 zum ersten Mal nach Chicago kam, weist das neue Gebäude zwar Bezüge zur Akropolis und zu Schinkels Schauspielhaus auf, blickt aber aufgrund eines glücklichen Zufalls auf den Mies van der Rohe Way. Dennoch zeigt sich etwas von Mies van der Rohes modernem Klassizismus auch in Kleihues' Entwurf, dessen schlichte, geometrische Innenraumaufteilung daneben auch Bezüge zu Louis Sullivans Carson, Pirie, Scott Store aufweist.

Le Chicago Museum of Contemporary Art a été fondé en 1967. En 1989, l'institution réussit à acquérir le terrain de la Chicago Avenue Armory où la garde nationale de l'Illinois était installée depuis 80 ans, et l'un des sites urbains américains les plus spectaculaires. Kleihues a été sélectionné sur une liste de six architectes (Emilio Ambaz, Tadao Ando, Fumihiko Maki, Christian de Portzamparc, et Thom Mayne de Morphosis) en 1991. Pour un coût de 46 millions de dollars, le nouveau MCA offre 4 000 m² de galeries, réparties presque à égalité entre les expositions permanentes et temporaires. Pour l'architecte qui a visité Chicago pour la première fois en 1981, les références historiques de ce nouveau bâtiment à l'Acropole et au Schauspielhaus de Schinkel sont implicites, mais c'est bien sûr par hasard que le musée se trouve face à la Mies van der Rohe Way. Le classicisme moderne de Mies est présent dans les projets de Kleihues, qui se réfère également au grand magasin Carson, Pirie, Scott de Louis Sullivan pour la simplicité géométrique de son plan intérieur.

The site of the new museum overlooks Lake Michigan to the east and Water Tower to the west, in the midst of two public parks in the heart of Chicago's most active retail, business and residential area.

Das Gelände des neuen Museums – mit Blick auf den Lake Michigan im Osten und den Water Tower im Westen – befindet sich inmitten zweier öffentlicher Parkanlagen, im Herzen von Chicagos belebtestem Einkaufs-, Geschäfts- und Wohnviertel.

Le site du nouveau musée donne sur le lac Michigan à l'est et Water Tower à l'ouest, entre deux parcs au centre du Chicago commercial et résidentiel.

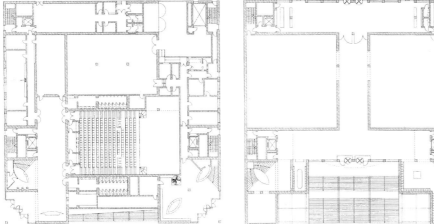

124 Josef Paul Kleihues: Museum of Contemporary Art, 1992–96

The strict, square plan of the Museum brings to mind neo-classical and modernist antecedents, with the main entrance stairway serving as a fitting introduction to a sort of contemporary temple.

Der strenge, quadratische Grundriß des Museums erinnert an klassizistische und moderne Vorläufer, wobei die Treppe zum Haupteingang als angemessene Einstimmung auf diesen zeitgenössischen »Tempel« dient.

Le plan orthogonal strict du musée rappelle certains antécédents néoclassiques et modernistes. Le grand escalier de l'entrée principale sert d'introduction à ce «temple» contemporain.

A geometric simplicity is conserved in interior detailing and design. This rather austere approach in fact seems very well suited to much of the contemporary art that the museum is called on to exhibit.

Die geometrische Schlichtheit setzt sich auch bei der Raumgestaltung und im Innenausbau fort. Dieser relativ strenge Ansatz ist hervorragend geeignet für die zeitgenössischen Kunstwerke, die das Museum beherbergt.

La simplicité géométrique a été conservée dans la conception et les finitions intérieures. Cette approche assez austère paraît en fait bien adaptée à l'art contemporain qu'abrite ce musée.

Hamburger Bahnhof

Berlin, Germany, 1992–1996

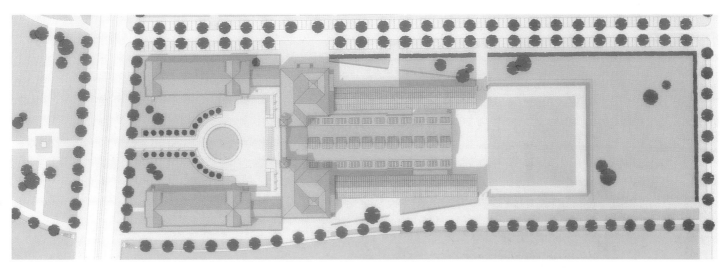

The Hamburger Bahnhof, lying just east of the line which divided East and West Berlin, was built in 1846–47 as a railroad station for the Berlin-Hamburg link, and was shut down in 1884. Transformed into a museum of transportation and building (1904–06), it was severely damaged during World War II and placed off bounds by the Allied Control Commission until it came under control of the West Berlin Senate in 1984. Restored in the 1980s as a location for temporary art shows, it was decided in 1989 that it would house the Erich Marx collection of works by Twombly, Rauschenberg, Kiefer, Warhol and Beuys. The competition winner, Josef Paul Kleihues decided to restore the central volume and flank it with two 80 meter long arched glass galleries. Because of financial restrictions, only the eastern gallery has thus far been built. Kleihues speaks of the "Hamburger Bahnhof identity" in describing his work, suggesting that one of his priorities was to retain the flavor of the original building together with its various mutations over time.

Der 1846–47 speziell für die Zugverbindung zwischen Berlin und Hamburg errichtete und 1884 wieder geschlossene Hamburger Bahnhof liegt auf einem Gelände, das sich direkt östlich der ehemaligen Demarkationslinie zwischen Ost- und Westberlin befindet. Das Gebäude wurde zwischen 1904 und 1906 in ein Museum für Transport- und Bauwesen umgewandelt, während des Zweiten Weltkriegs stark beschädigt und von der Alliierten Kontrollkommission zum Sperrgebiet erklärt, bevor man es 1984 der Aufsicht des Westberliner Senats unterstellte. Während der 80er Jahre diente das Gebäude als Veranstaltungsort für verschiedene Kunstausstellungen, und 1989 fiel der Beschluß, die Räumlichkeiten als Ausstellungsfläche für die Sammlung Erich Marx (mit Werken von Twombly, Rauschenberg, Kiefer, Warhol und Beuys) zu nutzen. Der Gewinner der Ausschreibung, Josef Paul Kleihues, entschloß sich, den zentralen Baukörper zu restaurieren und mit zwei je 80 m langen Galerien mit verglastem Deckengewölbe zu flankieren. Aus Kostengründen konnte bisher nur die östliche der beiden Galerien fertiggestellt werden. Bei der Beschreibung dieses Bauwerks spricht Kleihues von der »Identität des Hamburger Bahnhofs« und seinem vorrangigen Bemühen, die Ausstrahlung des ursprünglichen Gebäudes und seiner zahlreichen Umwandlungen im Laufe der Zeit zu bewahren.

La gare de Hambourg, juste à l'est de l'ancienne ligne de séparation entre Berlin Est et Ouest, a été construite en 1846–47 pour la ligne de chemin de fer Berlin-Hambourg, fermée en 1884. Transformée en musée des transports et de la construction (1904–06), elle fut sévèrement endommagée pendant la Seconde Guerre mondiale, et placée en zone hors limites par la commission de contrôle des Alliés avant de revenir au Sénat de Berlin Ouest en 1984. Restaurée dans les années 80 pour abriter des expositions temporaires, il fut décidé en 1989 qu'elle accueillerait la collection Erich Marx d'œuvres de Twombly, Rauschenberg, Kiefer, Warhol et Beuys. Le lauréat du concours, Josef Paul Kleihues a choisi de restaurer le volume central et de le flanquer de deux galeries de verre voûtées de 80 m de long. Pour des raisons financières, seule la galerie a jusqu'ici été construite. Kleihues décrit son intervention en citant «l'identité de la Hamburger Bahnhof», et en suggérant que l'une de ses priorités était de préserver la personnalité du bâtiment original et de ses multiples variations au cours des années.

While wishing to retain the "spirit" of the original Hamburger Bahnhof, the architect has created a vast new exhibition gallery (page 128 bottom). As the plan reveals, his intention is that this added space should have a symmetrical counterpart, now delayed for budgetary reasons.

In dem Bestreben, den »Geist« des ursprünglichen Hamburger Bahnhofs zu bewahren, schuf der Architekt eine riesige, neue Ausstellungshalle (Seite 128 unten). Wie der Plan zeigt, sollte dieser zusätzliche Raum ein symmetrisches Pendant erhalten, dessen Bau aber aus Kostengründen verschoben wurde.

Tout en souhaitant conserver l'esprit de la gare d'origine, l'architecte a créé une vaste galerie d'exposition (page 128 en bas), qui aurait dû avoir son pendant symétrique (comme l'indique le plan ci-dessus), malheureusement supprimé pour des raisons budgétaires.

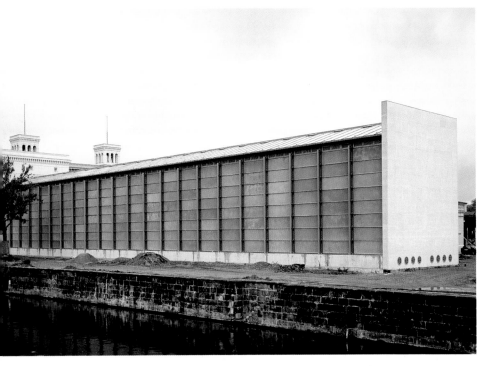

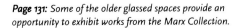

Page 131: Some of the older glassed spaces provide an opportunity to exhibit works from the Marx Collection.

Seite 131: Einige der älteren, verglasten Räume dienen als Ausstellungsfläche für Kunstwerke der Sammlung Marx.

Page 131: Certains espaces vitrés anciens ont été retenus pour la présentation de la collection Marx.

Page 130: In the context of 19th century glass and iron architecture, Kleihues has introduced a spare rigor which seems to suit the contemporary art displayed in the building very well. The rather austere exterior of the new wing is visible above.

Seite 130: In Anlehnung an die Glas- und Stahlarchitektur des 19. Jahrhunderts entwickelte Kleihues einen sparsamen, strengen Entwurf, der gut zu der ausgestellten zeitgenössischen Kunst paßt. Oben, das eher strenge Erscheinungsbild des neuen Flügels.

Page 130: Dans ce contexte d'architecture de fer et de verre du XIXᵉ siècle, Kleihues a introduit une rigueur austère qui convient parfaitement aux œuvres d'art contemporain présentées dans le bâtiment. L'extérieur de la nouvelle aile est plutôt austère (en haut).

Works by Anselm Kiefer, Richard Long and Mario Merz seem to occupy the space quite naturally. The architect has obviously reduced extraneous detail to its minimum expression while retaining the overall forms of the former station.

Die Kunstwerke von Anselm Kiefer, Richard Long und Mario Merz scheinen den Raum auf ganz natürliche Weise in Besitz zu nehmen. Der Architekt reduzierte die Verwendung unwesentlicher Details auf ein Minimum und behielt gleichzeitig die Grundformen des ehemaligen Bahnhofes bei.

Les œuvres d'Anselm Kiefer, Richard Long ou Mario Merz semblent occuper naturellement cet espace. L'architecte a réduit les détails ornementaux au minimum tout en conservant la forme générale de l'ancienne gare.

Jean Nouvel

Jean Nouvel has something of a reputation as a "bad boy" of contemporary architecture. Not always easy to get along with, he initiated a protracted legal action when he was not granted the Grand Stade project in Saint Denis on the outskirts of Paris, despite the fact that he had been selected by the jury. In many respects, Nouvel, author of the Institut du Monde Arabe (Paris, 1981–87, with Architecture Studio) and of the Fondation Cartier (Paris, 1991–95), is the most powerful and original French architect currently working. His sense of volumes and of materials, particularly glass, is unequaled, though the function of some spaces, like the main exhibition area of the Fondation Cartier, may not always be sufficiently in tune with the needs of the client. His largest current commission is for a cultural center in Lucerne, scheduled for 1998 completion.

Jean Nouvel genießt den Ruf eines »enfant terrible« der zeitgenössischen Architektur und gilt als nicht sehr umgänglich. Als man ihm den Auftrag für das Grand Stade-Projekt in St. Denis am Stadtrand von Paris verweigerte, obwohl ihn die Jury ausgewählt hatte, ging er gegen diese Entscheidung gerichtlich vor. In vielerlei Hinsicht zählt Nouvel, der das Institut du Monde Arabe in Paris (1981–87, in Zusammenarbeit mit Architecture Studio) und die Fondation Cartier in Paris (1991–95) entwarf, zu den expressivsten und originellsten französischen Architekten der heutigen Zeit. Sein Gefühl für Baukörper und Baumaterialien, insbesondere für Glas, ist unerreicht, obwohl die Funktion einiger Räume – wie etwa die Hauptausstellungsfläche der Fondation Cartier – nicht immer in ausreichender Übereinstimmung mit den Bedürfnissen des Auftraggebers steht. Zur Zeit beschäftigt sich Jean Nouvel mit dem Entwurf für ein Kulturzentrum in Luzern, das 1998 fertiggestellt werden soll.

Jean Nouvel est un peu le *bad boy* de l'architecture contemporaine. De contact parfois difficile, il s'est lancé dans un procès pour contester ne pas avoir obtenu le projet du Grand Stade de Saint-Denis, alors qu'il avait été choisi par le jury. À de nombreux égards, Nouvel, auteur de l'Institut du Monde arabe, Paris (1981–87, avec Architecture Studio), et de la Fondation Cartier, Paris (1991–95) est le plus créatif et le plus original des architectes français actuels. Son sens des volumes et des matériaux, en particulier du verre, est inégalé, bien que la fonction de certains de ses espaces, comme celui du rez-de-chaussée réservé aux expositions de la Fondation Cartier, ne répondent pas toujours aux attentes de ses clients. Son plus important projet actuel est un centre culturel pour Lucerne, qui devrait être achevé en 1988.

Jean Nouvel, Galeries Lafayette, Berlin, Germany, 1993–96.

Jean Nouvel, Galeries Lafayette, Berlin, Deutschland, 1993–96.

Jean Nouvel, Galeries Lafayette, Berlin, Allemagne, 1993–96.

Galeries Lafayette
Berlin, Germany, 1993–1996

Jean Nouvel's Galeries Lafayette building is situated at the corner of Friedrichstrasse and Französische Strasse in the Mitte area of Berlin. Located one block from the site of the former Wall, the new structure is clad in glass, which is in itself something of a departure from Berlin traditions. Nouvel points out that both Mies van der Rohe and Erich Mendelsohn had also opposed "the necessity of designing every building in Berlin in the same manner, with brick facades, opaque walls and little punch windows." Connected by an arcade to buildings designed by Harry Cobb of Pei Cobb Freed & Partners and O.M. Ungers, the Galeries Lafayette department store, which also includes office space located in the corners, is rendered distinct not only by the curvilinear glass facade, but also by the hollowed-out cones that plunge through the interior, giving an even greater sense of transparency.

Jean Nouvels Galeries Lafayette befindet sich an der Ecke Französische Straße – Friedrichstraße in Berlin-Mitte. Das nur einen Straßenblock von der ehemaligen Mauer entfernt gelegene Bauwerk ist vollständig mit Glas verkleidet und stellt dadurch eine Art Abkehr von den Berliner Bautraditionen dar. Nouvel erklärt, daß sowohl Ludwig Mies van der Rohe als auch Erich Mendelsohn sich ebenfalls dagegen verwehrten, »jedes Gebäude in Berlin auf die gleiche Art und Weise, mit Ziegelsteinfassaden, lichtundurchlässigen Wänden und kleinen, ausgestanzten Fenstern zu entwerfen.« Die durch die Friedrichstadtpassagen mit Gebäuden von Harry Cobb (von Pei Cobb Freed & Partners) und O.M. Ungers verbundene Galeries Lafayette, die in den Eckbereichen auch Büroräume beherbergt, gilt nicht nur aufgrund der geschwungenen Glasfassade als außergewöhnlich, sondern auch wegen der hohlen Kegel, die die Innenräume durchbrechen und so den Eindruck noch größerer Transparenz vermitteln.

L'immeuble des Galeries Lafayette de Jean Nouvel est situé à l'angle de la Friedrichstrasse et de la Französische Strasse, au centre de Berlin. À un bloc de l'ancien mur, la nouvelle construction est tendue d'une façade de verre, qui est en soi une rupture d'avec les traditions berlinoises. Nouvel fait remarquer que Mies van der Rohe et Erich Mendelsohn s'étaient également opposés à la «nécessité de concevoir tout immeuble berlinois de la même manière, avec des façades de brique, des murs opaques et de petites fenêtres découpées.» Réunies par une arcade à des immeubles de Harry Cobb de Pei Cobb Freed & Partners et d'O.M. Ungers, les Galeries Lafayette, qui comprennent également des bureaux dans leurs angles trouvent leur personnalité non seulement dans la façade courbe en verre, mais également dans les cônes qui plongent dans leurs entrailles, donnant un sentiment de transparence encore plus affirmé.

Although he describes his building as rejecting the prevailing stone architecture of Berlin, the Galeries Lafayette structure in fact has a rather classical and inoffensive bearing which makes it fit in well with its surroundings.

Obwohl Nouvel sein Gebäude als Absage an die vorherrschende Steinarchitektur Berlins beschreibt, zeichnet sich die Galeries Lafayette tatsächlich durch eine eher klassische und zurückhaltende Konstruktionsweise aus, wodurch sie sich hervorragend in die bebaute Umgebung einpaßt.

Même si l'architecte décrit sa réalisation comme un rejet de l'architecture de pierre qui domine à Berlin, l'impact de la structure de ses Galeries Lafayette est assez classique et inoffensif, ce qui lui permet de bien s'intégrer à son environnement.

Cone-shaped voids punctuate the building creating an unexpected feeling of transparency and visual contact with the rest of the inhabitants of the store.
Page 138 bottom: A plan of level 7.

Mehrere, das Gebäude durchbrechende kegelförmige Hohlräume erzeugen einen unerwarteten Eindruck von Transparenz und sorgen für einen visuellen Kontakt zwischen den Menschen in der Galeries Lafayette.
Seite 138 unten: Grundriß des 7. Obergeschosses.

Des vides en forme de cônes ponctuent le bâtiment en créant des transparences ainsi que des rapports inhabituels entre les visiteurs.
Page 138 en bas: Plan du septième niveau.

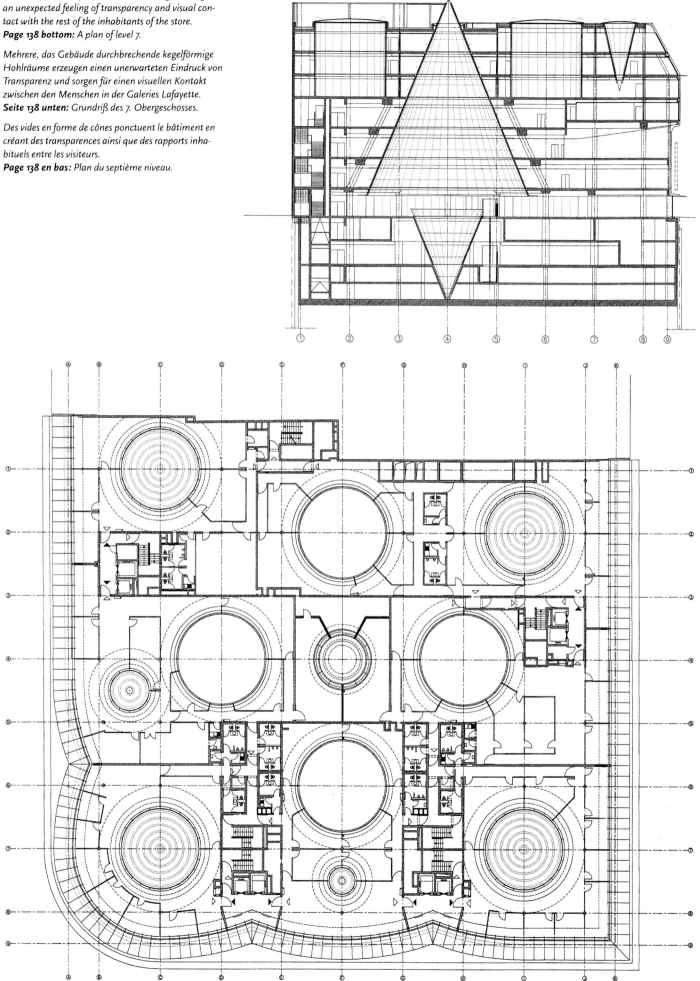

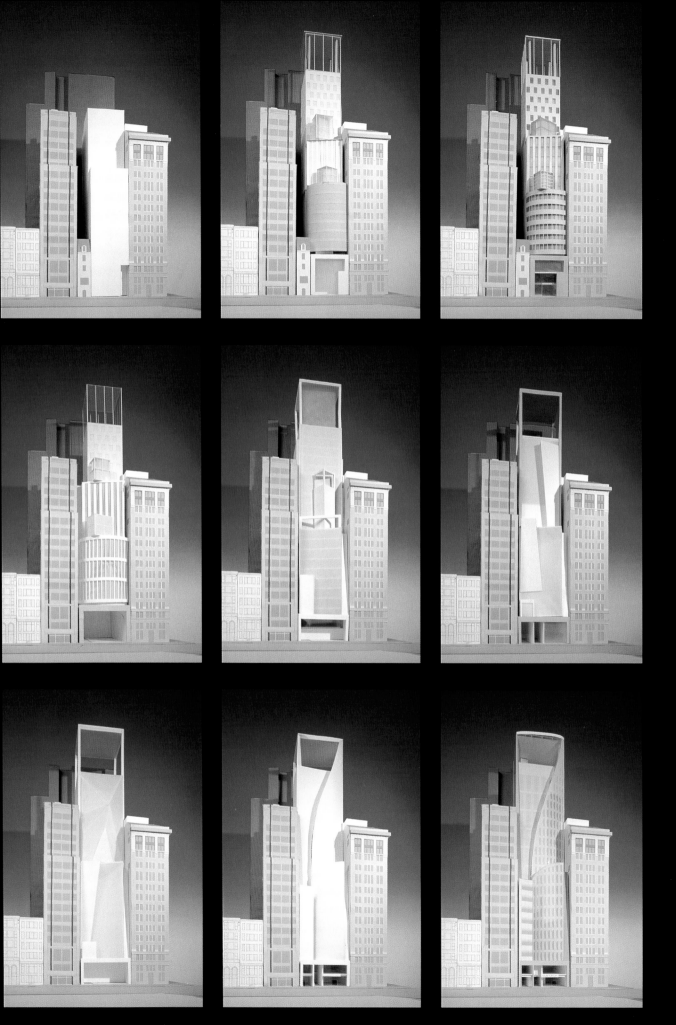

Christian de Portzamparc

Born in Casablanca in 1944, Christian de Portzamparc studied at the École des Beaux-Arts in Paris from 1962 to 1969. He won the competition for the Cité de la Musique on the outskirts of Paris, his largest project to date, in 1984, completing the second phase in 1995. He was awarded the 1994 Pritzker Prize, which may have had some bearing on his selection for the design of the new LVMH Tower on 57th Street in New York. He had already participated in the Euralille project with a tower built over the new Lille-Europe railway station in Lille, and built housing for the Nexus World project in Fukuoka, Japan (1992). Quite different from Nouvel's more brutal approach, Portzamparc's brand of lyrical modern architecture is closely linked to his feeling for the urban environment. For an area of new housing in Paris, he proposed what he calls an "open island" (îlot ouvert) approach, varying the heights of the buildings, and above all leaving a large opening between structures so that residents do not feel closed in.

Christian de Portzamparc wurde 1944 in Casablanca geboren und studierte von 1962–69 an der École des Beaux-Arts in Paris. 1984 gewann er den Architekturwettbewerb für die Cité de la Musique am Rande von Paris (sein bisher größtes Projekt), die er 1995 fertigstellte. Ein Jahr zuvor (1994) verlieh man ihm den Pritzker Preis, was möglicherweise die Entscheidung für seinen Entwurf des neuen LVMH Tower an der 57th Street in New York positiv beeinflußte. Darüber hinaus war Portzamparc mit einem Turm über dem neuen Bahnhof Lille-Europe am Euralille-Projekt beteiligt und errichtete eine Wohnanlage für das Nexus World-Projekt in Fukuoka (1992). Im Gegensatz zu Nouvels eher brutalistischem Ansatz ist Portzamparcs lyrische, moderne Architektur eng mit seinem Gefühl für die urbane Umgebung verbunden. Für ein neues Wohnbauprojekt in Paris entwarf er ein sogenanntes »offene Insel«-Konzept (îlot ouvert), mit Gebäuden von unterschiedlicher Höhe und besonders großen Freiflächen zwischen den einzelnen Komplexen, so daß sich die zukünftigen Bewohner nicht eingeschlossen fühlen würden.

Né à Casablanca en 1944, Christian de Portzamparc a fait ses études à l'École des Beaux-Arts à Paris (1962–69). Il a remporté le concours pour la Cité de la Musique – son plus important projet à ce jour – en 1984. La seconde phase a été achevée en 1995. Il a reçu en 1994 le Pritzker Prize, qui a peut-être joué un rôle dans sa sélection pour le projet de la tour LVMH sur la 57th Street, à New York. Il a déjà réalisé une tour pour le projet Euralille, au-dessus de la gare Lille-Europe, et construit des logements pour le projet Nexus World à Fukuoka (1992). Assez différente de celle de Nouvel, d'une approche plus brutale, l'architecture moderne lyrique de Portzamparc est étroitement liée à sa conception de l'environnement urbain. Pour un ensemble de logements à Paris, il a proposé ce qu'il appelle un «îlot ouvert», variant la hauteur des immeubles, et surtout laissant de vastes espaces entre les constructions pour que les habitants ne se sentent pas enfermés.

Christian de Portzamparc, LVMH Tower, New York, New York, 1995–98.

LVMH Tower

New York, New York, 1995–1998

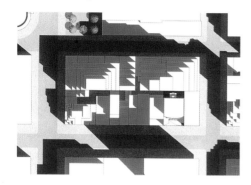

This twenty-three-story skyscraper is located directly across 57th Street from the imposing black IBM Building, and directly next to the new Chanel Tower. Given these factors, together with a narrow site and the obligation to respect strict zoning regulations, Portzamparc found an ingenious solution that permitted him to make his tower considerably taller than the neighboring building within the same envelope of requirements. A facade of clear and opalescent glass is articulated in a stylized flower form, which will be lit at night by neon tubes varying in color from soft gold to green. A crowning touch on the building will be a three-story glass cube to be used for fashion shows or receptions. Despite the proximity of this site to Philip Johnson's former AT&T building, or Edward Durell Stone's General Motors Building, towers by well-known and talented architects are rare in mid-town Manhattan. Given the enthusiastic reviews published by *The New York Times*, the LVMH Building promises to become a notable exception to that rule.

Dieser 23-geschossige Wolkenkratzer befindet sich an der 57th Street, gegenüber dem eindrucksvollen schwarzen IBM Building und direkt neben dem neuen Chanel Tower. Portzamparc gelang in Anbetracht dieser Lage, einem sehr schmalen Baugelände, und strenger Bebauungsauflagen eine geniale Lösung, die es ihm erlaubte, seinen Turm beträchtlich über die umliegenden Gebäude mit den gleichen Anforderungen und Auflagen hinausragen zu lassen. Die Fassade aus Klar- und Opalglas ist in eine stilisierte Blütenform gegliedert, die in der Nacht durch Neonröhren in unterschiedlichen Farben (von sanftem Gold bis hin zu Grün) beleuchtet wird. Den krönenden Abschluß des Gebäudes bildet ein dreigeschossiger Glaswürfel, der für Modeschauen und Empfänge genutzt werden kann. Trotz der Nähe des Geländes zu Philip Johnsons ehemaligem AT&T Building und Edward Durell Stones General Motors Building sind Wolkenkratzer bekannter und talentierter Architekten im Zentrum Manhattans eine Seltenheit. Angesichts der begeisterten Kritiken in der »New York Times« verspricht der LMVH Tower, eine bemerkenswerte Ausnahme dieser Regel zu bilden.

Ce gratte-ciel de 23 étages est situé 57th Street, juste en face de l'imposant immeuble noir d'IBM, et directement à côté de la nouvelle tour Chanel. Confronté à ces voisins, à un terrain étroit, et à l'obligation de respecter une stricte réglementation de zoning, Portzamparc a trouvé une solution ingénieuse qui lui a permis de monter sa tour beaucoup plus haut que les immeubles avoisinants tout en respectant la réglementation. La façade en verre transparent et opalescent s'articule en une forme de fleur stylisée qui sera éclairée la nuit par un système d'éclairage variable allant du doré au vert. Au sommet, un cube de verre de trois étages servira aux défilés de mode ou aux réceptions. Malgré la proximité de l'ancien immeuble AT&T de Philip Johnson, ou du General Motors Building d'Edward Durell Stone, les tours signées de grands architectes sont rares au centre de Manhattan. Les critiques enthousiastes du «New York Times» augurent sans doute que cette tour LVMH constituera une exception notable à cette règle.

Page 142: The complex massing of the tower permitted the architect to reach higher than neighboring structures.
Page 143: A montage shows the completed tower with the former IBM Building in the foreground and the GM Building to the right rear.

Seite 142: Das komplexe Volumen des Towers ermöglichte es dem Architekten, seinen Turm über die umliegenden Gebäude hinausragen zu lassen.
Seite 143: Eine Fotomontage zeigt den fertiggestellten Tower mit dem ehemaligen IBM Building im Vordergrund und dem GM Building rechts im Hintergrund.

Page 142: La répartition complexe des masses de la tour a permis à l'architecte de l'élever plus haut que les constructions voisines.
Page 143: Montage photographique de la tour achevée, avec l'ancien IBM Building au premier plan, et le GM Building à droite.

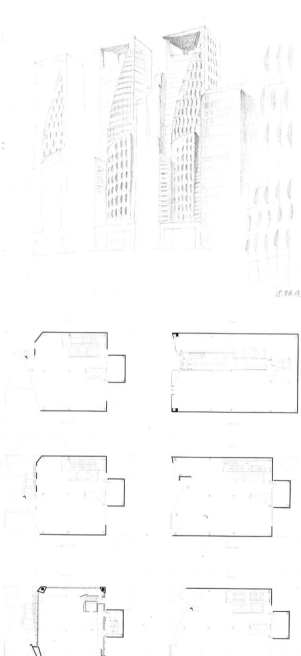

Indentations on the street side render the typical floor plans somewhat more complex than a simple rectangle. The sweeping glass facade resolves a number of fragments into a lyrical whole unlike almost any other tall building in New York.

Einbuchtungen zur Straßenseite lassen die Grundrisse etwas komplexer als ein schlichtes Rechteck erscheinen. Im Gegensatz zu den meisten hohen Bauwerken in New York vereint die gekrümmte Glasfassade eine Reihe von Fragmenten zu einem lyrischen Ganzen.

L'indentation de la façade sur rue enrichit le plan intérieur de chaque niveau. La façade de verre mouvementée réunit un certain nombre de fragments en un tout lyrique très différent des immeubles de grande hauteur new-yorkais.

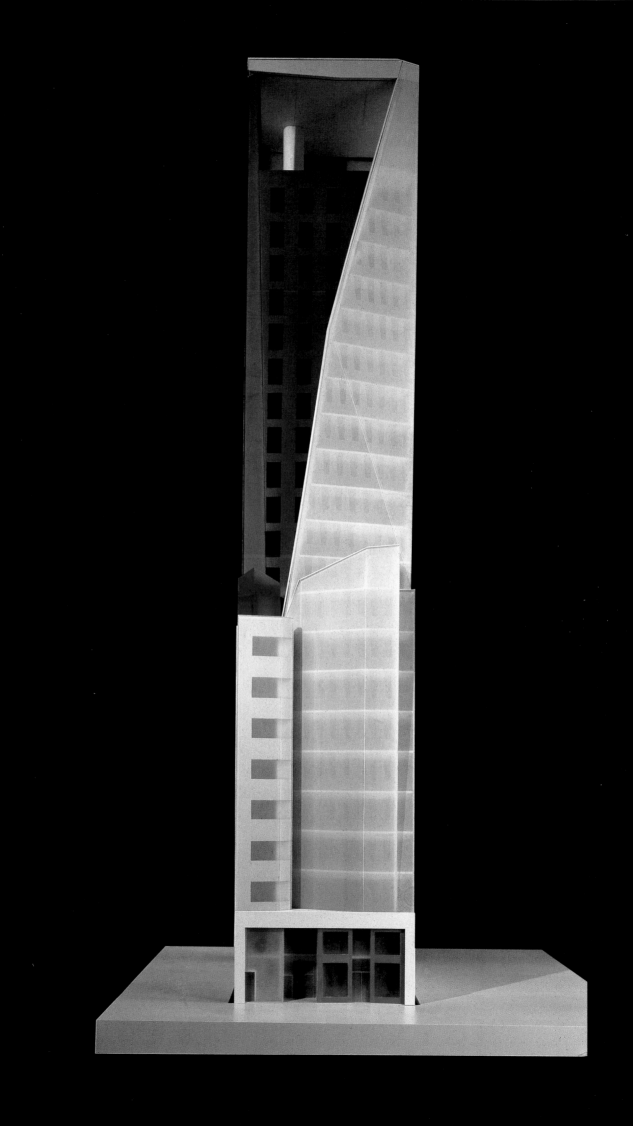

Reichen & Robert

Bernard Reichen   *Philippe Robert*

Over the past twenty years, Bernard Reichen and Philippe Robert have built a solid reputation in France, most notably for the renovation of old industrial facilities, like the Grande Halle de la Villette, Paris (1985) or the Halle Tony Garnier, Lyon, France (1988). They have also completed a number of new buildings, such as the French Embassy in Qatar (1987) or the American Museum in Giverny, France (1992). Their success is undoubtedly due to the fact that they have been able to carry out such renovations for costs below that of new construction. When the clients take into account the inherent quality of older buildings, they need hardly hesitate about deciding in favor of rehabilitation. Reichen & Robert have also shown that they are sensitive to the spatial characteristics of industrial architecture, and they do not attempt to artificially create tightly packed modern offices within the existing shells, preferring to make use of the ceiling heights as they were originally conceived where possible, for example.

In den vergangenen zwanzig Jahren haben sich Bernard Reichen und Philippe Robert in Frankreich einen Namen geschaffen – hauptsächlich im Zusammenhang mit Umwandlungen alter Industrieanlagen wie etwa der Grande Halle de la Villette in Paris (1985) und der Halle Tony Garnier in Lyon (1988). Darüber hinaus errichteten Reichen & Robert auch diverse Neubauten wie die Französische Botschaft in Qatar (1987) und das American Museum in Giverny (1992). Ihr Erfolg begründet sich zweifellos auf der Tatsache, daß die Kosten für ihre Umwandlungs- und Sanierungsprojekte unter dem Preis eines Neubaus liegen. Wenn der Auftraggeber die inhärente Qualität der alten Bausubstanz mit in Betracht zieht, besteht kaum noch ein Grund, sich gegen eine Umwandlung auszusprechen. Reichen & Robert haben darüber hinaus auch ihr Gefühl für die räumlichen Besonderheiten von Industriebauten bewiesen, und sie versuchen keineswegs, die bestehende Bauhülle mit eng geschachtelten, modernen Büroräumen zu füllen. Statt dessen bemühen sie sich beispielsweise, die ursprüngliche Deckenhöhe weitestgehend beizubehalten.

Au cours de ces 20 dernières années, Bernard Reichen et Philippe Robert se sont construit une solide réputation en France, en particulier à travers la rénovation d'anciens bâtiments utilitaires comme la Grande Halle de la Villette, Paris (1985), ou la Halle Tony Garnier, Lyon (1988). Ils ont également achevé un certain nombre d'immeubles nouveaux comme l'ambassade de France au Quatar (1987) ou l'American Museum de Giverny (1992). Leur succès est sans aucun doute dû à leur capacité à mener à bien ces importants chantiers de rénovation à un coût inférieur à celui d'une construction neuve. Lorsque le client prend en compte la qualité inhérente de certains bâtiments anciens, il n'hésite pas longtemps à se décider en faveur d'une réhabilitation. Reichen & Robert ont également montré qu'ils étaient sensibles aux caractéristiques spatiales de l'architecture industrielle, et ne tentent pas de «bourrer» ces structures de bureaux modernes, préférant, par exemple, respecter la hauteur des plafonds telles qu'elles avaient été conçues à l'origine lorsque c'est possible.

Page 147: *Reichen & Robert, Nestlé Center, Noisiel, France, 1993–95, restored façade of the "Moulin," Jules Saulnier (1865–72).*

Seite 147: *Reichen & Robert, Nestlé-Zentrum, Noisiel, Frankreich, 1993–95. Restaurierte Fassade der Mühle von Jules Saulnier (1865–72).*

Page 147: *Reichen & Robert, Centre Nestlé, Noisiel, France, 1993–95. La façade restaurée du moulin de Jules Saulnier (1865–72).*

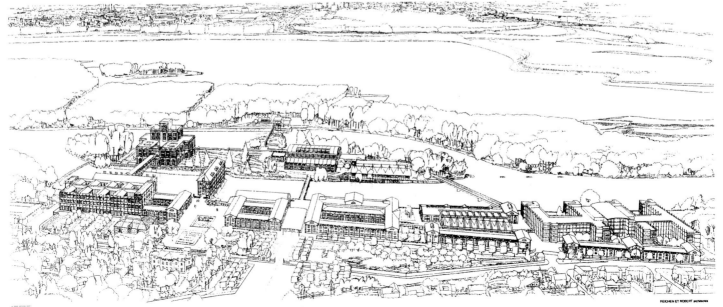

148 Reichen & Robert: Nestlé Center, 1993–95

Nestlé Center
Noisiel, France, 1993–1995

On a 14 hectare site along the banks of the
Marne River about 25 kilometers outside of
Paris, Reichen & Robert have rehabilitated
some 41,000 square meters of old buildings
belonging to the former Menier Chocolate
factory. Included in this group of buildings
are the famous "Moulin" by Jules Saulnier
(1865–72), a listed building (Monument
Historique) that is thought to be the first complete iron-framed structure ever erected, as
well as the "Cathédrale" by Stephen Sauvestre
(1906–08), one of the first reinforced concrete
buildings. A further 19,000 square meters of
new buildings were inserted into the Menier
grounds by the architects, together with some
40,000 square meters of gardens. The total
budget for the project was 800 million francs,
of which 620 million were spent on the construction. The overall cost of 10,000 francs per
square meter obviously compares very favorably to that of any equivalent new buildings.
About 1,800 people work in the complex,
which has retained its historical flavor while
become resolutely modern.

Auf einem 14 ha großen Gelände am Ufer der
Marne (etwa 25 km vor Paris) gelang es Reichen & Robert, einen Teil der alten Gebäude
der ehemaligen Menier-Schokoladenfabrik
mit etwa 41 000 m² Grundfläche zu sanieren.
Zu diesen Gebäuden gehören die berühmte
Mühle von Jules Saulnier (1865–72) – ein denk-
malgeschütztes Bauwerk (Monument Historique), das als eines der ersten vollständig in
Stahlskelettbauweise errichteten Gebäude gilt
– sowie die »Cathédrale« von Stephen Sauvestre (1906–08), einer der ersten Stahlbeton-
bauten. Darüber hinaus schufen die Architekten auf dem Gelände der Fabrik neue Gebäude
mit 19 000 m² Grundfläche sowie eine etwa
40 000 m² umfassende Gartenanlage. Das
Budget für das gesamte Projekt belief sich auf
eine Summe von 800 Millionen Francs, von
denen etwa 620 Millionen Francs auf die
Kosten für die Sanierung und Neubauten ver-
wandt wurden. Mit einem Gesamtpreis von
10 000 Francs pro Quadratmeter schneidet
das Projekt im Vergleich zu einem gleicharti-
gen Neubau durchaus günstig ab. Heute arbeiten etwa 1 800 Mitarbeiter in dem Komplex,
der inzwischen zwar von Grund auf moderni-
siert ist, aber sein historisches Flair behalten
hat.

Sur un terrain de 14 ha au bord de la Marne,
à 25 km environ à l'est de Paris, Reichen &
Robert ont réhabilité les quelque 41 000 m² de
bâtiments de l'ancienne chocolaterie Menier.
Ceux-ci comprennent le fameux moulin de
Jules Saulnier (1865–72), classé monument
historique, qui est probablement la première
construction à structure métallique jamais
érigée, ainsi que la «cathédrale» de Stephen
Sauvestre (1906–08), l'un des premiers bâtiments en béton armé. 19 000 m² supplémen-
taires de bâtiments neufs ont été insérés dans
cet ensemble, ainsi que 40 000 m² de jardins.
Le budget total du projet s'est élevé à 800
millions de Francs, dont 620 millions pour la
construction. Le coût global de 10 000 F le
mètre carré se compare très favorablement à
celui de n'importe quel immeuble neuf. 1 800
personnes environ travaillent dans ce complexe qui a conservé sa personnalité historique
tout en étant résolument moderne.

*An overall view of Saulnier's "Moulin" converted
into the offices of the Directors of Nestlé-France by
Reichen & Robert. Below, an overall drawing of
the site, with the "Moulin" left of center.*

*Eine Gesamtansicht von Saulniers Mühlengebäude,
das von Robert & Reichen zu Verwaltungsräumen der
Direktion von Nestlé-Frankreich umgewandelt wurde,
darunter eine Zeichnung des gesamten Geländes, mit
der Mühle in der Mitte des Flusses.*

*Vue d'ensemble du moulin de Noisiel de Jules Saulnier,
transformé en bureaux pour la direction de Nestlé-France
par Reichen & Robert. En bas, une perspective d'ensemble du site, avec le moulin au milieu de la rivière.*

Below: Reichen & Robert have succeeded in blending modern glass and steel structure such as an entrance pavilion into the prevailing 19th and early 20th century architectural environment. **Left:** The "Cathedral" (1906–08) by Stephen Sauvestre, who also worked on the Eiffel Tower.

Unten: Reichen & Robert gelang es, moderne Glas- und Stahlkonstruktionen wie etwa den Eingangspavillon in die hauptsächlich aus dem 19. und frühen 20. Jahrhundert stammende architektonische Umgebung zu integrieren. **Links:** Die »Cathédrale« (1906–08) von Stephen Sauvestre, der auch am Bau des Eiffelturms beteiligt war.

Ci-dessous: Reichen & Robert ont réussi à marier des constructions modernes en verre et en acier, comme le pavillon d'entrée, à un environnement essentiellement XIXᵉ et début XXᵉ siècles. **À gauche:** La «cathédrale» (1906–08) de Stephen Sauvestre, qui avait également collaboré aux plans de la Tour Eiffel.

Reichen & Robert: Nestlé Center, 1993–95 **151**

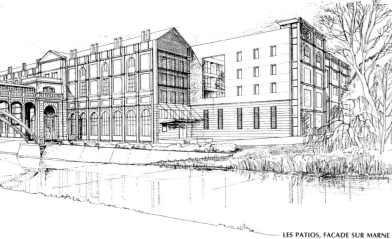

LES PATIOS, FACADE SUR MARNE

Above: The soaring glass and iron spaces of the original architecture of the Menier Chocolate Factory are echoed in the large glass atrium of one of the new buildings added by Reichen & Robert. **Right:** Glass-covered walkways link many parts of the complex.

Oben: Das große Glasatrium in einem der von Reichen & Robert neu hinzugefügten Gebäude nimmt die emporstrebenden Glas- und Stahlflächen der ursprünglichen Architektur der ehemaligen Menier-Schokoladenfabrik noch einmal auf. **Rechts:** Glasüberdachte Passagen verbinden verschiedene Teile des Komplexes miteinander.

Ci-dessus: Les vastes espaces de fer et de verre de l'architecture d'origine de la chocolaterie Menier trouvent un écho contemporain dans le grand atrium vitré de l'une des nouvelles constructions de Reichen & Robert. **À droite:** Des passerelles vitrées réunissent de nombreux éléments de ce complexe.

152 Reichen & Robert: Nestlé Center, 1993–95

Rudy Ricciotti

Born in 1952 in Algiers, Rudy Ricciotti attended the École supérieure technique in Geneva, from which he graduated in 1975. He received his degree as an architect after studies in Marseille in 1980. He created his own office in Bandol in the South of France in 1980. He has worked on a Center for Young People in Bandol, (1986); an office building in Bandol (1993); and the Côte Bleue High School in Sausset-les-Pins (1994). Current work includes the Selestat Theater and rock concert hall in Strasbourg, to be completed in 1998; a Philharmonic Concert Hall in Potsdam, Berlin, Germany, to be completed in 1999; and a 600 seat cinema to be built in Pierre-latte. He has also worked extensively on hospital projects including the Hospital Center in Carpentras, for which he won the competition in August 1996. Ricciotti belongs to the generation of French architects that came into its own just as the wave of government-led spending on architecture subsided dramatically, obliging the younger designers to be at once inventive and very much aware of budgetary restrictions.

Rudy Ricciotti wurde 1952 in Algier geboren und besuchte die École supérieure technique in Genf, an der er 1975 seinen Abschluß machte. 1980 graduierte er als Diplomarchitekt in Marseille. Im gleichen Jahr gründete er sein Architekturbüro im südfranzösischen Bandol, wo er ein Jugendzentrum (1986) und ein Bürogebäude (1993) errichtete. 1994 stellte Ricciotti die École Côte Bleue in Sausset-les-Pins fertig. Zu seinen aktuellen Bauvorhaben gehören: Theater- und Rockkonzerthalle Selestat, Straßburg (geplante Fertigstellung 1998); Philharmonie, Potsdam (geplante Fertigstellung 1999) sowie ein Kino mit 600 Plätzen in Pierrelatte. Darüber hinaus beschäftigt er sich intensiv mit Krankenhausbauten: 1996 gewann er eine Ausschreibung für ein Krankenhaus in Carpentras. Ricciotti gehört zu einer Generation französischer Architekten, die zu einem Zeitpunkt bekannt wurden, als die Welle regierungsgeförderter Architekturprojekte dramatisch zurückging und die jungen Designer gezwungen waren, innovative Entwürfe innerhalb eng gesteckter Budgetpläne zu entwickeln.

Né en 1952 à Alger, Rudy Ricciotti a suivi les cours de l'École supérieure technique de Genève dont il sort diplômé en 1975. Il passe son diplôme d'architecte à Marseille en 1980. Il a conçu le Centre municipal des Jeunes de Bandol (1986), un immeuble de bureaux à Bandol (1993), et le collège de la Côte Bleue à Sausset-les-Pins (1994). Il travaille actuellement sur le théâtre et salle de rock de Sélestat, à Strasbourg qui sera achevé en 1998, une salle philharmonique à Potsdam (Allemagne), terminée en 1999, et un cinéma de 600 places à Pierrelatte. Il a également beaucoup travaillé sur des projets d'hôpitaux dont le Centre hospitalier de Carpentras, remporté à l'issue d'un concours en août 1996. Ricciotti appartient à la génération d'architectes français qui se sont installés au moment où les pouvoirs publics ont dramatiquement réduit leurs investissements, obligeant ces jeunes praticiens à être à la fois inventifs et beaucoup plus conscients des contraintes budgétaires.

Rudy Ricciotti, Le Stadium, Vitrolles, France |
Frankreich, 1994–95.

Le Stadium
Vitrolles, France, 1994–1995

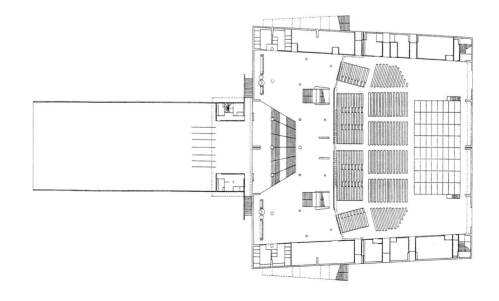

Rudy Ricciotti has more than a passing interest in contemporary art, which may explain something of the rather brutal, yet sculptural form of his rock concert hall Le Stadium, located on the site of a former garbage dump, and near bauxite mines in Vitrolles, an industrial and commercial town with about 35,000 inhabitants in the Bouches-du-Rhône area of France. The 6,000 square meter building, erected for a budget of 65 million francs allotted by the city of Vitrolles, is essentially made of concrete, tinted black for the exterior and polished for the floors. This powerful mass is studded with small red lights, and the architect chose to use the entire exterior planting budget on an aluminum palm tree, a sign of a sense of humor that tempers what could easily have been an overly brutalist concrete volume. With its implied reference to a film such as Stanley Kubrick's "2001, A Space Odyssey," the "Stade" succeeds in keeping roots in the popular culture that it is intended to house.

Rudy Ricciottis Interesse an zeitgenössischer Kunst erklärt möglicherweise die eher grobe und dennoch skulpturale Form seiner Konzerthalle Le Stadium. Das Bauwerk steht auf einer ehemaligen Mülldeponie, in der Nähe der Bauxitminen in Vitrolles – einer Industrie- und Handelsstadt mit 35 000 Einwohnern im Gebiet Bouches-du-Rhône in Frankreich. Das 6 000 m² große Gebäude wurde im Auftrag der Stadt Vitrolles mit einem Budget von 65 Millionen Francs errichtet und besteht hauptsächlich aus schwarz gestrichenem Beton für die Fassaden und poliertem Beton für die Böden. Es ist mit kleinen roten Lichtern übersät. Der Architekt verwendete das gesamte Budget für die Bepflanzung der Außenanlagen für eine Aluminiumpalme – Kennzeichen seines Sinns für Humor –, die die Ausstrahlung des massiven Betonbaukörpers, der sonst einen übermäßig brutalistischen Eindruck erzeugt hätte, etwas mildert. Aufgrund der implizierten Bezüge zu Filmen wie Stanley Kubricks »2001 – Odyssee im Weltraum« ist Le Stadium fest verwurzelt mit der populären Kultur, der es als Forum dienen soll.

Rudy Ricciotti s'intéresse réellement à l'art contemporain, ce qui explique en partie la forme assez brutale et sculpturale de sa salle de rock. Le Stadium, situé à Vitrolles à l'emplacement d'une ancienne décharge, et non loin d'une mine de bauxite à Vitrolles (Bouches-du-Rhône), ville industrielle et commerciale de 39 000 habitants. Ce bâtiment de 6 000 m², édifié pour un budget de 65 millions de francs accordé par la municipalité est essentiellement en béton teinté noir à l'extérieur et poli pour les sols intérieurs. Cette masse puissante est ponctuée la nuit de petites lumières orangées, et l'architecte a décidé de consacrer la totalité du budget de plantations à un arbre d'aluminium, signe d'humour qui tempère ce que ce massif volume de béton pourrait avoir de trop brutaliste. Avec ses références implicites au film de Stanley Kubrick «2001, odyssée de l'espace», le Stadium a réussit à pousser ses racines dans la culture populaire à laquelle il est destiné.

The bunker-like atmosphere of the Stadium is reinforced by the recessed entrance area. The heaviness of the black concrete is lightened in some areas by gestures such as the aluminum tree or a star-burst shaped opening in a wall (page 156 top).

Die bunkerartige Atmosphäre von Le Stadium wird durch den tiefergelegten Eingangsbereich zusätzlich betont. Die massive Schwere des schwarzen Betons ist an manchen Stellen durch Gesten wie die Aluminiumpalme oder eine sternförmige Wandöffnung (Seite 156 oben) aufgelockert.

L'atmosphère de bunker du Stadium est renforcée par une entrée en partie enterrée. La lourdeur du béton noir est allégée à certains endroits par des gestes esthétiques comme l'arbre d'aluminium ou une ouverture en étoile (page 156 en haut).

Rudy Ricciotti: Le Stadium, 1994–95 **157**

As might be expected from its external appearance, the Stadium has an intentional roughness in its materials and in its finishing. The orange-red lights set into the otherwise blank facades heighten the eerie, monolithic appearance of the building at night.

Wie das äußere Erscheinungsbild bereits vermuten läßt, zeichnet sich Le Stadium durch eine bewußt belassene Natürlichkeit der Materialien und der Verarbeitung aus. Die orangeroten Lichter auf der ansonsten undurchbrochenen Fassade verstärken den unheimlichen, monolithischen Eindruck, den das Gebäude bei Nacht erzeugt.

Comme le laisse prévoir son aspect extérieur, le Stadium fait appel à des matériaux et des finitions brutes. La nuit, les lumières orangées insérées dans les façades autrement aveugles soulignent l'apparence monolithique et mystérieuse du bâtiment.

Thomas Spiegelhalter

Born in 1959 in Freiburg, Thomas Spiegelhalter is something of an exception in a book dedicated to architects, because he would just as soon consider himself a sculptor or a "communications designer." His curriculum vitae makes as many references to art exhibitions as it does to building projects, and where architecture is involved, it is often associated closely with his interest in abandoned gravel pits and redevelopment schemes for disused industrial sites. Works such as the house in Breisach published here emerges not only from Spiegelhalter's interest in sculpture and recycling, construction or industrial landscapes, but also from his insistence on "direct physical experience" as opposed to what he sees as the threat of a digital society that "diminishes the body to a cerebral nervous system." This stance is not, however, indicative of a reactionary rejection of modern technology in general, as amply demonstrated, in the example of this house, by his use of sophisticated, environmentally-friendly systems and of CAD in planning the architectural details. "I think," he says, "that the traditional division into art on this side and architecture on the other is quite obsolete and stifles communication between the various media. We have to form different categories nowadays, and we have to think and act more in terms of networking."

Thomas Spiegelhalter, 1959 in Freiburg geboren, stellt insofern eine Ausnahme in einem Buch über Architekten dar, als er sich auch als Bildhauer und »Kommunikationsdesigner« bezeichnet. Sein Lebenslauf enthält ebenso viele Hinweise auf Kunstausstellungen wie auf Bauprojekte. Und wenn es sich doch einmal um Architektur handelt, dann steht sie häufig in engem Zusammenhang mit seinem Interesse für stillgelegte Kiesgruben und neu zu belebende Industrieanlagen. Spiegelhalters Werke, wie etwa das hier vorgestellte Haus in Breisach, entstehen nicht nur aus seinem Interesse an Bildhauerei und an der Wiederverwertbarkeit von verbrauchtem Material, Konstruktion und Landschaft der Industriegesellschaft, sondern auch aus seinem Beharren auf »direkter körperlicher Erfahrung« – im Gegensatz zu dem, was er als Drohung der digitalen Gesellschaft auffaßt, die »den Körper auf ein zerebrales Nervensystem reduziert«. Dennoch ist diese Haltung nicht kennzeichnend für eine generelle Ablehnung moderner Technologie, wie die ausgeklügelte Umwelttechnik und mit CAD-geplanten Details in Spiegelhalters Haus beweisen. Er erklärt dazu: »Ich glaube, daß die traditionelle Trennung von Kunst auf der einen und Architektur auf der anderen Seite ziemlich überholt ist und die Kommunikation zwischen den verschiedenen Medien im Keim erstickt. Wir müssen heute ganz andere Kategorien bilden und mehr in Vernetzungen denken und handeln.«

Né en 1959 à Freiburg, Thomas Spiegelhalter représente une sorte d'exception dans un ouvrage consacré à des architectes, puisqu'il se considère plutôt lui-même comme un sculpteur ou un «communications designer». Son curriculum vitae fait autant référence à des expositions artistiques qu'à des projets de construction. Dans la mesure où l'architecture est concernée, il montre son intérêt pour les gravières abandonnées et la reconversion d'installations industrielles. Une réalisation comme la maison de Breisach reproduite ici trouve ses racines à la fois dans son goût pour la sculpture et le recyclage de matériaux, de constructions et de paysages abandonnés, et dans sa défense de «l'expérience physique directe» opposée à ce qu'il voit comme une menace de la société numérique qui «réduit le corps à un système nerveux cérébral». Cette position ne reflète pas pour autant un rejet réactionnaire de la technologie moderne en général, comme le montrent amplement les systèmes sophistiqués et écologiques qui équipent cette maison et les détails techniques traités par CAO. «Je pense,» dit-il, «que la division traditionnelle entre l'art d'un côté et l'architecture de l'autre est assez obsolète, et étouffe la communication entre les différents médias. Nous devons constituer aujourd'hui des catégories différentes, et penser et agir davantage en termes de réseaux.»

Thomas Spiegelhalter, Breisach House, Germany, 1992–93.

Thomas Spiegelhalter, Haus in Breisach, Deutschland, 1992–93.

Thomas Spiegelhalter, Maison à Breisach, Allemagne, 1992–93.

House
Breisach, Germany, 1992–93

This house is located on the outskirts of Breisach, a town of 5,000 inhabitants located on the Rhine in Bad-Wurtemberg. On a 1,715 square meters property, it includes an enclosed area of 2,127 cubic meters. The mixed space for living and working of 613 square meters is divided into no less than sixteen levels, which are arranged in a spiral pattern around a central stairway. Intended to allow occasional concerts or small exhibitions as well as day-to-day living, the house, which was subsidized by the German government as an experimental residence with integrated solar cells, has an environmental design. Tubular vacuum collectors on the roof for hot water supply, and 54 square meters of photovoltaic cells provide energy, although a natural gas engine can take over if the sun does not shine enough. Incorporating some fragments from Freiburg's gravel pits, the house makes considerable use of prefabricated building components. Though it may not be appealing in the immediate esthetic sense, the house offers a variety of spatial experiences, which are not in the usual spectrum of household architecture.

Spiegelhalters Haus befindet sich am Rand von Breisach, einer am Rhein gelegenen Kleinstadt mit 5 000 Einwohnern in Baden-Württemberg. Das 1 715 m² große Gelände umfaßt einen umbauten Raum von 2 127 m³. Die 613 m² großen, gemischten Wohn- und Arbeitsbereiche sind auf 16 verschiedene Ebenen verteilt, die sich spiralförmig um ein zentrales, verglastes Treppenhaus gruppieren. Das sowohl für gelegentliche Konzerte und kleinere Ausstellungen als auch für das tägliche Leben konzipierte Gebäude, das als Experimentalhaus mit integrierten Solarzellen Fördergelder erhielt, zeichnet sich durch ein umweltfreundliches Design aus. Röhrenförmige Vakuumkollektoren auf dem Dach für die Warmwassergewinnung und eine 54 m² große Solarzellenfläche versorgen das Haus mit Energie, wobei eine Erdgasanlage die Versorgung übernehmen kann, falls die Sonne nicht genügend Strom liefert. Neben einigen Fragmenten aus den Freiburger Kiesgruben verwendete Spiegelhalter für dieses Haus hauptsächlich Fertigbauteile. Obwohl die ästhetische Ausstrahlung des Hauses nicht unmittelbar ansprechend wirken mag, bietet es eine Vielzahl von Raumerfahrungen außerhalb des normalen Spektrums herkömmlicher Hausarchitektur.

Cette maison est située dans les environs de Breisach, une ville de 5 000 habitants au bord du Rhin dans le Land du Bade-Wurtemberg. Sur un terrain de 1 715 m², elle enclôt un volume de 2 127 m³. L'espace mixte – travail et vie – de 613 m² est divisé en pas moins de 16 niveaux disposés en spirale autour d'un escalier central. Conçu aussi bien pour la vie quotidienne que pour accueillir à l'occasion des concerts ou des expositions, cette maison expérimentale à cellules solaires integrées a été subventionnée par le gouvernement allemand. Des collecteurs tubulaires à vide sur le toit pour l'eau chaude, et 54 m² de cellules photovoltaïques fournissent l'énergie, et peuvent être relayés par un générateur à gaz si l'ensoleillement est insuffisant. En dehors de quelques récupérations de matériaux des gravières environnantes, la maison fait un usage considérable d'éléments préfabriqués. Bien qu'elle ne soit pas forcément séduisante au premier abord, elle offre une multiplicité d'expériences spatíales rares dans l'architecture domestique habituelle.

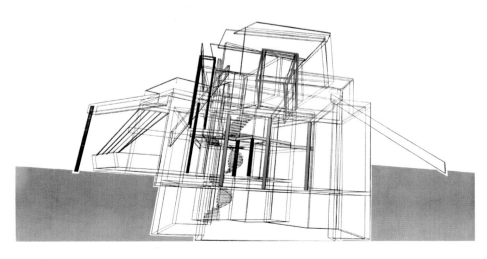

The complex forms of this house are in part derived from the architect's interest in the machinery and architecture of local gravel mining pits. Beyond its ecologically sensitive design, the building must be considered a kind of sculpture at the same time as it is a place to live and work.

Die komplexen Formen dieses Hauses lassen sich zum Teil von dem Interesse des Architekten für den Maschinenpark und die Architektur der örtlichen Kiesgruben ableiten. Unabhängig von seinem umweltbewußten Design muß das Gebäude als eine Art Skulptur und zugleich als Wohn- und Arbeitsplatz betrachtet werden.

La complexité des formes de cette maison vient en partie de l'intérêt de l'architecte pour l'architecture et les machines des gravières de la région. De conception écologique, cette construction peut être considérée à la fois comme une sculpture et un lieu pour vivre et travailler.

Ordinary building materials such as corrugated siding heighten the impression that this house is "handmade" much as a contemporary sculpture would be. According to the architect, it is divided into no less than sixteen levels with a total of 613 square meters of usable space.

Herkömmliche Bauteile wie die Außenwandverklei-dungen aus Wellblech verstärken den Eindruck, daß dieses Haus »von Hand gefertigt« wurde – vergleichbar einer zeitgenössischen Skulptur. Laut Architekt ist das Gebäude in nicht weniger als 16 Ebenen mit einer Nutzfläche von insgesamt 613 m² unterteilt.

Les matériaux de construction ordinaires, comme le bardage en tôle ondulée, soulignent l'impression de «fait main» de cette maison, un peu comme une sculpture contemporaine. Selon l'architecte, elle est divisée en pas moins de 16 niveaux et offre 613 m² de surface utile.

"We have to form different categories nowadays, and we have to think and act more in terms of networking," says the architect. Colliding spaces with often indeterminate or multiple functions are the rule in this house.

»Wir müssen heute ganz andere Kategorien bilden und mehr in Vernetzungen denken und handeln«, erklärt der Architekt. Miteinander kollidierende Räume von häufig unbestimmter oder multipler Funktion bilden in diesem Haus die Regel.

« Nous devons constituer aujourd'hui des catégories différentes, et penser et agir davantage en termes de réseaux », fait remarquer l'architecte. La collision d'espaces aux fonctions multiples et souvent indéterminées est de règle dans cette maison.

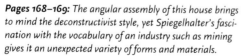

Pages 168–169: The angular assembly of this house brings to mind the deconstructivist style, yet Spiegelhalter's fascination with the vocabulary of an industry such as mining gives it an unexpected variety of forms and materials.

Seite 168–169: Die winkelförmige Konstruktion dieses Hauses erinnert an den Dekonstruktivismus. Spiegelhalters Begeisterung für die Formensprache der Industrie (wie etwa im Falle der Kiesgruben) zeigt sich durch eine unerwartete Vielfalt an Formen und Materialien.

Pages 168–169: Cet assemblage anguleux fait penser au style déconstructiviste. La fascination de Spiegelhalter pour le vocabulaire industriel, en particulier celui des mines, l'a amené à utiliser une étonnante variété de formes et de matériaux.

Wiel Arets architect & associates
d'Artagnanlaan 29
6213 CH Maastricht, The Netherlands
Tel: + 31 43 351 2200
Fax: + 31 43 321 2192

Wiel Arets

Born in Heerlen, The Netherlands, 1955. Graduated from Technical University, Eindhoven, 1983. Established Wiel Arets Architect & Associates, Heerlen, 1984. Traveled in Russia, Japan, America, Europe (1984–89). Taught at Academy of Architecture, Amsterdam, and Rotterdam, 1986. His interest in architectural theory led him to create the publisher Wiederhall in 1987. Diploma Unit Master at Architectural Association, London (1988–92); Visiting Professor, Columbia University, New York (1991–92); Dean, Berlage Institute, Postgraduate Laboratory of Architecture, Amsterdam (1995–98), where he is the succesor of Herman Hertzberger. Projects include: House and Pharmacy, Schoonbroodt, Brunssum (1985–86); Barbershop and House Mayntz, Heerlen (1986–87); Fashionshop Beltgens, Maastricht (1987); Academy of Art and Architecture, Maastricht (1989–93); Headquarters, AZL Pensionfund, Heerlen (1990–95); 67 apartments, Tilburg (1992-94); Police Station, Vaals (1993–96); 104 apartments, Jacobsplaats, Rotterdam (1995–97), all in the Netherlands.

Der 1955 in Heerlen (Niederlande) geborene Wiel Arets beendete 1983 sein Architekturstudium an der Technischen Hochschule Eindhoven und gründete 1984 in Heerlen das Büro Wiel Arets Architect & Associates. Von 1984–89 bereiste Arets Rußland, Japan, Amerika und Europa. 1986 lehrte er an der Akademie für Architektur in Amsterdam sowie in Rotterdam. Aufgrund seines Interesses für Architekturtheorie gründete Arets 1987 den Verlag Wiederhall. Diploma Unit Master der Architectural Association, London (1988–92); Gastprofessor an der Columbia University, New York (1991–92); Dekan des Berlage Postgraduierteninstituts für Architektur, Amsterdam (1995–98, als Nachfolger von Herman Hertzberger). Zu seinen Projekten zählen: Privathaus & Apotheke Schoonbroodt, Brunssum (1985–86); Friseursalon und Privathaus Mayntz, Heerlen (1986–87); Modegeschäft Beltgens, Maastricht (1987); Akademie für Kunst und Architektur, Maastricht (1989–93); Zentrale AZL Pensionskasse, Heerlen (1990–95); 67 Appartements, Tilburg (1992–94); Polizeiwache, Vaals (1993–96); 104 Appartements, Jacobsplaats, Rotterdam (1995–97), alle in den Niederlanden.

Né à Heerlen, Pays-Bas, en 1955. Diplômé de l'Université technique d'Eindhoven. Fonde Wiel Arets Architect & Associates, Heerlen, en 1984. Voyages en Russie, au Japon, en Amérique et en Europe (1984–89). Enseigne à l'Académie d'architecture d'Amsterdam et de Rotterdam, en 1986. Son intérêt pour la théorie architecturale l'amène à créer la maison d'édition Wiederhall en 1987. Responsable de la classe de diplôme de l'Architectural Association, Londres (1988–92); professeur invité, Columbia University, New York (1991–92); doyen, Institut Berlage, Laboratoire post-universitaire d'architecture, Amsterdam (1995–98), où il succède à Herman Hertzberger. Parmi ses réalisations: maison et pharmacie Schoonbroodt, Brunssum (1985–86); maison et salon de coiffure Mayntz, Heerlen (1986–87); boutique de mode Beltgens, Maastricht (1987); Académie d'art et d'architecture, Maastricht (1989–93); siège de AZL Pensionfund, Heerlen (1990–95); 67 appartements, Tilburg (1992–94); poste de police, Vaals (1993–96); 104 appartements, Jacobsplaats, Rotterdam (1995–97), tous aux Pays-Bas.

Van Berkel & Bos, architectuur bureau bv
Gebouw De Metropool Weesperstraat 97
1018 VN Amsterdam, The Netherlands
Tel: + 31 20 620 2350
Fax: + 31 20 620 7199

Ben van Berkel

Ben van Berkel was born in Utrecht in 1957 and studied at the Rietveld Academie in Amsterdam and at the Architectural Association (AA) in London, receiving the AA Diploma with honors in 1987. After working briefly in the office of Santiago Calatrava, in 1988, he set up his practice in Amsterdam with Caroline Bos. Visiting professor at Columbia, New York and visiting critic at Harvard (1994). Diploma Unit Master, AA, London (1994–95). As well as the Erasmus Bridge in Rotterdam (inaugurated in 1996), Van Berkel & Bos Architectural Bureau has built the Karbouw and ACOM (1989–93) office buildings, and the REMU electricity station (1989–93), all in Amersfoort, The Netherlands; housing projects and the Aedes East gallery for Kristin Feireiss (now Director of the Netherlands Architecture Institute, Rotterdam) in Berlin. More recent projects include a new museum for Nijmegen and an extension for the Rijksmuseum Twente in Enschede, the Netherlands (1992–96).

Ben van Berkel wurde 1957 in Utrecht geboren und studierte an der Rietveld Academie in Amsterdam und der Architectural Association (AA) in London (AA Honors Diploma 1987). Er arbeitete kurze Zeit im Büro von Santiago Calatrava und gründete 1988 in Amsterdam zusammen mit Caroline Bos sein eigenes Büro. Gastprofessor an der Columbia University, New York, Gastkritiker in Harvard 1994; Diploma Unit Master an der AA (1994–95). Neben der Erasmusbrücke in Rotterdam (1996 eingeweiht) entwarfen Van Berkel & Bos im niederländischen Amersfoort Bürogebäude für Karbouw und ACOM (1989–93) sowie das REMU-Umspannwerk (1989–93); in Berlin entstanden Wohnbauten und die Aedes East-Galerie für Kristin Feireiss (Direktorin des Niederländischen Architekturinstituts, Rotterdam). Zu den aktuellen Projekten zählen ein neues Museum für Nijmegen sowie die Erweiterung des Rijksmuseums Twente in Enschede (1992–96).

Ben van Berkel naît à Utrecht en 1957, et étudie à l'Académie Rietveld d'Amsterdam et à l'Architectural Association de Londres. Diplômé avec mention de l'AA (1987). Après avoir brièvement travaillé pour Santiago Calatrava, en 1988, il ouvre son agence à Amsterdam, en association avec Caroline Bos. Professeur invité à Columbia University, New York, et critique invité à Harvard University, en 1994. Responsable de la classe de diplôme de l'AA, Londres (1994–95). Parallèlement au pont Érasme de Rotterdam (inauguré en 1996), Van Berkel & Bos Architectural Bureau a construit à Amersfoort les immeubles de bureaux Karbouw et ACOM (1989–93), et la station électrique REMU (1989–93); des logements et la galerie Aedes East pour Kristin Feireiss (actuellement directrice de l'Institut néerlandais d'architecture, Rotterdam), à Berlin. Parmi ses récents projets, un nouveau musée pour Nimègue et une extension du Rijksmuseum Twente à Enschede, Pays-Bas (1992–96).

Mario Botta
Via Ciani 16
6904 Lugano, Switzerland
Tel : + 41 91 97 28 625
Fax : + 41 91 97 01 454

Mario Botta

Born in 1943 in Mendrisio, Switzerland, Mario Botta left school at the age of fifteen to become an apprentice in a Lugano architectural office. He designed his first house the following year. After completing his studies in Milan and Venice, Botta worked briefly in the entourage of Le Corbusier, Louis Kahn and Luigi Snozzi. He built numerous private houses in Cadenazzo (1970–71); Riva San Vitale (1971–73) and Ligornetto (1975–76), all in Switzerland. The Cultural Center in Chambéry, France (1982–87) and the Médiathèque in Villeurbanne, France (1984–88) followed. More recent projects include the Évry Cathedral, France (1988–1995); the San Francisco Museum of Modern Art, completed in 1995; the Tamaro Chapel, located above Rivera, Switzerland; the Tinguely Museum in Basel, inaugurated in October 1996; a church in Mogno, Switzerland, and a telecommunications center in Bellinzona, Switzerland.

Der 1943 im schweizerischen Mendrisio geborene Mario Botta verließ die Schule bereits mit 15 Jahren, um als Lehrling in einem Architekturbüro in Lugano zu arbeiten. Im darauffolgenden Jahr entwarf er sein erstes Haus. Nach seinem Studium in Mailand und Venedig war er kurzfristig für Le Corbusier, Louis Kahn und Luigi Snozzi tätig. Botta errichtete zahlreiche Privathäuser in der Schweiz, in Cadenazzo (1970–71); Riva San Vitale (1971–73) und Ligornetto (1975–76), denen das Kulturzentrum in Chambéry, Frankreich (1982–87) und die Médiathèque in Villeurbanne, Frankreich (1984–88) folgten. Zu seinen aktuellen Bauprojekten zählen die Cathédrale d'Évry in Frankreich(1988–95); das San Francisco Museum of Modern Art (1995 fertiggestellt); die Tamaro-Kapelle oberhalb von Rivera in der Schweiz; das Tinguely-Museum in Basel (im Oktober 1996 eröffnet); eine Kirche in Mogno sowie ein Fernmeldezentrum in Bellinzona (beide in der Schweiz).

Né en 1943 à Mendrisio (Suisse), Mario Botta quitte l'école à 15 ans pour devenir apprenti dans une agence d'architecture de Lugano. Il dessine sa première maison l'année suivante. Après avoir complété ses études à Milan et à Venise, il travaille brièvement dans l'entourage de Le Corbusier, Louis Kahn, et Luigi Snozzi. Il construit de nombreuses résidences privées à Cadenazzo (1970–71); Riva San Vitale (1971–73) ou Ligornetto (1975–76), tous en Suisse; puis édifie la Maison de la culture de Chambéry (1982–87), et la Médiathèque de Villeurbanne (1984–88) en France. Parmi ses réalisations récentes, la cathédrale d'Évry, France (1988–1995), et le San Francisco Museum of Modern Art, terminé en 1995; la Chapelle de Monte Tamaro (Rivera); le musée Tinguely à Bâle, inauguré en octobre 1996; une église à Mogno, et un centre de télécommunications à Bellinzona, tous en Suisse.

Coop Himmelb(l)au
Prix & Swiczinsky GmbH
Seilerstätte 16/11, A–1010 Vienna, Austria
Tel: + 43 1 512 0284
Fax: + 43 1 513 4754

Coop Himmelb(l)au

Coop Himmelb(l)au was founded in 1968 in Vienna, Austria by Wolf D. Prix and Helmut Swiczinsky. In 1988 they opened a second office in Los Angeles. Wolf D. Prix was born in 1942 in Vienna, and educated at the Technische Universität, Vienna, the Southern California Institute of Architecture (SCI-Arc), and the Architectural Association (AA), London. He is currently a Professor of the Masterclass of Architecture at the University of Applied Arts, Vienna, and an Adjunct Professor at SCI-Arc. Helmut Swiczinsky, born in 1944 in Poznan, Poland, was raised in Vienna, and educated at the Technische Universität, Vienna and at the AA, London. Completed projects of the group include the Rooftop Remodeling in Vienna; masterplan for Mélun-Sénart, France, and a pavilion of the Groninger Museum, Groningen, The Netherlands. They also remodeled the Austrian Pavilion in the Giardini, Venice, Italy. Current work includes the Museum of Health, Dresden; the Academy of Fine Arts, Munich, and the UFA Cinema Center, Dresden (all in Germany); the SEG Apartment Tower, Vienna to be completed in 1997; a second studio for Anselm Kiefer in the South of France, and two residential projects in Los Angeles.

Die Architektengemeinschaft Coop Himmelb(l)au wurde 1968 in Wien von Wolf D. Prix und Helmut Swiczinsky gegründet; 1988 eröffneten sie ein zweites Büro in Los Angeles. Der 1942 in Wien geborene Wolf D. Prix studierte an der Technischen Universität Wien, am Southern California Institute of Architecture (SCI-Arc) und an der Architectural Association (AA) in London. Er ist Professor an der Hochschule für angewandte Kunst in Wien, Meisterklasse für Architektur und außerordentlicher Professor am SCI-Arc. Helmut Swiczinsky wurde 1944 in Poznan (Polen) geboren und wuchs in Wien auf. Er studierte an der Technischen Universität Wien und der AA in London. Zu den fertiggestellten Bauten von Coop Himmelb(l)au zählen der Dachausbau einer Anwaltskanzlei in Wien; der Bebauungsplan für Mélun-Sénart, Frankreich sowie ein Pavillon für das Groninger Museum in Groningen (Niederlande). Darüber hinaus gestalteten sie den österreichischen Pavillon auf dem Gelände der Biennale in Venedig. Zu ihren aktuellen Bauprojekten zählen: Deutsches Hygiene-Museum, Dresden; Akademie der Schönen Künste, München; Filmtheater UFA-Palast, Dresden; SEG-Apartmentturm, Wien (geplante Fertigstellung 1997); ein zweites Studio für Anselm Kiefer in Südfrankreich und zwei Wohnbauprojekte in Los Angeles.

Coop Himmelb(l)au a été fondé en 1968 à Vienne (Autriche), par Wolf D. Prix et Helmut Swiczinsky. En 1988, il ouvrent une seconde agence à Los Angeles. Wolf D. Prix est né en 1942 à Vienne, et a étudié à la Technische Universität de cette ville, au Southern California Institute of Architecture (SCI-Arc), et à l'Architectural Association, Londres. Il est actuellement professeur de la Masterclass d'architecture à l'Université des arts appliqués de Vienne, et professeur adjoint au SCI-Arc. Helmut Swiczinsky est né en 1944 à Poznan, Pologne, a grandi à Vienne ou il à fait ses études à la Technische Universität et à l'AA de Londres. Parmi les projets réalisés du groupe: le réaménagement de la toiture d'un immeuble de bureaux à Vienne; le plan directeur de Melun-Sénart, France; un pavillon du musée de Groningue, Pays-Bas. Ils ont également remodelé le pavillon australien des Giardini à Venise. Ils travaillent actuellement sur le Musée de la santé, à Dresde; l'Académie des Beaux-Arts, Munich; un complexe de cinémas UFA à Dresde (tous en Allemagne); la tour d'appartements SEG, à Vienne, qui sera achevée en 1997; un second atelier pour Anselm Kiefer dans le sud de la France, et deux projets de résidences à Los Angeles.

Sir Norman Foster and Partners
Riverside Three, 22 Hester Road
London SW11 4AN, UK
Tel: + 44 171 738 04 55
Fax: + 44 171 738 11 07/08

Sir Norman Foster

Born in Manchester in 1935, Norman Foster studied architecture and city planning at Manchester University. After graduating in 1961 he was awarded a Henry Fellowship to Yale University, where he received an M. Arch. degree, and met Richard Rogers, with whom he created Team 4. In 1983 Norman Foster received the Royal Gold Medal for Architecture and in 1990 he was knighted. Since 1991 he has received the Mies van der Rohe Award, and the Gold Medal of the French Academy of Architecture. In 1994 he was given the American Institute of Architects Gold Medal for Architecture. Sir Norman Foster has notably built: IBM Pilot Head Office, Cosham, Great Britain (1970–71); Sainsbury Centre for Visual Arts and Crescent Wing, University of East Anglia, Norwich, Great Britain (1976–77; 1989–91); Hongkong and Shanghai Banking Corporation Headquarters, Hong Kong (1981–86); London's Third Airport, Stansted, Great Britain (1987–91); Faculty of Law, University of Cambridge, UK, Cambridge (1993–95); Commerzbank Headquarters, Frankfurt am Main, Germany (1994–97). Current projects: Airport at Chek Lap Kok, Hong Kong (1995–98); New German Parliament, Reichstag, Berlin, Germany (1995–99); British Museum Redevelopment, London (1997–2000).

Norman Foster wurde 1935 in Manchester geboren und studierte Architektur und Städteplanung an der University of Manchester. Nach seiner Abschlußprüfung 1961 erhielt er ein Stipendium (Henry Fellowship) für die Yale University, wo er 1963 seinen Master's Degree in Architektur erlangte und Richard Rogers kennenlernte, mit dem er das »Team 4« gründete. 1983 erhielt Foster die Royal Gold Medal for Architecture, und 1990 wurde er in den Adelsstand erhoben. Seit 1991 gewann er den Mies van der Rohe Award for European Architecture und die médaille d'or der Académie française d'architecture. Im Jahre 1994 bekam er die Gold Medal for Architecture des AIA. Zu den herausragendsten Bauten Fosters zählen das IBM Pilot Head Office, Cosham, Großbritannien (1970–71); das Sainsbury Centre for Visual Arts and Crescent Wing der University of East Anglia in Norwich, Großbritannien (1976–77; 1989–91); das Gebäude der Hongkong and Shanghai Bank in Hongkong (1981–86); der Terminal des Stansted Airport, London (1987–91); die Faculty of Law der Universität Cambridge, Großbritannien (1993–95) und die Hauptverwaltung der Commerzbank in Frankfurt am Main (1994–97). Zur Zeit arbeitet sein Büro an der Fertigstellung des Chek Lap Kok-Flughafens in Hongkong (1995–98), des Deutschen Bundestags im Reichstag in Berlin (1995–99) und am Umbau des British Museum in London (1997–2000).

Né à Manchester en 1935, Norman Foster fait ses études d'architecture et d'urbanisme à l'Université de cette ville. Diplômé en 1961, il reçoit une bourse Henry de Yale University où il passe son Master en architecture, et rencontre Richard Rogers avec lequel il fonde Team 4. En 1983, il reçoit la Royal Gold Medal for Architecture, et est anobli en 1990. Depuis 1991, il a reçu le Mies van der Rohe Award et la médaille d'or de l'Académie française d'architecture. En 1994, il reçoit la médaille d'or pour l'architecture de l'American Institute of Architects. Il a construit en particulier: le siège social pilote d'IBM, Cosham, Grande-Bretagne (1970–71); le Sainsbury Centre for Visual Arts et Crescent Wing, de l'Université d'East Anglia, Norwich, Grande-Bretagne (1976–77, 1989–91); le siège social de la Hongkong and Shanghai Banking Corporation, Hongkong (1981–86); le terminal du troisième aéroport londonien, Standsted, Grande-Bretagne (1987–91); la Faculté de droit de Cambridge University, Cambridge, Grande-Bretagne (1993–95); le siège social de la Commerzbank, Francfort-sur-le-Main, Allemagne (1994–97). Il travaille actuellement sur les projets de l'aéroport de Chek Lap Kok, Hongkong (1995–98); le Reichstag à Berlin pour le parlement allemand, Allemagne (1995–99), la rénovation du British Museum, Londres (1997–2000).

von Gerkan, Marg und Partner
Elbchaussee 139
22763 Hamburg, Germany
Tel: +49 040 88 1510
Fax: +49 040 88 151 177/178

Meinhard von Gerkan, Volkwin Marg

Meinhard von Gerkan was born in 1935 in Riga, Latvia. In 1939 he moved to Posnan, Poland. By the time he fled to Lower Saxony at the age of ten, both of his parents had been killed. He studied architecture in Berlin and Braunschweig, obtaining his degree in 1964. He has worked with Volkwin Marg since 1965, teaching at the Freie Akademie der Künste, Hamburg, Germany; the Technische Universität Braunschweig, Germany; the Nihon University, Tokyo, Japan; and the University of Pretoria, South Africa. He is an Honorary Fellow of the American Institute of Architects (AIA). Volkwin Marg was born in 1936 in Königsberg, fleeing to Thüringen in 1945, and to West Berlin in 1956. He studied architecture in Berlin and Braunschweig, and urban planning in Delft, Holland. He has been both vice-President (1979) and President (1983) of the Bund Deutscher Architekten BDA. The office of von Gerkan, Marg and Partner employs approximately 200 people. Their completed work includes: the Music and Congress Hall, Lübeck (1990); the Saar-Galerie, Saarbrücken (1991); 747 Servicing Facilities and a workshop for Lufthansa, Hamburg (1992); Zürich-Haus, Hamburg (1993); Deutsche Revision AG, Frankfurt am Main (1994); Galeria Duisburg, Duisburg (1994), all in Germany. Major projects include the Lehrter Bahnhof, Berlin.

Meinhard von Gerkan wurde 1935 in Riga, Lettland geboren. 1939 zog seine Familie nach Poznan in Polen; als er im Alter von zehn Jahren nach Niedersachsen fliehen mußte, hatte er bereits beide Eltern verloren. Von Gerkan studierte Architektur in Berlin und Braunschweig und machte 1964 seinen Abschluß. Er lehrte an der Freien Akademie der Künste in Hamburg, an der Technischen Universität Braunschweig, an der Nihon University in Tokio und an der University of Pretoria in Südafrika; seit 1965 arbeitet er mit Volkwin Marg zusammen. Von Gerkan ist Ehrenmitglied des American Institute of Architects (AIA). Volkwin Marg wurde 1936 in Königsberg geboren, floh 1945 nach Thüringen und 1956 nach Westberlin. Er studierte Architektur in Berlin und Braunschweig und Städtebau in Delft (Niederlande). Marg war sowohl Vize-Präsident (1979) als auch Präsident (1983) des Bund Deutscher Architekten (BDA). Das Architekturbüro Von Gerkan, Marg und Partner beschäftigt etwa 200 Mitarbeiter. Zu den fertiggestellten Bauten zählen: Musik- und Kongreßhalle, Lübeck (1990); Saar-Galerie, Saarbrücken (1991); ein 747-Instandhaltungsgebäude und eine Werkshalle für die Lufthansa, Hamburg (1992); Zürich-Haus, Hamburg (1993); Deutsche Revision AG, Frankfurt am Main (1994); Galeria Duisburg, Duisburg (1994). Zur Zeit beschäftigt sich das Büro u.a. mit dem Bau des Lehrter Bahnhofs in Berlin.

Meinhard von Gerkan est né en 1935 à Riga, Lettonie. En 1939, sa famille s'installe à Poznan, Pologne. Ses parents tués, il fuit en Basse-Saxe à l'âge de dix ans. Il étudie l'architecture à Berlin et Brunswick. Diplômé en 1964. Il travaille avec Volkwin Marg depuis 1965, enseignant à la Freie Akademie der Künste, Hambourg, à la Technische Universität de Brunswick, à l'Université Nihon de Tokyo, et à l'Université de Prétoria, Afrique du Sud. Il est membre honoraire de l'American Institute of Architects (AIA). Volkwin Marg naît en 1936 à Königsberg, fuit en Thuringe en 1945, et à Berlin-Ouest en 1956. Il étudie l'architecture à Berlin et Brunswick, et l'urbanisme à Delft, Pays-Bas. Il a été vice-président (1979) et président (1983) du Bund Deutscher Architekten (BDA). L'agence de gmp emploie environ 200 personnes. Parmi leurs réalisations: salle de congrès et auditorium, Lübeck (1990); la Saargalerie, Sarrebruck (1991); les ateliers pour 747 et un atelier pour la Lufthansa, Hambourg (1992); Zürich-Haus, Hambourg (1993); Deutsche Revision AG, Francfort-sur-le-Main (1994); Galeria Duisburg, Duisburg (1994), tous en Allemagne. Un de leurs plus importants projets est la gare centrale de Lehrter, Berlin.

Zvi Hecker
Oranienburger Strasse 31
10117 Berlin, Germany
Tel: + 49 30 282 69 14
Fax: + 49 30 282 73 22

Zvi Hecker

Born in 1931 in Krakow, Poland. Grew up in Krakow and Samarkand before moving to Israel in 1950. Studied architecture at Krakow Polytechnic (1949–50); Technion, Israel Institute of Technology, Haifa (1950–54); degree in engineering and architecture, 1955. Studied painting at Avni Academy of Art, Tel Aviv (1955–57). Two years' military service in Corps of Engineers, Israeli Army. Set up private practice in 1959, working with Alfred Neumann until 1966 and Eldar Sharon until 1964. Buildings include: City Hall, Bat-Yam, Israel (1960–63); Club Mediterranée, Ahziv, Israel (1961–62); Aeronautic Laboratory, Technion Campus, Haifa, Israel (1963–66); Ramot Housing, Jerusalem, Israel (Phase 1, 1974–76; Phase 2, 1981–85); Spiral Apartment Building, Ramat Gan, Israel (1986–90). Recent projects aside from the Heinz-Galinski-School, Berlin, include the Palmach Museum of History, Tel Aviv, Israel; and the Berlin Mountains residential neighborhood, East Berlin, Germany.

Zvi Hecker wurde 1931 in Krakau, Polen, geboren, wuchs in Krakau und Samarkand auf und zog 1950 nach Israel. Er studierte Architektur an der Polytechnischen Universität Krakau (1949–50) und am Technion, Israel Institute of Technology, Haifa (1950–54), wo er 1955 sein Diplom für Ingenieurwesen und Architektur erhielt. Von 1955–57 studierte er Malerei an der Avni Academy of Art, Tel Aviv und leistete danach zwei Jahre Militärdienst im Corps of Engineers der iraelischen Armee. 1959 gründete er ein Architekturbüro und arbeitete bis 1964 bzw. 1966 mit Eldar Sharon und Alfred Neumann zusammen. Bekannteste Bauten: Rathaus, Bat-Yam, Israel (1960–63); Club Mediterranée, Ahziv, Israel (1961–62); Aeronautic Laboratory, Technion Campus, Haifa, Israel (1963–66); Ramot Wohnungsbauten in Jerusalem, Israel (Phase 1, 1974–76, Phase 2, 1981–85); Spiral Apartment Building, Ramat Gan, Israel (1986–90). Zu Heckers aktuellen Projekten zählen die Heinz-Galinski-Schule in Berlin, das Palmach Museum of History, Tel Aviv und der Siedlungskomplex Berliner Berge in Ostberlin.

Né en 1931 à Cracovie, Pologne. Grandit à Cracovie et à Samarcande avant d'émigrer en Israël en 1950. Étudie l'architecture à l'École polytechnique de Cracovie (1949–50) et au Technion, Institut israélien de technologie, Haïfa (1950–54), dont il sort diplômé en ingénierie et architecture en 1955. Étudie la peinture à la Avny Academy of Art, Tel Aviv (1955–57). Deux années de service militaire dans le corps des ingénieurs de l'armée israélienne. Ouvre son agence en 1959, collaborant avec Alfred Neumann jusqu'en 1966, et Eldar Sharon jusqu'en 1964. Parmi ses réalisations: hôtel de ville de Bat-Yam, Israël (1960–63); Club Mediterranée, Ahziv, Israël (1961–62); Laboratoire d'aéronautique, Campus du Technion, Haïfa, Israël (1963–66); immeuble de logements Ramot, Jérusalem (Phase 1: 1974–76, Phase 2: 1981–85); immeuble d'appartements «Spiral», Ramat Gan, Israël (1986–90). Parmi ses récents projets en dehors de l'école Heinz-Galinski, à Berlin, le musée d'histoire Palmach à Tel Aviv, Israël, et le quartier résidentiel des «montagnes berlinoises», dans l'ancien Berlin-Est.

Herman Hertzberger
Gerard Doustraat 220
1073 XB Amsterdam, The Netherlands
Tel: + 31 20 676 5888
Fax: + 31 20 673 5510

Herman Hertzberger

Born in Amsterdam in 1932, Herman Hertzberger studied at the Technical University of Delft, from which he graduated in 1958. He opened his own office in 1958. Editor of *Forum* magazine with Aldo van Eyck from 1959 to 1963, he has been a Professor at the Technical University of Delft since 1970. He was Chairman of the Berlage Institute, Amsterdam from 1990 to 1995, where he was succeeded by Wiel Arets. His built work includes eight experimental houses, Gebbenlaan, Delft (1969–70); Vredenburg Music Center, Utrecht (1973–78); Kindergarten/primary School "De Evenaar," Amsterdam (1984–86); office building for the Ministry of Social Welfare and Employment, The Hague (1979–90); Theater Center Spui, The Hague (1986–93); Chassé Theater, Breda (1992–95); Theater Markant, Uden (1993–96), all in The Netherlands. Projects in preparation or under construction include: residential buildings, Amsterdamse Buurt, Haarlem, The Netherlands; MediaPark building with housing/studios/offices, Cologne, Germany; and a House on Borneo Isle, Amsterdam, The Netherlands.

Herman Hertzberger wurde 1932 in Amsterdam geboren und studierte an der Technischen Hochschule Delft, an der er 1958 sein Diplom erhielt. Im gleichen Jahr eröffnete er sein eigenes Architekturbüro. Zusammen mit Aldo van Eyck war er von 1959–63 als Herausgeber der Architekturzeitschrift »Forum« tätig; seit 1970 ist er Professor an der Technischen Hochschule Delft. Von 1990–95 war Hertzberger Dekan des Berlage Instituts für Architektur in Amsterdam (sein Nachfolger ist Wiel Arets). Zu seinen fertiggestellten Bauten zählen (alle in den Niederlanden): Acht experimentelle Häuser, Gebbenlaan, Delft (1969–70); Vredenburg Musikzentrum, Utrecht (1973–78); Kindergarten/Grundschule »De Evenaar« in Amsterdam (1984–86); Verwaltungsgebäude für das niederländische Arbeits- und Sozialministerium, Den Haag (1979–90); Theaterzentrum Spui, Den Haag (1986–93); Chassé Theater, Breda (1992–95) und das Theater Markant in Uden (1993–96). Zur Zeit beschäftigt sich sein Büro u.a. mit: Wohnbauten in der Amsterdamse Buurt in Haarlem, Niederlande; einem Bauprojekt im MediaPark in Köln mit Wohnungen/Studios/Büroräumen und einem Haus auf der Borneokade in Amsterdam, Niederlande.

Né à Amsterdam en 1932, Herman Hertzberger suit les cours de l'Université technique de Delft, dont il sort diplômé en 1958. Il ouvre sa propre agence la même année. Éditeur du magazine «Forum» avec Aldo van Eyck, de 1959 à 1963, il enseigne à l'Université technique de Delft depuis 1970. Il est président de l'Institut Berlage, Amsterdam, de 1990 à 1995, succédant à Wiel Arets. Son œuvre construit comprend huit maisons expérimentales, Gebbenlaan, Delft (1969–70); le Centre de musique Vredenburg, Utrecht (1973–78); un jardin d'enfants/école primaire «De Evenaar», Amsterdam (1984–86); un immeuble de bureaux pour le Ministère des affaires sociales et de l'emploi, La Haye (1979–90); le théâtre Center Spui, La Haye (1986–93); le Chassé Theater, Bréda (1992–95); le Théâtre Markant, Uden (1993–96), tous aux Pays-Bas. Il travaille actuellement à divers chantiers, dont des immeubles d'appartements, Amsterdamse Buurt, Haarlem, Pays-Bas; immeuble d'appartements, ateliers, bureaux à MediaPark, Cologne, Allemagne; et une maison sur Borneo Isle, Amsterdam, Pays-Bas.

Josef Paul Kleihues
Helmholtzstrasse 42
10587 Berlin, Germany
Tel: + 49 30 399 7790
Fax: + 49 30 39 97 79 77

Josef Paul Kleihues

Born in 1933 in Rheine, Westphalia, J. P. Kleihues studied architecture at the Technische Universität Stuttgart and the Technische Universität Berlin from which he obtained a diploma (1955–59). Scholarship at the École des Beaux-arts, Paris, 1959–60. He worked afterwards with Hans Scharoun. Founded his own office in 1962. Professor at the University of Dortmund, Chair for Architectural Design and Theory (1973–94) where he created the Dortmund Architecture Days. Planning Director for the 1984 Bauausstellung, Berlin (1979–84), and subsequently Consultant to the Senate for Housing and Construction in Berlin. Selected buildings: Berlin Cleansing Department, Main Workshop, Berlin-Tempelhof (1970–78); Block 270, Berlin (1975–77); Residential and Shopping Center, Neue Stadt Wulfen (1975–81); Hospital, Berlin-Neukölln (1975–86); Building 7, Block 7, Berlin (1988–89); Kant Triangle, Berlin-Charlottenburg (1992–94); Hamburger Bahnhof, Berlin (1992–96), all in Germany; Museum of Contemporary Art, Chicago, Illinois (1992–96).

Der 1933 im westfälischen Rheine geborene Josef Paul Kleihues studierte Architektur an der Technischen Universität Stuttgart und an der Technischen Universität Berlin (1955–59), an der er seinen Abschluß machte. Von 1959–60 erhielt er ein Stipendium für die École des Beaux-Arts in Paris; danach arbeitete er mit Hans Scharoun zusammen. 1962 gründete Kleihues sein eigenes Architekturbüro. Von 1973–94 war er Professor für Architekturdesign und -theorie an der Universität Dortmund, wo er die Dortmunder Architekturtage ins Leben rief. Kleihues war Planungsdirektor der »Internationalen Bauausstellung Berlin 1984« (1979–84) und danach Berater des Berliner Senators für Bauen, Wohnen und Verkehr. Zu seinen wichtigsten Bauten zählen: Hauptwerkstatt der Berliner Stadtreinigung, Berlin-Tempelhof (1970–78); Block 270, Berlin (1975–77); Wohn- und Einkaufszentrum, Neue Stadt Wulfen (1975–81); Krankenhaus in Berlin-Neukölln (1975–86); Gebäude 7, Block 7, Berlin (1988–89); Bürohaus »Kant-Dreieck«, Berlin-Charlottenburg (1992–94); Hamburger Bahnhof, Berlin (1992–96); Museum of Contemporary Art, Chicago, Illinois (1992–96).

Né en 1933 à Rheine, Westphalie, J. P. Kleihues étudie l'architecture à la Technische Universität de Stuttgart et à la Technische Universität de Berlin dont il est diplômé (1955–59). Bourse d'étude pour l'École des Beaux-Arts de Paris (1959–60). Travaille ensuite pour Hans Scharoun. Fonde son agence en 1962. Professeur à l'Université de Dortmund, chaire de design architectural et de théorie (1973–94) où il crée les Journées d'architecture de Dortmund. Directeur de la programmation pour la Bauaustellung 1984 de Berlin (1979–84), à la suite de quoi il est nommé consultant pour le Sénat de Berlin pour le logement et la construction. Parmi ses réalisations: Atelier principal du département de la voirie de Berlin, Berlin-Tempelhof (1970–78); Block 270, Berlin (1975–77); Centre résidentiel et commercial, Neue Stadt Wulfen (1975–81); Hôpital, Berlin-Neukölln (1975–86); Immeuble 7, Block 7, Berlin (1988–89); Kant Triangle, Berlin-Charlottenburg (1992–94); Hamburger Bahnhof, Berlin (1992–96), tous en Allemagne; Museum of Contemporary Art, Chicago, Illinois (1992–96).

Architectures Jean Nouvel
10, Cité d'Angoulême
75011 Paris, France
Tel: +33 1 49 23 83 83
Fax: +33 1 43 55 35 61

Jean Nouvel

Born in 1945 in Sarlat, Jean Nouvel was admitted to the École des Beaux-Arts in Bordeaux in 1964. In 1970, he created his first office with François Seigneur. His first widely noticed project was the Institut du Monde Arabe in Paris (1981–87 with Architecture Studio). Other works include his Nemausus housing, Nîmes, (1985–87); offices for the CLM/BBDO advertising firm, Issy-les Moulineaux (1988–92); Lyon Opera House, Lyon (1986–93); Vinci Conference Center, Tours (1989–93); Euralille Shopping Center, Lille (1991–94); Fondation Cartier, Paris (1991–95), all in France; Galeries Lafayette, Berlin (1992–96), and his unbuilt projects for the 400 meter tall "Tour sans fins," La Défense, Paris, France (1989); Grand Stade for the 1998 World Cup, Paris (1994), and Tenaga National Tower, Kuala Lumpur, Malaysia (1995). His largest current commission is for a music and conference center in Lucerne, Switzerland, scheduled for 1998 completion.

Jean Nouvel, der 1945 in Sarlat geboren wurde, nahm 1964 sein Studium an der École des Beaux-Arts in Bordeaux auf. 1970 gründete er zusammen mit François Seigneur sein erstes Architekturbüro. Das Institut du Monde Arabe in Paris (1981–87, in Zusammenarbeit mit Architecture Studio) war sein erstes Bauprojekt, das international Aufsehen erregte. Zu seinen kürzlich fertiggestellten Bauprojekten zählen: »Nemausus«-Wohnanlage, Nîmes (1985–87); Verwaltungsgebäude der Werbeagentur CLM/BBDO, Issy-les Moulineaux (1988–92); Opernhaus, Lyon (1986–93); Palais des Congrès, Tours (1989–93); Euralille Einkaufszentrum, Lille (1991–94); und die Fondation Cartier, Paris (1991–95) alle in Frankreich; Galeries Lafayette, Berlin (1992–96); sein (nicht ausgeführter) 400 m hoher Turm »Tour sans fins« im Pariser Viertel La Défense (1989) sowie seine Konstruktionspläne des Grand Stade, Paris (1994) für die Fußballweltmeisterschaft 1998 in Frankreich und des Tenaga National Tower, Kuala Lumpur, Malaysia (1995). Zur Zeit beschäftigt sich Jean Nouvel mit einem Projekt für ein Musik- und Kongreßzentrum in Luzern, Schweiz (geplante Fertigstellung 1998).

Né en 1945 à Sarlat, Jean Nouvel est admis à l'École des Beaux-Arts de Bordeaux en 1964. En 1970, il crée une première agence avec François Seigneur. Son premier projet vraiment remarqué est l'Institut du Monde Arabe, à Paris, (1981–87, avec Architecture Studio). Parmi ses autres réalisations: les immeubles d'appartements Nemausus, à Nîmes (1985–87); les bureaux de l'agence de publicité CLM/BBDO, Issy-les-Moulineaux (1988–92); l'opéra de Lyon (1986–93); le Palais des Congrès Vinci, Tours (1989–93); le centre commercial Euralille, Lille (1991–94); la Fondation Cartier, Paris (1991–95); les Galeries Lafayette, Berlin (1992–96). Projets non réalisés: tour de 400 m de haut, «La tour sans fin», La Défense, Paris (1989); le Grand Stade de la Coupe du monde de football 1998, Paris (1994), et la Tenaga National Tower, Kuala Lumpur, Malaisie (1995). Son chantier actuel le plus important est le Centre de musique et de conférences de Lucerne (Suisse) qui devrait être achevé en 1998.

Christian de Portzamparc
1, rue de l'Aude
75014 Paris, France
Tel: +33 1 40 64 80 00
Fax: +33 1 43 27 74 79

Christian de Portzamparc

Born in Casablanca in 1944, Christian de Portzamparc studied at the École des Beaux-Arts in Paris from 1962 to 1969. Early projects include a water tower at Marne-la-Vallée, France (1971–74); Hautes-Formes public housing, Paris (1975–79). He won the competition for the Cité de la Musique on the outskirts of Paris in 1984, completing the project in 1995. He was awarded the 1994 Pritzker Prize. He participated in the Euralille project with the Crédit Lyonnais Tower (1992–95) built over the new Lille-Europe railway station in Lille, France, and built housing for the Nexus World project in Fukuoka, Japan (1989–92). He also has completed an extension for the Bourdelle Museum, Paris, France (1988–92), and a housing complex in the ZAC Bercy, Paris (1991–94). Current work, aside from the LVMH Tower on 57th Street in New York, includes an addition to the Palais des Congrès in Paris; a tower for the Bandai toy company in Tokyo, and a courthouse for Grasse in the south of France.

Christian de Portzamparc wurde 1944 in Casablanca geboren und studierte von 1962–69 an der École des Beaux-Arts in Paris. Zu seinen ersten Projekten zählten der Wasserturm in Marne-la-Vallée bei Paris (1971–74) und die städtische Wohnanlage Hautes-Formes in Paris (1975–79). 1984 gewann er den Architekturwettbewerb für die Cité de la Musique am Rande von Paris, die er 1995 fertigstellte. Ein Jahr zuvor (1994) verlieh man ihm den Pritzker Preis. Darüber hinaus war Portzamparc mit einem Turm über dem neuen Bahnhof Lille-Europe am Euralille-Projekt beteiligt und errichtete eine Wohnanlage für das Nexus World-Projekt in Fukuoka, Japan (1989–92); einen Erweiterungsbau für das Bourdelle-Museum in Paris, Frankreich (1988–92) sowie einen Wohnkomplex in Paris-Bercy (1991–94). Zur Zeit arbeitet er an dem LVMH Tower an der 57th Street in New York; einem Erweiterungsbau für das Palais des Congrès in Paris; einem Turm für den Spielzeughersteller Bandai in Tokio und einem Gerichtsgebäude für die Stadt Grasse in Südfrankreich.

Christian de Portzamparc naît à Casablanca en 1944, et fait ses études à l'École des Beaux-Arts de Paris, de 1962 à 1969. Parmi ses premières réalisations: les châteaux d'eau de Marne-la Vallée (1971–74), et les H.L.M. des Hautes-Formes, à Paris (1975–79). Il remporte le concours pour la Cité de la Musique, à Paris (1984), dont la construction est achevée en 1995. En 1994, il reçoit le Prix Pritzker. Il participe au projet Euralille, à Lille, où il élève la tour du Crédit Lyonnais au-dessus de la gare Lille-Europe, et construit un immeuble d'appartements pour Nexus World, à Fukuoka, Japon (1989–92). Il est également responsable de l'extension du musée Bourdelle, Paris (1988–92), et d'un immeuble de logements dans la ZAC Bercy, Paris (1991–94). Actuellement, en dehors de la tour LVMH à New York, il travaille à la restructuration du Palais des Congrès de Paris; à une tour pour la société de jouets Bandai, à Tokyo, et au futur palais de justice de Grasse, en Provence.

Reichen & Robert Architectes
17, rue Brézin
75014 Paris, France
Tel: +33 1 45 41 47 48
Fax: +33 1 45 41 47 44

Reichen & Robert

Bernard Reichen graduated from the École spéciale d'architecture, Paris, in 1965. He spent two years in the Congo working with a prefectural urban service. He created the office of Reichen & Robert in 1973 with Philippe Robert, who graduated from the École spéciale d'architecture, Paris in 1966. He then worked for two years with Paolo Soleri in the United States. He also worked with Richard Rogers and Renzo Piano on the Centre Georges Pompidou. He has taught at the University of Illinois and the University of Technology of Sydney, Australia, and wrote a book on reconversion of old buildings for the Éditions du Moniteur, Paris. Philippe Robert is an Honorary Fellow of the AIA. Aside from the rehabilitation of the Menier Chocolate factory for Nestlé, the office has worked on a number of reconversions of industrial buildings such as the Leblan factory, Lille, France (1980); the Grande Halle de la Villette, Paris (1985), and the Halle Tony Garnier, Lyon, France (1988). They have also built new structures such as the French Embassy, Qatar (1987), and the American Museum in Giverny, France (1992), or the Chomette Favor Headquarters, Grigny, France (1993).

Bernard Reichen erhielt 1965 sein Diplom an der École spéciale d'architecture in Paris. Er verbrachte zwei Jahre im Kongo, wo er für ein staatliches Amt für Stadtver- und -entsorgung arbeitete. 1973 gründete er zusammen mit Philippe Robert (Diplom an der École spéciale d'architecture, Paris 1966) das Architekturbüro Reichen & Robert. Danach arbeitete er zwei Jahre mit Paolo Soleri in den Vereinigten Staaten sowie mit Richard Rogers und Renzo Piano am Centre Georges Pompidou. Reichen lehrte an der University of Illinois und an der University of Technology of Sydney und verfaßte für die Éditions du Moniteur in Paris ein Buch zum Thema Umwandlung alter Bauwerke. Philippe Robert ist Ehrenmitglied des American Institute of Architects (AIA). Neben der Sanierung der Menier-Schokoladenfabrik für Nestlé beschäftigte sich das Architekturbüro mit zahlreichen Umwandlungen industrieller Bauten wie etwa der Fabrik Leblan in Lille, Frankreich (1980); der Grande Halle de la Villette in Paris (1985) und der Halle Tony Garnier in Lyon, Frankreich (1988). Darüber hinaus errichteten Reichen & Robert auch diverse Neubauten wie die Französische Botschaft in Qatar (1987); das American Museum in Giverny, Frankreich (1992) und die Zentrale von Chomette Favor in Grigny, Frankreich (1993).

Bernard Reichen est diplômé de l'École spéciale d'architecture de Paris (1965). Il passe deux ans au Congo dans un service d'urbanisme de préfecture, et crée l'agence Reichen & Robert en 1973, avec Philippe Robert, également diplômé de l'École spéciale (1966). Il travaille ensuite deux ans avec Paolo Soleri aux États-Unis, puis avec Richard Rogers et Renzo Piano sur le chantier du Centre Pompidou. Il a enseigné à l'Université de l'Illinois, et l'Université de technologie de Sydney, Australie, et a rédigé un ouvrage sur la reconversion des bâtiments anciens paru aux Éditions du Moniteur, Paris. Philippe Robert est membre honoraire de l'AIA. En dehors de la réhabilitation de la chocolaterie Menier pour Nestlé, leur agence a travaillé sur un certain nombre de reconversions de bâtiments industriels comme l'usine Leblanc, Lille (1980); la Grande halle de la Villette, Paris (1985), et la Halle Tony Garnier, Lyon (1988). Ils ont également construit des bâtiments neufs comme l'Ambassade de France au Quatar (1987), ou l'American Museum à Giverny (1992), ainsi que le siège de Chomette-Favor, Grigny (1993).

Agence Rudy Ricciotti Architecte
3, place d'Estienne d'Orves
83150 Bandol, France
Tel: +33 4 94 29 52 61
Fax: +33 4 94 32 45 25

Atelier Prof. Spiegelhalter+Assoziierte
Postfach 5107
79018 Freiburg, Germany
Tel: + 49 761 47 46 11 / 47 46 21
Fax: + 49 761 47 46 12

Rudy Ricciotti

Born in 1952 in Algiers. Attended the École supérieure technique in Geneva, from which he graduated in 1975. Graduated from the UP-AM, Marseille in 1980, architecte DPLG. He created his office in Bandol in 1980. His office employs a total of five architects. His early work included a number of private houses apparently influenced by architects such as Richard Meier or Arquitectonica. Aside from the Stade in Vitrolles, he has worked on a Center for Young People, Bandol, 1986; an office building in Bandol, France, 1993, and the Côte Bleue High School in Sausset-les-Pins, France, 1994. Current work includes the Sélestat theater and rock concert hall, (Alsace), France, to be completed in 1998; a Philharmonic Concert Hall, Potsdam, Berlin, Germany, to be completed in 1999, and a 600-seat cinema to be built in Pierrelatte, France. He has also worked extensively on hospital projects including the Hospital Center, Carpentras, France, for which he won the competition in August 1996.

Rudy Ricciotti wurde 1952 in Algier geboren und besuchte die École supérieure technique in Genf, an der er 1975 seinen Abschluß machte. 1980 graduierte er als Diplomarchitekt (DPLG) an der UPAM in Marseille. Im gleichen Jahr gründete er sein Architekturbüro in Bandol, das zur Zeit fünf Architekten beschäftigt. Zu seinen frühen Werken zählen eine Reihe von Privathäusern, die deutlich von Architekten wie Richard Meier oder Arquitectonica beeinflußt sind. Danach errichtete Ricciotti in Frankreich neben einer Konzerthalle (Le Stadium) in Vitrolles ein Jugendzentrum in Bandol (1986); ein Bürogebäude in Bandol (1993) sowie die École Côte Bleue in Sausset-les-Pins (1994). Zu seinen aktuellen Bauvorhaben gehören: Theater- und Rockkonzerthalle Sélestat, (Elsaß, geplante Fertigstellung 1998); Philharmonie, Potsdam (geplante Fertigstellung 1999) und ein Kino mit 600 Plätzen in Pierrelatte, Frankreich. Darüber hinaus beschäftigt er sich intensiv mit Krankenhausbauten: 1996 gewann er eine Ausschreibung für ein Krankenhaus in Carpentras, Frankreich.

Né en 1952 à Alger. Études à l'École supérieure technique de Genève, dont il sort diplômé en 1975. Diplômé de l'UPAM, Marseille, en 1980, architecte DPLG. En 1980, il ouvre son agence à Bandol, qui emploie cinq architectes. Il commence par réaliser des maisons individuelles, apparemment influencées par des confrères comme Richard Meier ou Arquitectonica. En dehors du Stadium de Vitrolles, il a réalisé un Centre municipal des Jeunes à Bandol (1986); un immeuble de bureaux à Bandol (1993), et le collège de la Côte Bleue à Sausset-les-Pins (1994). Actuellement, il travaille sur le théâtre et salle de rock de Sélestat (Alsace), qui sera achevé en 1998; une salle de concerts philharmoniques, à Postdam, Allemagne, prévue pour 1999, et un cinéma de 600 places à Pierrelatte en France. Il est également beaucoup intervenu sur des projets d'hôpitaux, comme le Centre hospitalier de Carpentras, dont il a remporté le concours en août 1996.

Thomas Spiegelhalter

Thomas Spiegelhalter was born in Freiburg, Germany, in 1959. He works in Freiburg as a "sculptor, architect and communications designer." In 1977 he received a Venice Scholarship to study sculpture. He obtained degrees in sculpture, 3-D visual communication and architecture in Bremen, Flensburg and from the Hochschule der Künste in Berlin. He has taught architecture and visual arts in Kaiserslautern and at the Technische Hochschule in Leipzig since 1990. His projects include a number of architectural and landscape sculptures, sometimes related to his interest in the revival and transformation of gravel pits and abandoned industrial architecture. Since 1989 he has been involved in developing multistory buildings which have low energy consumption and make use of passive energy systems.

Thomas Spiegelhalter wurde 1959 in Freiburg/Brsg. geboren, von wo aus er als »Bildhauer, Architekt und Kommunikationsdesigner« tätig ist. 1977 erhielt er ein Stipendium in Venedig für das Studium der Bildhauerei. Danach studierte er in Bremen, Flensburg und an der Hochschule der Künste in Berlin Bildhauerei, Visuelle Kommunikation und Architektur. Spiegelhalter lehrt seit 1990 Architektur und Visuelle Künste in Kaiserslautern und an der Technischen Hochschule in Leipzig. Seine Arbeiten umfassen eine Reihe von Architektur- und Landschaftsskulpturen, die teilweise im Zusammenhang mit seinem Interesse für die Revitalisierung und Transformation von Kiesgrubenanlagen und stillgelegter Industriearchitektur stehen. Seit 1989 beschäftigt er sich intensiv mit der Entwicklung von mehrgeschossigen Niedrigenergie- und Passivhäusern.

Thomas Spiegelhalter est né à Freiburg, Allemagne, en 1959. Il travaille dans cette ville comme «sculpteur, architecte et designer en communication». En 1977, il reçoit une bourse pour étudier la sculpture à Venise et obtient des diplômes en sculpture, communication visuelle en trois dimensions, et architecture à Brême, Flensburg, et à l'École des Beaux-Arts de Berlin. Dès 1990, il enseigne l'architecture et les arts visuels à Kaiserslautern et à la Technische Hochschule de Leipzig. Ses projets comprennent un certain nombre de sculptures architecturales ou d'interventions sur le paysage, parfois liées à l'intérêt qu'il porte à la revitalisation et à la transformation de gravières ou d'installations industrielles abandonnées. Depuis 1989, il travaille sur la mise au point et la conception de maisons à faible consommation ou à accumulation d'énergie.

Bibliography | Bibliographie

"Ben van Berkel." *El Croquis*, 72(I), Madrid, 1995.

Bertoni, Franco: *Philippe Starck, L'architecture.* Mardaga, Liège, 1994.

Boissière, Olivier: *Jean Nouvel.* Terrail, Paris, 1996.

Bosman, Jos (editor): *Wiel Arets. Strange Bodies.* Birkhäuser, Basel, 1996.

van Dijk, Hans: "Conjugal cunning. Recent work by Wiel Arets," *Archis*, 4.96.

Feireiss, Kristin (editor): *The Heinz-Galinski-School in Berlin.* Ernst Wasmuth Verlag, Berlin, 1996.

Foster, Norman: *Sir Norman Foster and Partners.* Sir Norman Foster and Partners Publications, London, 1993.

Frei, Fritz: "Solar Gain," *The Architectural Review*, October, 1996.

Futagawa, Yukio (editor): "Jean Nouvel," *GA Document Extra 07*, A.D.A. Edita, Tokyo, 1996.

Galloway, David: "A New Focus for Berlin's Art Landscape," *International Herald Tribune*, December 7, 1996.

Goulet, Patrice: *Jean Nouvel.* Éditions du Regard, Paris, 1994.

Kahn-Rossi, Manuela: *Mario Botta, Enzo Cucchi, La Cappella del Monte Tamaro.* Umberto Allemandi & C., Torino, 1994.

Kent, Cheryl: "Kleihues Defies Skepticism to Create Chicago Landmark," *Architectural Record*, August, 1996.

Le Dantec, Jean-Pierre: *Christian de Portzamparc.* Éditions du Regard, Paris, 1995.

Machado, Rodolfo, and Rodolphe el-Khoury: *Monolithic Architecture.* The Heinz Architectural Center, The Carnegie Museum of Art, Prestel Verlag, Munich, 1995.

Marg, Volkwin: *Neue Messe Leipzig, New Trade Fair Leipzig.* Birkhäuser Verlag, Basel, 1996.

Mesecke, Andrea, and Thorsten Scheer (Editors): *Josef Paul Kleihues, Themes and Projects.* Birkhäuser Verlag, Basel, 1996.

Muschamp, Herbert: "A Temple to the Present Leans Heavily on the Past," *The New York Times*, June 30, 1996.

Muschamp, Herbert: "An Elegant Blow Against Kitsch, Vuitton and Chanel Towers Tilt the Balance on 57th Street," *The New York Times*, July 23, 1996.

Muschamp, Herbert: "A Pair of Skyscrapers, Opposites That Attract," *The New York Times*, August 11, 1996.

Pélissier, Alain: *Reichen & Robert, architectures contextuelles.* Éditions du Moniteur, Paris, 1993.

Petit, Jean: *Botta, traces d'architecture.* Fidia Edizioni d'Arte, Lugano, 1994.

Portzamparc, Christian de, et al.: "Christian de Portzamparc," *L'Architecture d'aujourd'hui*, December 1995.

Range Ross, Peter: "Reinventing Berlin," *National Geographic*, December 1996.

Scheer, Thorsten: *Museum Hamburger Bahnhof Berlin.* Verlag der Buchhandlung Walther König, Cologne, 1996.

Philippe Starck. Benedikt Taschen Verlag, Cologne, 1996.

Tonka, Hubert and Jeanne-Marie Sens: *Rouge & Noir, Le Stadium à Vitrolles de Rudy Ricciotti.* Sens & Tonka, Éditeurs, 1995.

Turner, Allen, et al.: *Collective Vision, Creating a Contemporary Art Museum.* Museum of Contemporary Art, Chicago, 1996.

Valentin, Marc, et al.: *Noisiel, La Chocolaterie Menier.* Inventaire général des Monuments et des Richesses artistiques de la France, Paris, 1994.

Werner, Frank: *Coop Himmelblau, The Power of the City.* Verlag der Georg Büchner Buchhandlung, Darmstadt, 1988.

Index

Adler and Sullivan 34, 35
Alberti, Leon Battista 121
Ambasz, Emilio 122
Ando, Tadao 8, 9, 53, 54, 122
Arets, Wiel 8, **8**, 9, 11, 46, 47, 50, **52**, 53, 54, **53–59**, 170, 172

Berkel, Ben van 6, **7**, 8, 9, 36, 38, **38**, 39–41, **41**, 42–44, 46, 47, 50, **60**, 61, **61**, 62, **62–65**, 170
Beuys, Joseph 14, 16, 17, 129
Bos, Caroline 170
Botta, Mario 18, 20, 21, **21**, 22, **22**, 23–25, 27, 47, 48, 50, **66**, 67, **67**, 68, 75, **68–79**

Calatrava, Santiago 40, 41, 43, 61, 170
Candela, Felix 61
Casson, Hugh 24, 27, 29
Cobb, Harry 36, 39, 40, 136
Coop Himmelb(l)au 8, 10, 11, **11**, 12, 13, 43, 44, 46, 47, 50, **80**, 81, **81**, 82, **82–87**, 170
Crämer & Petschler 12, 13, 15
Cucchi, Enzo 20, 22–24

Eisenman, Peter 28–30, 32, 35, 36, 38, 39, 43
Eyck, Aldo van 115, 172

Foster, Sir Norman 24, **25**, 27–31, 33, 34, 47, 48, 50, **88**, 89, **89**, 90, **90–95**, 96, **96–97**, 171

Gehry, Frank O. 18, 20, 21, 26, 29, 30, 32, 35, 36
von Gerkan, Marg und Partner 12, 13, **13**, 14, **98**, 99, **99**, 100, **100–105**, 171
Gropius, Walter 18, 20, 21

Hadid, Zaha 36, 39, 40, 61
Hecker, Zvi 24, 26, **26**, 27, 29, 30, 43, 44, 46, 47, 50, **106**, 107, **107**, 108, **108–113**, 171

Hertzberger, Herman 30, **32**, 33, 34, **114**, 115, **115**, 116, **116–119**, 170, 172
Hollein, Hans 18, 20, 21

Isozaki, Arata 18, 20, 21

Johnson, Philip 142

Kahn, Louis 67, 170
Kiefer, Anselm 14, 16, 17, 129, **132**
Kleihues, Josef Paul 14, **14**, 15–17, 32–35, **35**, 36, 39, 43, 44, 47, 99, **120**, 121, **121**, 122, **123–129**, 129, **130–133**, 172
Koolhaas, Rem 28–30, 36, 38–40, 43, 61

Le Corbusier 67, 170
Libeskind, Daniel 26, 29, 30
Long, Richard **132**

Maki, Fumihiko 122
Mayne, Thom 122
Meier, Richard 115, 173
Mendelsohn, Erich 26, 29, 30, 136
Mendini, Alessandro 10, 12, 13
Merz, Mario **132**
Mies van der Rohe, Ludwig 34–36, 39, 40, 122, 136
Moneo, Rafael 28–30
Morphosis 122

Nervi, Pier Luigi 61
Neumann, Alfred 171
Nouvel, Jean 28–30, **31**, 36, 39, 40, **51**, **134**, 135, **135**, 136, **136–139**, 172

Palladio, Andrea 121
Paxton, Josef 12, 15

Pelli, Cesar 30, 31, 34
Piano, Renzo 173
Portzamparc, Christian de 44, 45, **45**, 46, **46**, 47, 48, 50, 122, **140**, 141, **141**, 142, **142–145**, 172

Rauschenberg, Robert 14, 16, 17, 129
Reichen & Robert 16, 17, **17**, 18, 19, 47, 48, 50, 146, **146–148**, 149, **150–153**, 173
Ricciotti, Rudy 34, 37, **37**, 39, 46, 47, **49**, 50, **154**, 155, **155**, 156, **156–159**, 173
Rogers, Richard 171, 173

Saint Phalle, Niki de 24, 25, 27
Saulnier, Jules 16, 19, **147**, **148**, 149
Sauvestre, Stephen 149
Scharoun, Hans 172
Schinkel, Karl Friedrich 32, 35, 36, 121, 122
Sharon, Eldar 171
Snozzi, Luigi 170
Soleri, Paolo 173
Spiegelhalter, Thomas 42, **42**, 43, 46, 47, 50, **160**, 161, **161**, 162, **162–169**, 173
Starck, Philippe 28, **28**, 29–31, 33
Stirling, James 24, 27, 29
Stone, Edward Durell 142
Sullivan, Louis 122

Tinguely, Jean 22, 24, 25, 27, 75, 170
Tschumi, Bernard 38, 39, 43
Twombly, Cy 14, 16, 17, 129

Ungers, Oswald Matthias 36, 39, 40, 99, 136

Warhol, Andy 14, 16, 17, 129
Wehberg, Eppinger, Schmidtke 100
Wright, Frank Lloyd 28, 31, 33, 34–36

Credits | Fotonachweis | Crédits photographiques

l. = left | links | à gauche
r. = right | rechts | à droite
t. = top | oben | en haut
c. = center | Mitte | centre
b. = bottom | unten | en bas

2	© Photo: Paul Raftery/Arcaid
7	© Photo: Richard Bryant/Arcaid
8	© Photo: Atelier kim zwarts
11	© Photo: Ralph Richter/Architekturphoto
13	© Photo: Busam+Richter/Architekturphoto
14	© VG Bild-Kunst, Bonn 1997 (Andy Warhol: Mao)/© Photo: Christian Richters
17/18	© Photo: Arnaud Carpentier
21	© Photo: Enrico Cano
22	© Photo: Arnaud Carpentier
25	© Photo: John Edward Linden
26	© Photo: Christian Richters
28	© Photo: Philip Jodidio
31	© Photo: Christian Richters
32	© Photo: Herman H. van Doorn
35	© Photo: Hedrich Blessing
37	© Photo: Paul Raftery/Arcaid
38	© Photo: Christian Richters
41	© Photo: Hélène Binet
42	© Photo: Friedrich Busam/Architekturphoto
45/46	© Christian de Portzamparc
49	© Photo: Paul Raftery/Arcaid
51	© Photo: Christian Richters
52/53	© Photo: Atelier kim zwarts
54 t.	© Photo: Atelier kim zwarts
54 b.	© Wiel Arets
55/56 t.	© Photo: Atelier kim zwarts
56 b.	© Wiel Arets
57–59	© Photo: Atelier kim zwarts
60	© Photo: Richard Bryant/Arcaid
61	© Photo: Hans-Jürgen Commerell
62 t.	© Photo: Richard Bryant/Arcaid
62 b.	© Ben van Berkel
63–65	© Photo: Richard Bryant/Arcaid
64–65 b.	© Ben van Berkel
66	© Photo: Enrico Cano
67	© Photo: Arnaud Carpentier
68	© Mario Botta
69 t.	© Photo: Enrico Cano
69 b.	© Mario Botta
70–73	© Photo: Enrico Cano
74 t.	© Photo: Arnaud Carpentier
74 b.	© Mario Botta
76–77	© Photo: Arnaud Carpentier
78 t.	© Mario Botta
78–79	© Photo: Arnaud Carpentier
78 b.	© VG Bild-Kunst, Bonn 1997 (Jean Tinguely: Hannibal No.1/Spirale/Isidor III)
79	© VG Bild-Kunst, Bonn 1997 (Jean Tinguely: Plateau agriculturel/Fatamorgana)
80	© Photo: Ralph Richter/Architekturphoto
81	© Photo: Gerald Zugmann

82 b.	© Coop Himmelb(l)au
82–87	© Photo: Ralph Richter/Architekturphoto
88	© Photo: Dennis Gilbert/VIEW
89	© Photo: 1994 Luca Zanetti/Lookat
90	© Sir Norman Foster and Partners
91/92	© Photo: John Edward Linden/Arcaid
93 t.	© Sir Norman Foster and Partners
93 c.	© Photo: John Edward Linden/Arcaid
93 b.	© Sir Norman Foster and Partners
94–95	© Photo: John Edward Linden/Arcaid
96	© Sir Norman Foster and Partners
97	© Photo: Richard Davies
98	© Photo: Busam+Richter/Architekturphoto
99	© gmp/Archiv
100–103	© Photo: Busam+Richter/Architekturphoto
101 b.	© VG Bild-Kunst, Bonn 1997 (Sol Lewitt: Wall drawing # 516)
103 b.	© gmp
104–105	© Photo: Busam+Richter/Architekturphoto
106	© Photo: Christian Richters
107	© Photo: Hans-Jürgen Commerell
108–111	© Photo: Christian Richters
112 t.	© Zvi Hecker
112–113	© Photo: Christian Richters
114	© Photo: Herman H. van Doorn
115 t.	© Photo: Atelier Kinold
115 b.	© Photo: Herman H. van Doorn
116	© Herman Hertzberger
117–119	© Photo: Herman H. van Doorn
120	© Photo: Hedrich Blessing
121	© Josef Paul Kleihues
123	© Photo: Hedrich Blessing
124 t.	© Photo: Hedrich Blessing
124 b.	© Josef Paul Kleihues
125–127	© Photo: Hedrich Blessing
127 t.	© VG Bild-Kunst, Bonn 1997 (Dan Flavin: The alternate diagonals of March 2, 1964/ Donald Judd: Untitled)
127 b.	© VG Bild-Kunst, Bonn 1997 (right: Donald Judd: Untitled)
128	© Photo: Christian Richters
128 b.	© VG Bild-Kunst, Bonn 1997 (Andy Warhol: Mao)
129	© Josef Paul Kleihues
130 t.	© Josef Paul Kleihues
130 c.	© Photo: Christian Richters
130 b.	© Josef Paul Kleihues
131	© Josef Paul Kleihues
132–134	© Photo: Christian Richters
132 c.	© VG Bild-Kunst, Bonn 1997 (Joseph Beuys: Richtkräfte)
135	© Photo: Jean Nouvel and Lewis Baltz

136/137	© Photo: Christian Richters
138	© Jean Nouvel
139	© Photo: Christian Richters
140	© Christian de Portzamparc
141	© Photo: Francesca Mantouani
142–144	© Christian de Portzamparc
145	© Nicolas Borel
146	© Photo: Studio LITTRE
147/148 t.	© Photo: Arnaud Carpentier
148 b.	© Reichen & Robert
150–151	© Photo: Arnaud Carpentier
152 b.l.	© Reichen & Robert
152–153	© Photo: Arnaud Carpentier
154	© Photo: Paul Raftery/Arcaid
155	© Photo: School of Architecture of Rennes/France
156 b.	© Rudy Ricciotti
156–159	© Photo: Paul Raftery/Arcaid
160	© Photo: Friedrich Busam/Architekturphoto
161	© Photo: Peter Gross
162	© Thomas Spiegelhalter
163–169	© Photo: Friedrich Busam/Architekturphoto
164 b./ 165–167	© VG Bild-Kunst, Bonn 1997 (Thomas Spiegelhalter: Breisach House, Interior)

The publisher and editor wish to thank each of the architects and photographers for their kind assistance.